MATTHEW ARNOLD:
Between Two Worlds

MATTHEW ARNOLD:
Between Two Worlds

edited by
Robert Giddings

VISION
and
BARNES & NOBLE

Vision Press Limited
Fulham Wharf
Townmead Road
London SW6 2SB

and

Barnes & Noble Books
81 Adams Drive
Totowa, NJ 07512

ISBN (UK) 0 85478 116 1
ISBN (US) 0 389 20625 3

Printed and bound in Great Britain by
A. Wheaton & Co. Ltd.,
Exeter, Devon.
Phototypeset by Galleon Photosetting,
Ipswich, Suffolk.
MCMLXXXVI

Contents

Introduction

by ROBERT GIDDINGS

1

There seems to have been something symbolic about the death of Matthew Arnold. On 15 April 1888 he fell dead running for a tramcar in a Liverpool street. Those who are tempted to romanticize the last century have read much into the manner of his passing:

> It was as if the spirit of the nineteenth century, symbolized by a noisy mechanical juggernaut grinding towards the docks between shabby prosperous warehouses, had finally vanquished the gallant exponent of a less inharmonious order.

Thus (and more) Peter Quennell.[1] This is to attribute to Matthew Arnold a far greater degree of order and harmony than the evidence will justify. Of course there have been those in the twentieth century whose very cause has required a prophet proclaiming and foretelling the coming of the Master, and having no better material to hand, they have had to work up something from Matthew Arnold as well as they could. The result of this construction is to make of Dr. Thomas Arnold's great son something considerably less interesting than he really was.[2] It is possible to perceive how damaging it was for Arnold to have been so conveniently manipulated by the products of the putative New English School at Cambridge, as a good man fallen among the Leavisites:

> [Leavis] was intensely and integrally British. Not Europeanized, not of the intelligentsia, not of the upper classes, not of

7

Bloomsbury, not of any group or set. . . . [He] comes to us from generations of decency and conscience and reasonableness and separateness, of private houses hidden behind hedges, along the road from Matthew Arnold and John Stuart Mill. . . .[3]

And there we have it, stated by no less an authority than Martin Green—Matthew Arnold as the prototypical Leavis. The passage is not without its latent (and probably quite unintentional) drollery. There is something so breathtakingly suburban about it, conjuring up as it does, the idea of Dr. Leavis residing in his smug little, neat little semi-detached house in Matthew Arnold Road, replete with its seclusion-granting hedges and possibly a fine collection of gnomes representing Coleridge, Ruskin, Carlyle and other luminaries of that mammoth British winge, the Condition of England Question. But to place Matthew Arnold in the apostolic succession which—it has been assembled to suggest—led inevitably to the author of *The Great Tradition* is a serious misjudgement. One of the things which makes Arnold such an interesting writer is that he lacked that supreme self-assurance, that neurotic confidence which—manifested either as literary demagoguery or puritan shrillness—sadly became typical of *Scrutiny* and its disciples.

Matthew Arnold was not sure. On 7 September 1851, the year of the Great Exhibition at Crystal Palace which seemed an act of faith in the new age of machinery and industrialism, he visited the French Alpine monastery of the Grande Chartreuse. It had been established by St. Bruno in the eleventh century, and its regimen of fasting and religious observation had remained almost unchanged. To Arnold it seemed a rock of certainty in a crumbling world.

He wrote of this experience that he felt as an ancient Greek might have felt had he stood before some ancient Teutonic monument carved with runes, commemorating a Nordic religion now extinct, and been reminded that his own Hellenic religion was dying and would soon be moribund:

> Forgive me, masters of the mind!
> At whose behest I long ago
> So much unlearnt, so much resign'd!
> I come not here to be your foe.
> I seek these anchorites, not in ruth,
> To curse and to deny your truth;

Not as their friend or child I speak!
But as on some far northern strand,
Thinking of his own Gods, a Greek
In pity and mournful awe might stand
Before some fallen Runic stone—
For both were faiths, and both are gone.

Wandering between two worlds, one dead,
The other powerless to be born,
With nowhere yet to rest my head,
Like these, on earth I wait forlorn.
Their faith, my tears, the world deride;
I come to shed them at their side.[4]

Matthew Arnold felt permanently displaced, belonging neither to the old world and its certainties, nor could he share the seeming confidence of the modern age into which he had been born. His alienation and doubt fuelled an astonishing and wide ranging intellect which probed the nature of religious experience and its relevance in a period increasingly dominated by scientific empiricism, the place of culture in society, the organization of education, the function of literature and its survival amid materialism. His mind had a richness and generosity which allowed these topics to overspill one into another, so that useful connexions were made against the tendency of the age to compartmentalize and bureaucratize the lived practices of life. Arnold began to get a bad press quite early. William Hurrell Mallock portrayed him in his novel *The New Republic* 1877 as Mr. Luke, a rather 'supercilious-looking man' who talks rather loudly and slowly, and is 'the great critic and apostle of culture'. He is given to making bold assertions and uttering powerful opinions. A character in the novel asks him why, if he has so clearly perceived the meaning of life, he is so melancholy? Mr. Luke answers that it is from that very knowledge that the melancholy springs:

We—the cultured—we indeed see. But the world at large does not. It will not listen to us. It thinks we are talking nonsense. Surely that is enough to sadden us. Then, too, our ears are perpetually being pained and deafened by the din of the two opposing Philistinisms—science and orthodoxy—both equally vulgar, and equally useless. But the masses cannot see this. It is impossible to persuade some that science can teach them nothing worth knowing, and others that the dogmatic utterances of the gospels are either ignorant mistakes or oriental metaphors.[5]

It is a gross injustice, and indeed, a slur upon Matthew Arnold's reputation, that it is for one moment possible to conceive that such hubristic utterances are remotely similar to the ideas or the expression of the author of *Culture and Anarchy*. Further damage was inflicted by the malicious cartoon of that little prick Max Beerbohm, which appeared in *The Poets' Corner* (1904). Beerbohm affected to admire Arnold,[6] but this cartoon, with its famous joke about his high seriousness, hardly does justice to Beerbohm's alleged high opinion of Matthew Arnold. Sadly, British Philistinism was ready (as ever) to consume such dismissive off-the-peg opinions, and it became received opinion that Arnold was a bit of a bore. In fact, Arnold's doubts and confusions made him a master ironist, poet and polemicist.

2

There is something very modern about Arnold, and yet, at the same time, the sense of looking backwards is very strong. These qualities do make him seem very much a man between two worlds, one dead, the other powerless to be born. We cannot fail to be impressed by the contemporary relevance of so much that he says about education, and we sense that he is striving for the same victory against the same enemies as may still be seen in the struggle today. Of Prussian education he wrote:

> In general, the Gymnasium is steadily to regard the *allgemeine wissenschaftliche Bildung* of the pupil, the formation of his mind and of his powers of knowledge, without prematurely taking thought for the practical applicability of what he studies. It is expressly forbidden to give this practical or professional turn to the studies of a pupil in the highest form of a gymnasium, even when he is destined for the army.[7]

He looked at the state of school education in Britain and found matters left to a chapter of accidents:

Seven years ago, having been sent by a Royal Commission to study the primary schools on the continent, I was so much struck by all I then saw . . . that looking beyond the immediate scope of my errand, I said to my countrymen . . . *organize your secondary instruction.* That advice passed perfectly unheeded, the hubbub of our sterile politics continued, ideas of social reconstruction had not a thought given to them, our secondary instruction is still the chaos it was; and yet now, so urgent and irresistible is the impression left upon me by what I have again seen abroad, I cannot help presenting myself once more to my countrymen with an increased demand: Organize your secondary and superior instruction.[8]

In our generation we have lived to experience a government which has revived the spirit of Thomas Gradgrind. It may be too easy simply to point to the materialism, the mammonism, the shopkeeper mentality of what passes for educational 'policy' in the mid-1980s, without realizing that it is really the full tide of a deep groundswell which was noticeable for several decades. A writer to the *Daily Telegraph* in 1957 lamented that:

. . . the average child leaves school having spent a considerable amount of time on subjects such as Latin, Greek, algebra and geometry, which may be of little subsequent practical value. Little or nothing is taught about the value of money, a bank account, what a company is, or an ordinary share or dividend— and nothing about the functions of capital in industry. So-called modern history is taught, probably including a boring account of the Industrial Revolution. . . .[9]

Apart from the reference to the boring old Industrial Revolution this sounds very like the kind of evidence which Arnold quoted so damningly from contemporary Victorian newspapers in *Culture and Anarchy* (1869). The infamous *Black Papers*, the monster of unbridled Philistinism released in James Callaghan's so-called Great Debate on education, the fulminations of Dr. Rhodes Boyson, the government's use of the National Advisory Board to restrict courses on arts, humanities and the social sciences in favour of professional, trade and vocational courses and the tendency of Sir Keith Joseph to blame schools for the nation's poor industrial performance are all examples of a state of affairs which would make Matthew Arnold feel—should he be brought to life and sent forth into modern Britain—that things had changed but little since his day. What would he make of an heir apparent who proclaims that the nation should turn itself into small businesses and shopkeepers? Prince Charles was elected president of the Scottish Business in the Community in November 1985. At the meeting which elected him he took occasion to draw public attention to what he saw as the splendid example of the United States. He urged Scottish businessmen to take a lead in telling people what to do. People had developed an 'employee-related' existence, he said. This nation, in the Prince's view, had always been a trading nation, but 'what appears to me to be the case is that our potential customers don't think we provide a service.' This is because: 'We don't deliver the goods on time and we don't deliver the goods they want. We can't go on in the same old way . . .' If this continues, he thinks, we shall never be able to pay for the things that we want. One solution to the problem as he saw it was to stimulate the growth and development of small businesses. The alternative was for Britain to end up as 'a fourth-rate country'. What he sought to unleash was good old individualism (a quality Matthew Arnold often wrote about):

> Those who have been employed in large industries for many years—coal mining, shipbuilding, steel and textiles . . . had got used to a completely employee-related existence. The problem is how to change people's attitudes so they realize they can make a contribution themselves towards the creation of jobs and enterprise. More enterprise and lots more small businesses are needed. The trouble is, of course, how to kindle a spirit of enterprise and determined individuality. . . . I long to know why, for example, it does not pay to do in this country what they do in the U.S., where each company can put aside a certain percentage of its pre-tax profit for community enterprise.[10]

Matthew Arnold must be spinning in his grave, as the likeness to the very targets he attacked in the middle of the last century—Philistinism, materialism, utilitarianism and the shopkeeper mentality—would strike him as risible. But at least Prince Albert was musical.

Our generation has also witnessed the taking up on a considerable scale of the parrot-cry for 'Victorian values'. These are taken to include sexual restraint, self-sufficiency, family life, thrift, hard work, the dignity of labour, etc., etc. The edifice of this immense value system is taken to stand firmly on a rock-bed of ideological stability. The glib propounders of this rag-bag of falsity and confusion have clearly been spared a serious study of their nation's recent history. This would have taught them that the nineteenth century—certainly after the accession of Queen Victoria—was rocked by uncertainties and conflicts. In Matthew Arnold's generation fundamentals of religious faith, beliefs in man's place in the universal scheme of things, of the principles by means of which the nation should govern itself, of the very foundations of the basic assumptions of our society, were questioned—often quite violently. What seems so secure to us, when we look back from our corner of the twentieth century, was to Arnold's contemporaries utterly insecure. Carlyle's oft expressed fear of revolution and anarchy voiced the anxieties of thousands in this country. A similar fear is latent in that magnificent outpouring of the Victorian soul, Tennyson's *Idylls of the King*. In Tennyson's treatment of the story of King Arthur society has just managed to emerge from a barbarous wasteland, into which it may again relapse at any moment. It is part of Tennyson's grand design that the cycle moves from the spring-time coming of the hero, through summer and autumn, and that the work culminates in the barren and bleak landscape in which the final battle is fought and which implies the collapse of the stability and idealism which Arthur's fellowship of the Round Table had achieved. Tennyson dedicated *Idylls of the King* to Prince Albert. The *Dedication* strongly suggests that Albert should be seen as a modern counterpart of King Arthur, with the suggested analogy that the civilization attained in Britain might similarly lapse back into barbarism: 'And indeed He seems to me/ Scarce other than my king's ideal knight. . . .'[11] The sense of loss is heavy in the closing sections of *The Passing of Arthur*, which pictures the decline of a whole world-order:

> The sequel of today unsolders all
> The goodliest fellowship of famous knights
> Whereof this world holds record. Such a sleep
> They sleep—the men I loved. I think that we
> Shall never more, at any future time,

Delight our souls with talk of knightly deeds,
Walking about the gardens and the halls
Of Camelot, as in the days that were.
I perish by this people which I made. . . .[12]

From where Matthew Arnold was looking at things this was
not such a fantastic view to take. It seemed to him and to
many of his contemporaries that the demonstrations in the
mid-1860s for an extension of the franchise, which included
violence in Hyde Park and the tearing down of railings, might
be a prelude to a more general break down of the social order,
followed by a collapse into atavistic barbarism. To read *Culture
and Anarchy*—Arnold's response to the agitation which pre-
ceded the 1867 Reform Act—is to sense fully Arnold's fear of
working-class anarchy. Culture was important because it
brought the possibility of harmony and respect for authority
nearer. It was not simply a matter of 'Sweetness and Light'
being good for the soul; it was good for the organization of
society as well, insofar as it reduced the possibility of tumult
and disorder, multitudinous processions in the streets of our
towns, mass meetings and other public manifestations of
political agitation which, he felt, were quite unnecessary in the
present course of British affairs. These things, he asserted,
should be expressly forbidden, and we should all encourage
and uphold the executives of power in our society who
attempted to prohibit such activities. If this does not sound all
that liberal, we should remind ourselves what he actually
wrote. Freedom to do as one liked was not a good thing. As far
as the British working classes were concerned it was more
socially threatening than mass alcoholism:

> Our prevalent notion is . . . that it is a most happy and
> important thing for a man merely to be able to do as he
> likes. . . . Our familiar praise of the British Constitution . . . is
> that it is a system of checks,—a system which stops and
> paralyses any power in interferring with the free action of
> individuals. To this effect Mr. Bright, who loves to walk in the
> old ways of the Constitution, said forcibly in one of his great
> speeches, what many other people are every day saying less
> forcibly, that the central idea of English life and politics is *the
> assertion of personal liberty*. Evidently this is so; but evidently, also,
> as feudalism, which with its ideas and habits of subordination

14

was for many centuries silently behind the British Constitution, dies out, and we are left with nothing but our system of checks, and our notion of its being the great right and happiness of an Englishman to do as far as possible what he likes, we are in danger of drifting towards anarchy. We have not the notion, so familiar on the Continent and to antiquity, of *the State* . . . entrusted with stringent powers for the general advantage, and controlling individual wills in the name of an interest wider than that of individuals.[13]

Arnold relates how he was informed by M. Michelet that France was a nation of barbarians who had been civilized by military conscription. He laments that when the Crimean war offered the opportunity of attempting the same 'civilizing' experience on our masses, rather than serve in the army the population ran away, and hid themselves in coal mines in Derbyshire.[14]

Culture and Anarchy was first published in book form in 1869, and when the author revised the text for the second edition of 1875 several passages were omitted or toned down. One such passage contained this comment about the way demonstrations should be handled; recalling his father's views when 'the political and social state of the country was gloomy and troubled and there were riots in many places' the good Dr. Thomas Arnold had opined that even when bearing in mind 'the badness and foolishness of the government' there was only one way to deal with the situation:

> As for rioting, the old Roman way . . . is always the right one; flog the rank and file, and fling the ringleaders from the Tarpeian Rock! And this opinion we can never forsake. . . .[15]

This may come as a bit of a shock from such a Christian gentleman scholar, but it may well give us a better insight into what our present leaders mean when they talk of a return to 'Victorian values'. It is a fact that the Prince of Wales, when visiting Consett, walked up to a group of skinheads and said to them: 'What are you yobbos doing behind that fence?'[16] We cannot precisely date this comment of Dr. Arnold's which so significantly remained in Matthew Arnold's mind, but it probably referred to the riots and disturbances of the late 1820s and early 1830s, when Matthew was about 10 years old.

To his father's generation the eruption of politics onto the streets was a constant nightmare and was regarded as a possibility. While Matthew was at Balliol College, Oxford in the mid-1840s, the figure of Chartism and the social disruption it connoted stalked the land.

These fears were real and they were firmly based on evidence which seemed valid at the time. The period from the end of the Napoleonic Wars until well into the second half of the nineteenth century was a time when revolution seemed imminent. The end of the war brought to an end the boom in many industries involved in the war effort. The slackening of production brought unemployment. The ranks of the unemployed were swelled by the returning sailors and soldiers. Discontent and hardship showed itself in riots and disturbances—Spa Fields, Peterloo, the March of the Blanketeers, the Cato Street Conspiracy.[17] The Combination Law of 1824 seemed to usher in a year of strikes and demonstrations.[18]

The Peace of Vienna 1815 brought to an end the artificial prosperity of the farmers, and a drastic decline in agricultural prices followed. Wheat slumped to 65/7d. a quarter in that year. The less efficient farmers were ruined. Difficulties were increased by a series of bad harvests. Many farms were abandoned and much land changed from arable land to pasture. Farmers in the Midlands suffered particularly as heavy clay land was less suitable for the obvious alternative crops, such as turnips of four course rotation; heavy land like this required more labour and horse-power as well as better drainage. They were thus costly to the farmer, and to this must be added the fact that crops like this were also subject to failure. There were several agricultural riots in the 1830s.[19] In December 1830 900 agricultural labourers were arrested.[20]

Lord Melbourne took a hard line on these disturbances and circulated a letter to Justices of the Peace urging them to exert all the authority in their power to suppress them. Almost at once it was being said of Melbourne that he was the one strong man in the government.[21] In three months he had cleared it up, by using soldiers and a special commission of judges with powers of immediate trial. By treating the symptoms and not the disease, all agitation was ended.[22] 450 labourers were transported.[23]

The infamous Corn Law of 1815—repealed, to the ruin of his political career and the cost of party's unity by Sir Robert Peel in 1846—was passed to protect the landed minority.[24] It was in the main wholly ineffective, and promoted rising opposition in the industrially minded middle classes. The worst of this depression in agriculture did not pass until the early 1840s.[25]

Manufacturing areas also showed signs of disorder. Cornwall and Wales experienced bad strikes in 1831[26] and at Manchester there was a particularly serious strike of cotton spinners during which a manufacturer's son was murdered.[27] When Matthew Arnold was a boy of about 10 there was a genuine fear of revolution in this country. The French revolution was fresh in the imagination and the threat of a public rising was re-awakened by the Revolution in July 1830 which brought Louis Philippe to power. The French revolution had started with an agricultural rising and had culminated in mobs at Paris. After the horrors occasioned by the mob in France in the disturbances of 1831 Wellington had commented to Philip Henry, fifth Earl of Stanhope: 'Our mob is not trained nor accustomed to regular direction as the French was . . . once let the mob loose, and you will see what it will do!'[28]

The failure of the First Reform Bill at the committee stage on 21 March 1831 seemed to presage a period of considerable public unrest. 'Before spring all Europe will be in war', wrote Sir William Napier to his wife, 'here in London men speak sedition openly in the clubs, and secretly in the streets. . . . Public opinion is ripe for a revolution.'[29]

Wellington had stated that he was opposed to any further reform and that he did not care who knew it,[30] and there were anti-Wellington demonstrations. The form these assemblies took is significant, several of them involving the display of *tricours*.[31] Elie Halevy comments of this period: 'After the events in France, English agitation for reform assumed a revolutionary character which no one could mistake.'[32] Bristol experienced terrible public riots in protest at the failure of the first Reform Bill[33] and feelings ran so high that William IV was prepared to leave the country for his own safety if necessary.[34] There were political riots at Derby and at

Nottingham, where the castle—owned by the hated Duke of Newcastle—was burned to the ground.[35]

As the campaign for parliamentary reform gradually formed itself into the ever-growing battalions which became the outstanding public manifestation of the people's politics in the Victorian period, Chartism, public attention was also focused on the dreadful case of the Tolpuddle martyrs.[36] The obvious pathos and drama of the case of the Dorset labourers in some ways overshadows other examples of unrest and oppression at the time, a combination of the economic instability of the period, the dreadful effects of the 1834 Poor Law Amendment Act and popular political agitation, which all found a focal point in Chartism.

Chartism was in many respects a bread-and-butter question. A contemporary newspaper carries the report of a meeting at Manchester in August 1839, where the Chartists tried to put into effect their plan for a stoppage of work, a 'National Holiday'. They visited mills and factories at the hour for starting work and before being prevented by the police these efforts were effective in about twenty places of work:

> One of the parties walked in procession, headed by a band of music and a man carrying a banner, having upon it the cap of liberty, with the inscriptions 'The earth and the right of Man' and 'He that will not work, neither shall he eat'.[37]

At St. Stephen's church in the same month some 600 Chartists took possession of the building where the Rev. Booth attempted to preach a sermon on St. Paul's words: 'I have learned in whatever station of life, therewith to be content.' He was barracked, voices bawling out: 'You get £200 a year! Come and weave bambazines!'[38] This is really the nub of the whole matter, Chartism *was* an attempt to mobilize working people—and it was this which so alarmed the economic and political establishment. William Lovett, one of the founders of the London Working Men's Association, said that working men had always previously had leaders from the educated middle classes, but he wanted a *new* kind of movement:

> The working classes had not hitherto evinced that discrimi-
> nating and independant spirit in the management of their
> political affairs, which we were desirous to see. . . . they were

18

always looking up to *leadership* of one description or another. . . .
The masses were taught to look up to great men . . . rather than
great principles. . . .[39]

The mid-nineteenth century was dominated by the spectre of
Chartism which refused all attempts at exorcism.[40] The
tearing down of the park railings which is so regularly and
famously asserted to be the signs of anarchy which prompted
Matthew Arnold to create *Culture and Anarchy* was not an
isolated, sudden or impromptu act, but just another example
of the groundswell of popular unrest which did not feel retiring
ebb but kept right on through the fabled 'stability' of Queen
Victoria's reign. As Bertrand Russell recorded in *Ideas and
Beliefs of the Victorians*, as his grandfather, John, first Earl
Russell, lay dying in 1878, he heard a loud noise in the street,
and believed that 'the revolution' had broken out.[41]

3

Matthew Arnold deeply believed in social harmony and
social order, and his faith may well have been strengthened by
the anxiety brought on by living through such a period of
social and political tensions. He felt that he was justified in
recognizing a considerable threat latent in the idea of its being
an Englishman's right to do as he liked. The modern spirit, he
wrote, had almost entirely dissolved those feudal habits of
respect for the social order and one's place in it, and the
contemporary worship of freedom was a gaderene rush to
anarchy:

> . . . this and that man, and this and that body of men, all over
> the country, are beginning to assert and put in practice an
> Englishman's right to do what he likes; his right to march
> where he likes, meets where he likes, enter where he likes, hoot
> as he likes, threatens as he likes, smash as he likes. All this, I say,
> tends to anarchy. . . .[42]

The terrible symptoms of social disintegration he affected to
perceive were the combined consequence of too much liberty,
weak 'liberal' policies, an aristocracy no longer capable of
leadership (the Barbarians), a middle class unfit for government (the Philistines) and a populace who were daily growing

more uncontrollable. If we read *Culture and Anarchy* properly, it is clear that one of the things he criticizes the most strongly is our failure of nerve in dealing with the crises he recognizes. We have nothing to fear from Fenianism, he asserts, 'fierce and turbulent as it may show itself' because against this threat to our stability 'our conscience is free enough to let us act resolutely and put forth our overwhelming strength. . . .'[43] But against the threats nearer home we seem to be powerless.

Arnold's answer was culture. Sweetness and light, if properly cultivated, would thrive and flourish, and social harmony would be restored:

> . . . how to organise this authority. . . . How to get your *State*, summing up the right reason of the community, and giving effect to it. . . .
>
> The *State*, the power most representing the right reason of the nation, and most worthy, therefore, of ruling,—of exercising, when circumstances require it, authority over us all,—is for Mr. Carlyle the aristocracy. For Mr. Lowe, it is the middle class with its incomparable Parliament. For the Reform League, it is the working class. . . .
>
> Now, culture, with its disinterested pursuit of perfection, culture, simply trying to see things as they are, in order to seize on the best and to make it prevail, is surely well fitted to help us to judge rightly, by all the aids of observing, reading, and thinking, the qualifications and titles to our confidence of these three candidates for authority. . . .[44]

In Arnold's view, culture would judge that the aristocracy would be unsuited to lead because they may have 'sweetness' but they lack 'light'. The middle classes were unfit to govern because of the vulgarity and hideousness the worship of machinery and mammonism produced.

The answer was inescapable—it lay in creating a cultivated élite. This was the only way to achieve social harmony, a harmony between the classes. Arnold's ambitions were simple and straightforward, despite all the Judaic-Hellenic-Oxbridge-school-inspectorish mumbo-jumbo they were tricked up in: he wanted an élite, an aristocracy of the enlightened; supported by a cultivated bourgeoisie; followed by an obedient proletariat.

In *Friendship's Garland* he says that the aristocracy administer, and the middle classes govern. He accepts the British class system in principle. The basis of his acclaimed attacks on it is that it does not do its job, that is to say, it is not *wrong*, but *inefficient*. The aristocracy is there, playing a leading rôle in what passes for 'theory' in Arnold's sermonizings. What is wrong with this class is that its interest in hunting, shooting and fishing has rendered it useless for its true social rôle.[45] The middle class, as perceived by Arnold, was incapable of rising to the rôle history was about to thrust upon it, because—to put it bluntly—it had been insufficiently prepared by its schooling. Hence the need for a massive injection of Hellenic culture into the school system, which will—in his words—link the middle class to 'the best culture of their nation' and give them 'a greatness and a noble spirit, which the tone of these classes is not of itself at present adequate to impart'.[46] The classics are seen here as something akin to a shot-in-the-arm to revitalize the bourgeoisie and render them painlessly and immediately physically fit for their true responsibilities. This enterprise, he argued:

> would really augment their self-respect and moral force; it would truly fuse them with the class above, and tend to bring about for them the equality which they are entitled to desire.[47]

Would it be such an exaggeration to say that as far as giving the middle class its Culture was concerned, Matthew Arnold was a fascist with his heart in the right place? After all, he once wrote to Arthur Clough: 'Those who cannot read Greek literature should read nothing but Milton and parts of Wordsworth: the state should see to it. . . .'[48] According to Arnold's view of history, the rot had set in during the Renaissance, which he saw as a moment of social and cultural disintegration. What was taken for mellifluousness and richness of expression in Elizabethan drama and poetry were the symptoms of a society in an advanced state of disorganization. The model to be studied—and imitated—was the highly organized period of Hellenic culture, with its apparent social and political stability and its splendid and coherent literature and drama. It has been claimed that when Arnold heard that John Wilkes Booth shouted in Latin about the death of tyrants at the moment he assassinated President Lincoln, he opined that there was hope for America.

Time and again Arnold's lack of democracy comes through. He had no faith in the public at large. Walt Whitman pointed out (while Arnold was giving a lecture tour in America) that he would not see the truth about America in its institutional and public world, but only in the factories and in the crowds:

> Arnold always gives you the notion that he hates to touch the dirt—the dirt is so dirty! But everything comes out of the dirt—everything: everything comes out of the people, the everyday people as you find them and leave them: not university people . . . people, people, people, just people. . . .[49]

In his scheme of things it was essential that the masses be prepared to follow the classes above them. The proletariate cannot be expected to follow a middle class so bereft of spiritual and intellectual qualities as Arnold considered the Victorian bourgeoisie to be:

> It is of itself a serious calamity for a nation that its tone of feeling and grandeur of spirit should be lowered or dulled, but the calamity appears far more serious still when we consider that the middle classes, remaining as they are now, with their narrow, harsh, unintelligent and unattractive spirit and culture, will almost certainly fail to mould or assimilate the masses below them, whose sympathies are at the moment actually wider and more liberal than theirs. They arrive, these masses, eager to enter into possession of the world, to gain a more vivid sense of their own life and activity. In this their irrepressible development, their natural educators and initiators are those immediately above them, the middle classes. If these classes cannot win their sympathy, or give them their direction, society is in danger of falling into anarchy.[50]

Arnold's belief in an élite, the Golden Few, the Gauleiters of Sweetness and Light, was everywhere implicit in his social thinking:

> Knowledge and truth, in the full sense of the words, are not attainable by the great mass of the human race at all. The great mass of the human race have to be softened and humanized through their hearts and imagination, before any soil can be found in them where knowledge may strike living roots.[51]

Although Arnold felt that the society he lived in had cut itself adrift from the true glories of the past, and was in danger

of ruining the present, he had some optimism for the future, if
we could only get ourselves organized in time. He put his faith
in culture and education 'which saves the future, as one may
hope, from being vulgarized, even if it cannot save the
present'.[52] His gloomy social vision offered itself two escape
routes—the retreat into an idyllic rural past, which we may
clearly detect as the main thrust of *The Scholar Gipsy*—or the
projection into an élitist future: the choice was between
organic nostalgia, and controlled new times.[53]

Although there is so much we of the last quarter of the
twentieth century may identify with in this eminent Victorian,
there is one considerable point of departure. He found the
present unacceptable, and preferred to look back, or to hope
that due organization undertaken in time would deliver a
worthwhile future. We regard the present as pretty unbearable
and believe we have a future which probably does not bear
thinking about. We have actually suffered 'this strange disease
of modern life' through its various stages—fever, delirium,
convulsions, aches, spasms and mortification—and are at a
loss to find an unconquerable hope which we may nurse with
any well founded confidence.[54]

NOTES

1. Peter Quennell, *The Singular Preference*, quoted in Justin Wintle and
   Richard Kenin, *The Dictionary of Biographical Quotation* (Routledge and
   Kegan Paul, 1978), p. 31.
2. Terry Eagleton, *Criticism and Ideology* (New Left Books, 1976), pp. 104–10;
   Lesley James, *The Cultural Critics* (Routledge and Kegan Paul, 1979), pp.
   18–34; Francis Mulher, *The Moment of Scrutiny* (New Left Books, 1979),
   pp. 128–29, 174–75, 253, 288 and of F. R. Leavis, 'Arnold as Critic' in
   Scrutiny, Vol. II (1938), reprinted in *A Selection From 'Scrutiny'*, edited by
   F. R. Leavis (Cambridge University Press, 1968), pp. 258 ff.
3. Martin Green, 'British Decency' in *Kenyon Review*, Vol. XXI, Number 4
   (Autumn 1959), pp. 505 ff.
4. Matthew Arnold, 'Stanzas From the Grande Chartreuse' in *The Poetical
   Works of Matthew Arnold* (Oxford University Press, 1945), p. 272.
5. See Alan Bold and Robert Giddings, *Who Was Really Who in Fiction*
   (Longman, 1986), p. 189.
6. David Cecil, *Max—A Biography* (Constable, 1964), p. 370 and cf. Max
   Beerbohm, *Around Theatres* (Heinemann, 1922), p. 174.

7. Matthew Arnold, *Schools and Universities on the Continent* (1868), p. 159.
8. Ibid., p. 296.
9. *Daily Telegraph*, Monday 13 October 1957.
10. 'Prince Sees United Kingdom in Fourth Division' in the *Guardian*, 27 November 1985.
11. Tennyson, 'A Dedication' to *Idylls of the King*, in *Poetical Works of Alfred, Lord Tennyson* (MacMillan, 1901), p. 308.
12. Tennyson, *Idylls of the King*, ibid., pp. 469–70.
13. Matthew Arnold, *Culture and Anarchy* (1869), edited by John Dover Wilson (Cambridge University Press, 1955), pp. 74–5.
14. *Culture and Anarchy*, ibid., pp. 75–6.
15. Quoted in Raymond Williams, *Problems in Materialism and Culture* (Verso, 1980), pp. 6–7.
16. Quoted in *New Society*, 6 December 1985, p. 403.
17. See F. O. Darvall, *Popular Disturbances and Public Order in Regency England* (1934), Pauline Gregg, *A Social and Economic History of Britain* (MacMillan, 1962), pp. 57–97; Donald Read, *Peterloo: The Massacre and its Background* (Manchester University Press, 1969).
18. Henry Pelling, *A History of British Trade Unions* (Penguin, 1966), pp. 30–1 and cf. G. D. H. Cole and A. W. Filson, *British Working Class Movements: Select Documents 1789–1875* (MacMillan, 1967), pp. 116 ff.
19. See E. J. Hobsbawm and George Rudé, *Captain Swing* (Lawrence and Wishart, 1970), pp. 72 ff.
20. *Carpenter's Political Register*, 4 December 1830, pp. 919 ff.
21. David Cecil, *Melbourne* (Constable, 1970), pp. 248–49.
22. Ibid., pp. 249 ff.
23. J. L. Hammond, *The Village Labourer* (MacMillan, 1920), p 284.
24. Norman Gash, *Politics in the Age of Peel* (W. W. Norton, New York, 1971), pp. 178, 184, 230 and 234–35.
25. E. P. Thompson, *The Making of the English Working Class* (Penguin, 1968), pp. 254–58 and Cole and Filson, op. cit., pp. 116 ff.
26. *Annual Register* (1831), *Chronicle*, 2 February.
27. Ibid., 3 January.
28. Elizabeth Longford, *Wellington: Pillar of State* (Weidenfeld and Nicolson, 1972), p. 150.
29. H. A. Bruce, *Life of Sir William Napier* (1864), Vol. I, p. 336.
30. *Wellington Dispatches*, Vol. VII, p. 423, quoted in Elie Halevy, *History of the English People in the Nineteenth Century* (1961), Vol. 3, p. 18.
31. Halevy, op. cit., p. 18.
32. Ibid., p. 16.
33. Keith Feiling, *A History of England* (MacMillan, 1969), pp. 824 ff.
34. Halevy, op. cit., p. 56.
35. *Political Register*, 5 October 1831, Vol. LXIV, pp. 179–80 and *Annual Register*, 8 October 1831 and 9 October 1833, pp. 161 ff.
36. Pelling, op. cit., pp. 41 ff., and Cole and Filson, op. cit., pp. 283–87.
37. *Observer*, 18 August 1839.
38. Ibid.
39. William Lovett, *The Life and Struggles of William Lovett in the Pursuit of*

Bread, Knowledge and Freedom (1876), pp. 91–2.

40. See Halevy, op. cit., pp. 283–301; G. D. H. Cole and Raymond Postegate, *The Common People 1746–1946* (Methuen, 1967), pp. 272–91; Mark Hovell, *The Chartist Movement* (Manchester University Press, 1920) and Cole and Filson, op. cit., pp. 345–422.

41. John, first Earl Russell (1792–1878) British statesman. He was long associated with Parliamentary reform. He was one of four members of the government entrusted with the drafting of the Reform Bill 1832, and it was Russell who proposed it to the Commons. After the crisis of the Corn Law repeal in 1846, and the eclipse of Sir Robert Peel, Russell was Prime Minister 1846–52. He proposed a further Reform Bill in 1854, which failed. On the death of Palmerston in 1865, Russell was again Prime Minister, but his third Reform Bill failed in June of the same year and he resigned. See his *Recollections and Suggestions* (1875) and Spencer Walpole, *Life of Lord John Russell*, two vols. (1891).

42. *Culture and Anarchy*, op. cit., p. 76.

43. Ibid., p. 79.

44. Ibid., pp. 82–3.

45. Cf. *Culture and Anarchy*, ibid., pp. 84 ff.

46. Matthew Arnold, 'The Popular Education of France' in *Democratic Education*, edited by R. H. Super (Michigan University Press, Ann Arbor, 1962), p. 22.

47. Ibid., p. 23.

48. Quoted in Lionel Trilling, *Matthew Arnold* (George Allen and Unwin, 1963), p. 33.

49. Walt Whitman, in an article in *The Critic*, quoted in Trilling, op. cit., p. 398.

50. Matthew Arnold, 'The Popular Education in France' in Super, op. cit., p. 26; cf. Terry Eagleton, *Criticism and Ideology*, op. cit., pp. 104–10, to whom I am particularly indebted.

51. Matthew Arnold, *Complete Prose Works*, edited by R. H. Super (University of Michigan Press, Ann Arbor, 1963), vol. 6, p. 72; cf. Kevin Harris, *Education and Knowledge* (Routledge and Kegan Paul, 1979), pp. 151 ff.; Richard Johnson, 'Notes on the Schooling of the English Working Class 1780–1850' in Roger Dale, Geoff England and Madeleine MacDonald (eds.), *Schooling and Capitalism: A Sociological Reader* (Routledge and Kegan Paul, 1976), pp. 44–54; Samuel Bowles and Herbert Gintis, *Schooling in Capitalist America* (Routledge and Kegan Paul, 1976), pp. 151 ff.; Madan Sarup, *Marxism and Education* (Routledge and Kegan Paul, 1978), pp. 129 ff. and Ralph Milliband, *The State in Capitalist Society* (Quartet Books, 1973), pp. 215–19.

52. *Culture and Anarchy*, op. cit., p. 52.

53. See Robert Giddings, 'The Chic of the Old' in the *Listener*, 24 January 1985.

54. Matthew Arnold, 'The Scholar Gipsy', ll. 202–11.

1

Arnold in Coketown

by ALAN CHEDZOY

Picture, if you will, the classroom of Coketown Elementary School, one winter morning in 1864. The coughing class of some sixty boys and girls is ranged around the room in clean tunics and pinafores. The children are of about 11 or 12 years of age, for they are in Standards V and VI. The centre of the room has been cleared by moving the desks to the sides. Desks are normally shared between three pupils so that only twenty children are seated with the rest standing. Their parents have paid 1d or 2d a week to send them to the school for education is still not compulsory and certainly not free. Today the children seem nervous and subdued. They glance occasionally at the two gentlemen in the middle of the room but take care not to catch the eye of either of them. Their schoolmaster, Mr. McCheerumchild, is perfectly familiar to them, and normally they would not be so careful to avoid his glance. At the moment, however, he is more agitated and snappish than usual, for his guest is one of Her Majesty's Inspectors, come to examine the children of Standards V and VI.

One of the children, a little girl, dares to steal a glance at the Inspector. He is a tall man dressed in a black frock coat; his dark hair is parted in the middle and he has mutton-chop whiskers. His manner is severe but not unkind, his voice low, and clearly that of a gentleman. Today he is listening to the pupils recite their portions of poetry as part of the examination in English. He has already heard six of them deliver

Mrs. Hemans's 'The Homes of England'. Sometimes he asks
the candidate a question or two about the poem, but this he
does in a low voice so that the others shall not hear the
answers. Jemima knows full well that the poem is full of hard
words and her heart thuds when she knows that it is her turn
next to go to the upturned box serving as the reciter's dais.

'Gal number twen . . er . . Jemima Jupe, come out.', intones
Mr. McCheerumchild (who has difficulty in remembering that
the children in the class are no longer addressed by number).
The Inspector regards her keenly and gestures that she should
take her place on the box.
'What is your name, child?'
'Jemima Jupe, Sir.'
'Schoolmaster, don't I know this girl?'
'No, Sir. Not possible. But you did examine her sister, Sissy,
when you were last here, Sir. It was in your first year as an
Inspector, Sir. This gel is most remarkable like her.'
'I see, Schoolmaster. Before we begin again, may we have
some more warmth in here?'
'Certainly, Sir. Benjamin Bitzer, the hod. But just you do it
quiet mind, so's not to drowned out Jemmy's poem.'[1]

So Jemima began to stammer out her verses while a boy,
remarkable in appearance for his white eyelashes, began to
heap coke into the stove, a feat he performed with remarkable
efficiency because he was almost entirely silent.

At the fourth verse of 'The Homes of England', Jemima was
clearly in trouble:
'The cottage homes of England!
By thousands on her plains
They are smiling o'er the silvery brooks,
And round the hamlet fanes.
Through glowing orchards forth they peep . . .
they peep. . . .
Each . . each fearless. . . .
Each from its nook! . . .'[2]
'Yes, you do not know the poem very well, do you, er,
Jemima?'
'Please, Sir, I *did* know 'er, Sir, leastways, I thinks I did, Sir,
but 'er all got jumbled, Sir, seeing you, Sir.'
'What does your father do, Jemima?'
'Sir?'

'His job, Jemima. What is his work?'

'Oh, he's in the horse-riding business, Sir. We've got the biggest horse-riding tent you ever did see. An' Merrylegs, he's mine, Sir. . . .'

'Yes, I see. Some sort of circus, McCheerumchild? I see. And Jemima, did you like the poem? I chose it myself especially for school use.'

'Oh, yes, Sir. It's very nice, Sir.'

'Good. And do you know what a "fane" is? . . . "They are smiling o'er the silvery brooks/around the hamlet fanes" . . . What is a "fane", Jemima?'

'Dunno, Sir.'

Bitzer dropped the coal bucket and burst forth: 'Please, Sir, "fane", Sir. Means "temple", Sir, from the Latin "fanum, a temple", Sir.'

'That's very good . . . er?'

'Bitzer, Sir.'

'Very good, Bitzer. Though you must not shout out and interrupt an examination. Do I know you, Bitzer?'

'No, Sir. Know me brother, Sir. 'E carries your case to Mrs. Collard's lodgings, Sir, last time you was here. You passed 'im, Sir; 'E give you "Casabianca", Sir.'

'Ah, very good. I seem to remember it. Thank you, Jemima. That will do. You must learn your hard words, you know, so that your poetry will be of use to you when you are a grown woman.'

This scene, or one very like it, was part of Matthew Arnold's professional life for thirty-five years. As one of Her Majesty's Inspectors, he examined pupils and pupil-teachers in regular inspections between 1851 and 1886. Few biographers and commentators on Arnold have sufficiently indicated that his work as an Inspector was his real work, while the writing of poetry and essays had to be fitted in to his spare time.

Arnold had drifted into the education service. After leaving Oxford, where he had been a student at Balliol and a fellow at Oriel, he became private secretary to Lord Lansdowne, the Whig politician, who was, at that time, President of the Council in Lord John Russell's administration. The Secretary to the Education Department was Ralph Lingen (afterwards Lord Lingen) who had been Arnold's tutor at Oxford. In 1846 the parliamentary grant to schools had been raised to

£100,000, and the government of the day decided that such a huge expenditure on schools should be matched by rising standards of education. Inspectors were to be appointed to ensure efficiency in the classroom and Lingen was determined that they should be drawn from young men of intelligence and vision. Accordingly, he petitioned Lansdowne for the services of his secretary and, on 14 April 1851, Matthew Arnold became an H.M.I.[3]

Arnold's motives for joining the education service were at first less than visionary. He was too fastidious for business or the law and the church was uncongenial to him. He wanted to get married to Frances Lucy Wightman, daughter of Mr. Justice Wightman and, accordingly, Lansdowne's suggestion that he should become an H.M.I. was a very welcome one in that it provided him with a profession which would enable him to keep a wife. They were married on 10 June 1851.

One of the first letters he wrote to his wife was addressed from 'Oldham Road Lancasterian School, Manchester' in October 1851, and sagely observes that 'I think I shall get interested in the schools after a little time. . . .' His work was, for the greater part of his career, restricted to nonconformist elementary schools and training colleges, and, to visit them, he travelled constantly, particularly in the north of England. At first his wife accompanied him, but she was no longer able to do so after the birth of their first child, Tom, between the prison and the workhouse in Derby. Much of Arnold's life was spent alone, either in coaches or, later, trains, traversing dreary industrial landscapes, or else in comfortless lodgings where he would read and scribble notes for essays, after indigestible dinners.

From the first, Arnold was imbued with an idea of the *political* significance of state education. The letter from the Oldham Road Lancasterian School continues:

> their [the schools'] effects on the children are so immense, and their future effects in civilising the next generation of the lower classes, who, as things are going, will have most of the political power of the country in their hands, may be so important.[5]

He dreaded the potential violence of an unenfranchized, uneducated, urban working class. In 1848, the year of revolutions, he wrote to his sister:

> the spectacle of France is likely to breed great agitation here, and such is the state of our masses that their movements now *can* only be brutal plundering and destroying. And if they wait, there is no one, as far as one sees, to train them to conquer, by their attitude and superior conviction. . . .[6]

Thus he conceived his task as an Inspector as one of helping to train the emergent working class to develop 'superior conviction', so that it might take its place in a democratic system rather than exercising its will by mob rule. For him the choice was between ever-increasing outbreaks of violence from a brutalized working-class, or an electorate of working-men, educated and civilized by their elementary schools. The urgency he attached to this civilizing process may be better understood by noting that, in 1867, the electorate of 1,057,000 was enlarged by 938,000 largely working-class voters. Third members of parliament were granted to Liverpool, Manchester, Birmingham, Leeds and, we may suppose, Coketown.

Arnold's views on the nature of the English social system were formulated in *Culture and Anarchy* (1869) and are probably too familiar to the reader to warrant close attention here. It is sufficient to say that, in that essay, he represents English society as one of three classes, each incomprehensible to the other. The aristocracy he refers to as the 'Barbarians', the middle classes as the 'Philistines' and the working class as the 'Populace'. It is the last named of these which is our interest here. He depicts the working class as that

> which, raw and half-developed, has long lain half-hidden amidst its poverty and squalor, and is now issuing from its hiding place to assert an Englishman's privilege of doing as he likes, and is beginning to perplex us by marching where it likes, meeting where it likes, bawling what it likes, breaking what it likes. . . .[7]

Arnold's notion of working-class people in the mass is always of a threatening mob. Behind each stammering Benjamin Bitzer or Jemima Jupe he glimpsed a potential rioter and looter.

His best hope in *Culture and Anarchy* is placed not in any class, but in those individuals who were able to transcend class interests and to consider their experiences in the light of truth. For them, party, class and nation were secondary influences on their thought and utterance; in framing their responses to life they consulted their 'best selves' rather than easy prejudices. Arnold calls such people 'aliens' and he believes that their number in any class is 'capable of being diminished or augmented'. One of his educational objectives is, therefore, the increasing of the number of aliens among the working classes, so that they might act as an ameliorating force among their workmates.

It is quite clear that Arnold has no belief in the general education of the working class to a high level. At best, he thought, the majority of its members might have their rough edges sanded down a little by their elementary school experience. He was of the opinion that 'The mass of mankind will never have any ardent zeal for seeing things as they are; very inadequate ideas will always satisfy them', but added significantly, 'On these inadequate ideas reposes, and must repose, the general practice of the world.'[8]

Nevertheless, he felt that the attempt must be made to ensure that the inadequate ideas that satisfied the Populace should, as far as possible, bear some relationship to things as they are, and the best way to bring this about was to give them some experience of the best that has been thought and said.

Such testimony is best found in literature, which study had a central rôle in Arnold's educational thought. In his *General Report for the Year 1871*, Arnold wrote of 'the mighty engine of literature in the education of the working classes'.[9] It was natural that Arnold should rate literature so highly in the educational process, for he was not only an Inspector of schools but also, from 1857–67, Professor of Poetry at Oxford. No man in English history has been better placed to promote the cause of literature among the common people. His claims for the significance of literature in human life far exceed those of any of his critical predecessors:

> More and more mankind will discover that we have to turn to poetry to interpret life for us, to console us, to sustain us. Without poetry, our science will appear incomplete; and most of what now passes with us for religion and philosophy will be replaced by poetry.[10]

31

Literature, then, was to play an important part in the new elementary school education, but Arnold was unable to find a model for procedure in his own education at school. Like all public schoolboys at the time, his schooldays were spent largely in the study of Greek and Latin literature, in translating, parsing and scanning the classical writers. Elementary school children were taught no Greek and Latin and therefore such activities, even if desirable, were not possible for them. The only comparable activity in which they could engage was the study of the 'classics' of English literature. Shakespeare and Milton could be studied in the same way as Homer and Ovid. Children could be required to learn long passages from the English poets and to subject these passages to grammatical analysis just as well as if they were writers in a dead language. In a letter to Clough, Arnold wrote: 'Those who cannot read Greek should read nothing but Milton and parts of Wordsworth: the state should see to it. . . .'[11]

Arnold's notion of literature as an educative force is restricted entirely to poetry, and it is poetry which is cast as his 'mighty engine' of education. Unfortunately, his critical writings nowhere offer an analysis of the nature of poetry and, because he has no distinctive conception of what kind of thing poetry is, his ideas on the study of the subject in schools are both limited and flawed. T. S. Eliot has remarked with brutal accuracy that Arnold 'was so conscious of what, for him, poetry was *for*, that he could not altogether see it for what it is'.[12]

The *Reports on Elementary Schools 1852–1882* enable us to glimpse Arnold's views on the teaching of poetry just as clearly by what they do not say as what they do. Arnold does not mention at any point the pleasurable element in reciting rhymes, in the repetition of homely jingles, in the sheer fun of much folk verse. For him, the significant educational characteristic of poetry is that it is noble and, therefore, an uplifting experience for humble scholars. The difference between Homer and the English ballad poets is that he is noble and they are not.

> Homer and they [the ballad poets] are both of them natural, and therefore touching and stirring; but the grand style, which

is Homer's is something more than touching and stirring; it can form the character, it is edifying.[13]

For this reason, Arnold prefers what Gerard Manley Hopkins has called 'Parnassian' poets in the schoolroom, those that offer uplifting sentiments and moral reflection. By the study of such verse even young Coketowners may be a little ennobled.

Yet the constraints of the educational system, which Arnold found himself superintending, were such as to minimize the spiritual and moral experience of poetry. In the first place, as Arnold frequently pointed out, elementary scholars left school at 13 which was the same age at which public schoolboys commenced their education. Secondly, Arnold was faced with administering the Revised Code, which was introduced to the education service by Robert Lowe, the Vice-President to the Department, in 1862. The Code set out the method by which children were to be tested in school to determine the educational efficiency of the institution. The schoolmaster's salary was determined partly by the grant awarded to each school, and this grant was calculated by a weighting of attendance and examination performances in a ratio of one to two. Consequently, the method was known as 'payment by results' and the schoolmaster was forced to consult his own interest by making the annual examination visit of an H.M.I. the focal point and goal of the year's work. There were seven 'Standards' with children of 7 years of age in Standard I and those of 13 years in Standard VII. There was a prescribed syllabus in English and arithmetic and also a number of optional subjects such as geography. Children from all grades were examined in all subjects by persistent questioning from the Inspector.

As always in an educational system designed to serve terminal examinations, the adoption of the Revised Code necessitated that the content of education should be restricted to that which was testable. The results looked for by the Inspectors were correct answers to questions of fact and the memorization of much detailed information. In literature, this meant that, in addition to material being learned by heart, children were required to answer questions about poems and, inevitably, these were mainly concerned with the definition of words in the text. Such a method, of course, lay no stress upon the *experience* of literature, because it was not possible to examine how far a poem had taken hold of the imagination of a child. There was little that was obviously civilizing or ennobling in the poetry lesson which consisted of the uniform chanting of the prescribed passage by pupils, who were warned that they must get it by heart if they were to please the Inspector.

The official requirements in English for each Standard were set down in the Code. 'Literature' does not appear as a heading, but there were literary elements in 'English'. Each child was required in his English examination to pass tests in reading, writing and speaking. The Standard I requirements were:

> *Reading.* To read (aloud) a short paragraph from a book not confined to words of one syllable.
> *Writing.* Copy in manuscript characters a line of print, and write from dictation not more than ten easy words, commencing with capital letters. Copy books (large of half text hand) to be shown.
> *English.* To repeat 20 lines of simple verse.[14]

Those for the twelve-year-old children of Standard VI (Jemima and Benjamin Bitzer's group) were:

> *Reading.* To read a passage (aloud) from one of Shakespeare's historical plays, or from some other standard author, or from a History of England.
> *Writing.* A short theme or letter on an easy subject: spelling, hand-writing, and composition to be considered. Copy books to be shown.
> *English.* To recite 150 lines from Shakespeare or Milton, or some other standard author, and to explain the words and allusions. To parse and analyse a short complex sentence, and to know the meaning and use of Latin prefixes in the formation of English words.

It will be seen that the main literary component of these studies was to learn lines of poetry by heart. If we total the twenty lines to be learned by a Standard I child with all those he was required to learn right up to Standard VII, we discover that he had to learn 600 lines of poetry with all the meanings of all the hard words, if he was to satisfy the Inspectors and 'pass

out' successfully from elementary school. Literature was a 600
pl (poetry line) engine in the education of the working classes.

The business of teaching and testing poetry as allowed for in
the Code was very much at odds with Arnold's grand
conception of the educative rôle of the subject and yet,
curiously, he proposed few amendments to the teaching
methods employed. Of the nineteen reports written between
the years 1852 and 1882, only six refer to literature at all, and
only one of these, the *Report for 1880*, considers literary
education at any length. Observations on the aims and objects
of literature teaching are merely scattered at random throughout the earlier reports. In the *Report for 1852* he repeats his view
that a study of English literature will tend to 'elevate and
humanize' young pupil-teachers who he seems to consider
badly need such treatment. In 1861 he recommends that the
exercise of learning passages by heart is especially valuable to
the young teacher and far more so than learning 'the rules of
good taste directly'.[15] (He does not stoop to defining these
rules.) In the *Report for 1874* he declares that the learning of
vocabulary is an especially useful activity and that in examining a school of some seventy children in poetry, he could not
find one scholar who was able to define the word 'feeble'. The
implication here is that poetry is valuable material for the
provision of hard words which the scholars may be set to learn.

The *Report for 1880* begins with the observation that Arnold
has found poetry to be by far the most popular subject in
school (though one may suspect that his method of sampling
pupil opinion may have helped to elicit this response).
Nevertheless, Arnold goes on to admit the inadequacy of the
approach to literary education which is: 'in plain truth the
learning by heart and reciting of a hundred lines or two of
standard English poetry'.[16] Yet he defends the memorizing
exercise strongly as the only one which 'cannot be spoiled by
pedantry and injudiciousness' on the part of the master. What
he seems to believe is that memorized poetry becomes a
permanent possession of the pupil and one which may be
activated by a trick of memory at any time in his adult life. In
this sense, he seems to believe that poetry committed to
memory may operate unconsciously and may provide moral
intuitions which inform the behaviour of the individual.

Characteristically, Arnold calls upon Wordsworth to justify the teaching of poetry by quoting his words: 'To be incapable of a feeling for poetry, in my sense of the word, is to be without love of human nature and reverence for God.' When we consider the vast number of human beings who manifest no particular interest in poetry, the quotation is rendered false to experience, unless we admit that the phrase 'in my sense of the word' allows of an interpretation of the word 'poetry' so all-embracing as to make the sentiment meaningless. Unfortunately, it is just this kind of talk which Arnold admired and imitated in such essays as *On Translating Homer*. It is especially unsuitable in educational discussion because it employs that most anti-educational of all devices—the argument from authority.

Arnold quotes Wordsworth's words as self-evidently true *because Wordsworth said them*. The argument put forward is as follows: 'If you love poetry you will revere Wordsworth. What Wordsworth writes is the work of a profound poetic insight and is, therefore, true. Wordsworth testifies to the value of poetry. Therefore you should love poetry.' Such an argument is not only circular but also inconclusive. It may be summed as 'If you love poetry then you will love poetry.' But the surly student-teacher whose imagination is better taken with engineering and the new steam locomotives might well reply that he still has not heard an argument as to why he *should* love poetry. In practice, very few student-teachers were prepared to admit to Inspector Arnold that they did not like poetry and *therefore* were without love of God or their fellow human beings. They might not have passed the examination had they done so.

Arnold's literary criticism is 'at bottom' authoritarian. It eschews analysis and argument for examples derived from the words of poets whom he regards as seers. His own worst prose combines wish-fulfilment with a sort of solemn noise:

> Good poetry does undoubtedly tend to form the soul and character; it tends to beget a love of beauty and truth in alliance together, it suggests, however indirectly, high and noble principles of action, and it inspires the emotion so helpful in making principles operative.[17]

The revealing features here are the hesitancies ('does undoubtedly', 'tend', 'tends to', 'beget', 'suggests', 'indirectly'), the indefinables ('*good* poetry', 'soul', 'character', 'beauty', 'truth') and the vagueness of phraseology ('inspires the emotions'). If we attempted to apply a test once in favour among the logical positivists, and asked how we might seek to negate this statement, we should find no answer, for its meaning, if it has any, is not sufficiently clear. Eliot declared with justice that 'In philosophy and theology he [Arnold] was an undergraduate....'[18]

The *Report* is more concerned with the practical than the theoretical issues of English teaching and Arnold has some words of advice on the choice of poetry to be memorized. It might be supposed that the fastidious author of *Essays in Criticism* would have a valuable contribution to make here, especially in the choice of 'some other standard author' than Shakespeare or Milton, permitted by the words of the Code. In fact he recommends the poetry of Mrs. Hemans, author of *The Graves of a Household, The Homes of England, Casabianca* ('The boy stood on the burning deck') and many other pieces of sentimental rhetoric. He argues that the poems have 'real merits of expression and sentiment' so that the children could feel them while committting them to memory. Presumably he felt that 'real' poetry, i.e. Shakespeare, Milton, or those poets which are the subject of his critical writing, were intellectually beyond the scholars of elementary schools. At least Mrs. Hemans was pious and moral and, above all, easy. She also presented sufficient 'poetic' words such as 'steed' and 'ford' to keep the scholars busy.

All this will no doubt come as a disappointment to the reader of Arnold's criticism who comes to his educational writings with a sense of excited expectation. The 'great engine' turns out to be a bit of old-fashioned clockwork. His recommended authors turn out to be crass. Nowhere does he sense the possibility of reading novels with advantage in the classroom. He has no suggestions for drama work and does not anticipate discussion in the classroom. Most serious of all is the fact that he nowhere anticipates that the pupil will want to bring his experiences of life into the articulated language of the classroom. The pupil, for Arnold, is there to be talked at like some memory machine.

Yet Arnold's wider critical writing is, very properly, the

dimension of much discussion on the nature of English in schools. A key book on the teaching of English in schools in a later generation is *English for the English* (1921), and its author, George Sampson, is quite clearly a disciple of Arnold in much that he writes. In the first place, Arnold is always humane in attitude to the pupils and this itself is a considerable factor in the linguistic matter of the way people talk to each other in the classroom. Secondly, it was Arnold himself who developed the notion of criticism as a 'free play of the mind' on objects looked at truly. If he himself did not grasp that this concept was capable of development in a humble way, even with working-class children, then others, such as Sampson, did. Thirdly, it was Arnold, in his splendid essay on Wordsworth (1888), who grandly identified the primary topic of all literature, and all criticism, and therefore of all English teaching:

> The question *how to live*, is itself a moral idea; and it is the question which most interests every man, and with which, in some way or other, he is perpetually occupied. A large sense is of course to be given to the term *moral*. Whatever bears upon the question 'how to live', comes under it.[19]

It is, perhaps, understandable, that Arnold should not have grasped the significance of his own ideas for English in the schools. He was a gentleman, to whom the working-class pupils of the elementary schools, whatever his kindness of feeling towards them, were essentially to be regarded as different creatures from himself. George Sampson, by contrast, spent his earlier life as a teacher in Poplar and Rotherhithe and had a much greater insight into the potential and aspirations of working-class pupils and parents. Then again, we might agree that the constraints upon English teaching in Arnold's own day were such that it is understandable that he did not envisage the developments in the English curriculum of later years. Classes of sixty pupils did not permit of much discussion or of drama. There was no money to buy sets of Dickens or other popular novelists. Many of the pupils were ill-fed and ill-clothed from desperately poor homes, with little sanitation, comfort or culture. The teachers were overworked and obliged to limit truly creative work by the pressures of the 'payment by results' system. Discussion, story-telling, play-acting, were just a waste of time for many of them.

We may prefer to take the view that Arnold's limitations as a writer on the teaching of English derive 'at bottom' from the fact that he expected little more of the working classes than a dutiful appreciation of their relatively humble place in the new democratic England. True culture was not for them, but shreds of Mrs. Hemans sounding in their ears would keep them on the right path.

That Arnold's pedagogic attitude is fundamentally élitist is to be expected from his technique of judging passages of poetry by comparison with certain 'touchstones'. These are choice but brief extracts from the works of Homer, Dante, Shakespeare and Milton, comparison with which Arnold employs to test the value of the work of other poets. With reference to his touchstone lines he declares that

> If we are thoroughly penetrated by their power, we shall find that we have acquired a sense enabling us, whatever poetry may be laid before us, to feel the degree in which a high poetical quality is present or wanting there.[20]

The touchstone technique is implicit in that it eschews any attempt to give reasons why one passage is held to be better or worse than another. Arnold's method depends upon flattering the reader so as to draw him into a critical coterie. What reader would deny that he has been 'thoroughly penetrated by the power of the poetry'? Once having assented to the description of himself, however, he will find that Arnold is then able to predict his responses ('we shall find'), and make his conclusions for him.

Crucial to Arnold's critical technique is his employment of the word 'we', by which he apparently admits his reader to an exclusive critical circle. The pronoun includes him among Balliol men, that community of civilized beings who, through an education in classical languages and literature, have experience of the best that has been thought and said, and are thus able to weigh the true worth of contemporary life and literature. To disagree with Arnold is always a risky thing. It involves the reader admitting that he has *not* been thoroughly penetrated by the power of a poem, or that he does *not* have a love of his fellow human beings and a reverence for God.

Arnold's social and educational attitudes are equally authoritarian. In his writings on education, Arnold welcomes the reader as a fellow Balliol man, with the same attitudes as himself, and puts his suggestions to his listener with a tone of sweet reasonableness. 'Look', he seems to say, 'These children will soon possess much power in the land and, therefore, must be civilized. How shall we do this? They cannot understand the classical languages and literature and barely anything of the superior literature of their own language. Let us provide them with a knowledge of some simple, moralistic verses which they may use as touchstones in making judgements in their own humble lives. If we do so efficiently, they will become a little more like us and, therefore, less of a threat to us.'

This, then, was Arnold's way with literature in the classroom—to provide the children with something bequeathed to them by posterity and which they could keep for ever in the vaults of memory. It was a concept which was very influential in English teaching for the next hundred years. A seminar of English and American educators met in Dartmouth, New England, in 1966 and agreed that there were three principle models for the teaching of the subject to be found in both countries:

> The first centred on *skills*; it fitted an era when initial literacy was the prime demand. The second stressed the *cultural heritage*, the need for civilizing and socially unifying content. The third (and current) model focuses on *personal growth*; on the need to re-examine the learning processes and the meaning to the individual of what he is doing in English lessons.[21]

The skills model identified here is, of course, the vestiges of the old payment by results system. Teachers aiming to improve their pupils' skills have largely restricted their activities to such things as spelling tests, punctuation, dictation and anything else which is thought to give a measurable indication of language competence.

Arnold's influence is still at work in the cultural heritage model. The chief emphasis of such teaching is placed on the experience of the child in reading literary 'classics'. The commonest metaphor employed by writers of this school has been that of inheritance; whole series of books for children were presented as items from a 'heritage', and Arnold's metaphor of the touchstone, which was taken from the techniques of gold assaying, was picked up in numerous references to silver and gold and treasuries, all of which were to be inherited by the reader on turning the pages.

The chief inadequacy of the inheritance model was that it left the pupil with nothing to do but passively receive his treasury of literature with gratitude. George Sampson was probably the first to grasp the significance for teachers of Arnold's heritage view, but found it necessary to develop a range of activities for the pupil, such as writing stories and even visiting theatres, which gave him a greater hold upon the treasure and occasionally, in a small way, an opportunity to add to the hoard, with a few coins from his own experience. Sampson also argued that the treasure might be spread among the nation as a whole. Arnold never expected that literature could be anything but a minority culture, but Sampson pointed out that it had never been a matter of investigation whether all pupils might benefit from contact with fine literature:

> No attempt has ever yet been made to give the whole English people a humane, creative education in and through the treasures of their own language and literature. The great educational reform now needed is to begin that universal education.[22]

Yet even Sampson's approach was, like Arnold's, élitist. It tacitly discounted the experience of the pupil in his own life as part of the necessary relationship between an active reader and the text. Neither of these well-meaning men considered, for one moment, that the stammering pupils in front of them had anything worth saying on their own account and experiences which were just as valid subjects for literature as those of their social betters. Because Arnold was such a profound classicist, he tended to overvalue the past at the expense of the present. The literature he wished to be presented to the pupil was of something already achieved. The over-emphasis upon touchstones from classical literature persuades the reader to observe, compare and then go away and do nothing.

The assumption of Arnold's educational writing is that his elementary pupils have no culture of their own. The *Reports* make no suggestions for getting the children to write or speak their own stories or poems. Such a dismissal of the possibility of working-class culture brought about a profound rejection in the methods employed by certain 'radical' English teachers in the 1970s. They were seeking:

> to move away from literature into classroom dicussion of social issues and the children's environment. Their unwillingness to teach literature stems mainly from their convictions about the richness of working-class culture.[23]

For such teachers, the cultural inheritance was both a symbol of bourgeois dominance of culture and also of the over-valuation of the past at the expense of contemporary experience. Such attitudes mark a final dethronement of Arnold's doctrine. The mighty engine of literature is to be dismantled. It was pointing the wrong way all the time.

But this history was not guessed at in that Coketown schoolroom on a winter's morning in 1864, and the present reader will want to know how the examinations went. Benjamin Bitzer passed, of course. He not only knew what a 'fane' was, but he could also define a 'ford'. He was clearly ready to pass into Standard VII where he would be required to recite next year for Mr. Arnold 150 lines from Shakespeare or Milton or some other standard author (Mrs. Hemans was already selected again), and to explain the words and allusions, as well as analyse the sentences and to develop an encyclopaedic knowledge of prefixes and suffixes.

Jemima failed. She broke down three times while trying to remember the fifth verse of *The Homes of England* and she could not define a 'steed'. At first she was rather castdown while walking home, but as she approached the horse-riding, she brightened when she heard Merrylegs neighing for his supper.

Mr. Matthew Arnold, H.M.I. left Mr. McCheerumchild to lock the schoolroom and walked the few paces to his lodgings at 1 Brigg Row, Coketown, while meditating how to live. It was raining again and the wind blew smuts in his face. That night, Mrs. Collard, his landlady, served him a supper of boiled cabbage and fatty mutton which he was obliged to wash down with two cups of milky tea. He sighed with relief when he stretched in front of the fire in his slippers. For a moment or two he gazed abstractedly into the flames, then, with the doggedness of an habitual writer, he reached into his pocket, produced a notebook, and began to scribble observations for his new essay on *The Function of Criticism at the Present Time*.

NOTES

1. Readers unfamiliar with Coketown School should consult the first two chapters of *Hard Times* by Charles Dickens (1854).
2. 'The Homes of England' by Mrs. Hemans is reprinted in *Parlour Poetry*, selected and introduced by Michael R. Turner (Pan Books, 1969). The opening line of the poem is 'The stately homes of England' and was, of course, pirated by Noel Coward.
3. See Herbert W. Paul, *Matthew Arnold* (Macmillan, 1902), pp. 30–1.
4. See P. J. Keating (ed.), *Matthew Arnold: Selected Prose* (Penguin, 1970), pp. 415–16.
5. Ibid., p. 416.
6. Letter to his sister, afterwards Mrs. Forster, in Keating, op. cit., 407–8.
7. See *Culture and Anarchy* (1869). reprinted in Keating, pp. 407–8.
8. *The Function of Criticism at the Present Time* (1865), in Keating 146–47.
9. See The 'General Report for 1871' in Sir Francis Sandford (ed.), *Reports on Elementary Schools 1852–1882* (MacMillan, 1889), p. 157.
10. *The Study of Poetry* (1888), in Keating, p. 340.
11. See the letter to A. H. Clough (1848–49) in Keating, p. 411.
12. See T. S. Eliot, *The Use of Poetry and the Use of Criticism* (Faber & Faber, 1933), p. 118.
13. *On Translating Homer* (1861) (Everyman Edition, 1907), p. 248.
14. See George Sampson, *English for the English* (1921; Cambridge University Press, 1970), pp. 36–8.
15. Sandford, op. cit., p. 94.
16. Ibid., p. 225.
17. Ibid., p. 226.
18. Eliot, op. cit., p. 105.
19. *Wordsworth*, in Keating, p. 375.
20. *The Study of Poetry*, in Keating, p. 349.
21. See John Dixon, *Growth Through English* (1967), N.A.T.F.H.E., p. 1.
22. See David Shayer, *The Teaching of English in Schools 1900–1970* (Routledge & Kegan Paul, 1972), p. 77.
23. See Margaret Mathieson, 'The Ideology of English Teaching', in *Education for Teaching*, Autumn, 1975.

2

Reading the Signs of the Times: Some Functions of Criticism—Arnold and Ruskin

by CHARLES SWANN

1

There is so much inviting us!—what are we to take? what will
nourish us in the growth towards perfection? That is the
question which, with the immense field of life and of literature
lying before him, the critic has to answer; for himself first, and
afterwards for others.

> *The demand for perfection is always a sign of a misunderstanding of
> the claims of art.*[1]

On 29 October 1864, Matthew Arnold lectured on 'The
Functions of Criticism' as Oxford Professor of Poetry. That
lecture was to become (losing an 's' on the way) the keynote
essay of *Essays in Criticism* (February 1865) after having
appeared in the *National Review* for November 1864 (and
receiving a notable rebuke from Fitzjames Stephen in the
Saturday Review). On 6 December 1864, Ruskin gave his lecture
'Of Kings' Treasuries' in Rusholme Town Hall near Manchester as—professor of things in general is perhaps the best
title (to recall the subtitle of Vol. III of *Modern Painters*—'Of

44

Many Things'—and to borrow Carlyle's description of Teufelsdröckh). He was speaking in aid of a fund to establish a public library. It was to become the first part of his best-seller (160,000 copies by 1905), *Sesame and Lilies* (June 1865). That work had a particular importance for Ruskin: it was the first volume of the 'collected edition' (1871–80) which attempted to bring together those works which Ruskin thought still valid and valuable—an argument he makes in the preface to that edition. The *Saturday Review* did not care for *Sesame and Lilies* any more than it had for Arnold's essay, though it felt the need to preface its attack with a reservation which almost seems to suggest that some of Arnold's points had been taken:

> The smug complacency which is continually dinning into our ears the perfection of our institutions, our matchless political wisdom, our boundless material prosperity, our profound social contentment, is both puerile and revolting. Of all tasks, that of habitually flattering national vanity is the meanest as well as the most injurious.

But the *Saturday* is recoiling the better to strike:

> But more hateful than an egregious conceit of one's nation is an egregious conceit of one's own private cleverness and goodness, combined with a rancorous disparagement of all the rest of mankind. . . .
>
> For some entirely inscrutable reason, . . . Mr. Ruskin has called his book *Sesame and Lilies, or Kings' Treasuries and Queens' Gardens*. Perhaps a more appropriate title for such a farrago would have been *Thistles and Sea Apples, or Fools' Paradises and Wise Men's Purgatories*. (15 July 1865, pp. 83, 85)

Arnold's tone was more urbane but his attitude was much the same as his dismissal of Ruskin's Shakespearian etymologies in 'The Literary Influence of Academies' shows. But though he rebuked Ruskin in 'The Function of Criticism', though their paths and swords had crossed before (as, for example, in Arnold's submerged references—or debts—to Ruskin in the attempt to define the grand style and in his explicit attack on Ruskin's interpretation of a passage from the *Iliad* in *On Translating Homer*), as far as I can discover there is no evidence that Ruskin had read either of the pieces that were to appear in *Essays in Criticism*. (And as Ruskin was not afraid to name those who had irritated him, one can be fairly confident that he had not when he gave his lecture.)

Yet the essays are, on one level, extraordinarily similar in structure. Both begin from a general discussion of reading, criticism, and literature and valuations of culture, both pivot on a critical reading of and commentary on a text that is, in exemplary fashion, not 'Literature' but from a newspaper— and move on to more general social criticism. Both, in short, imply that literary criticism must lead to cultural/social criticism. But for all these similarities, the essays are radically different in their conceptions of the functions of literary and political criticism. Juxtaposing the two pieces provides an exemplary way of seeing the clashes in Victorian debates about the nature and function of cultural criticism, of pointing to fissures and rifts within what is too often seen as a coherent ideological class position. Both texts were produced in the middle of a decade which saw an intense debate about the function of education—a debate explicitly related to the arguments about where political power was to be located, where there are connections between Lowe's 'Twice-Revised Code' and Disraeli's leap in the dark. The signs of the times remain ambiguous and have to be re-read and re-interpreted.[2] And Ruskin at least saw literature and criticism as anything but pacifying influences. This is to argue against one model of cultural history best set out recently by Terry Eagleton (in *Literary Theory* and, ironically enough, in *his Function of Criticism*):

> As religion progressively ceases to provide the social 'cement', affective values and basic mythologies by which a socially turbulent class-society can be welded together, 'English' is constructed as a subject to carry this ideological burden from the Victorian period onwards. The key figure here is Matthew Arnold, always preternaturally sensitive to the needs of his social class, and engagingly candid about being so. . . . Literature was in several ways a suitable candidate for this ideological enterprise. As a liberal, 'humanizing' pursuit, it could provide a potent antidote to political bigotry and ideological extremism. . . . Literature would rehearse the masses in the habits of pluralistic thought and feeling, persuading them to acknowledge that more than one point of view than theirs existed—namely, that of their masters. It would communicate to them the moral riches of bourgeois civilization,

> impress upon them a reverence for middle-class achievements, and, since reading is an essentially solitary, contemplative activity, curb in them any disruptive tendency to collective political action. (*Literary Theory* (Basil Blackwell: Oxford, 1983), pp. 23–4, 25)

Eagleton may indeed be right about Arnold—though Arnold's strategy, that clubman's tone is dependent as much on exclusion as incorporation. Witness his mistrust of Colenso's effect upon the ignorant and his celebration of Spinoza's tact in writing in the decent obscurity of a learned language. (*'Pas devant les enfants'* might have been the motto of Arnold's academy.) But the suggestion that Arnold is representative evades the fact that it is hard to generalize about the effects of literacy and literature. That the *intended* effect of teaching literature may be as Eagleton argues may be true; that it was the effect one may well doubt. The real history is more complex and contradictory—and Eagleton's statement simply not true:

> From the writings of the later Coleridge, through to Carlyle, Kingsley, Ruskin, Arnold and others, literature is extricated from the arena of Realpolitik and elevated to a realm where, in the words of one Victorian commentator, 'all might meet and expatiate in common. (*The Function of Criticism* (New Left Books: London, 1984), pp. 39–40)

This statement would considerably astonish Arnold—who would be deeply uncomfortable about the company he is made to keep. One function of Arnold's 'Function of Criticism' is precisely to remove criticism from the company of such roughs as Carlyle and Ruskin. The fate of *Unto This Last* and *Munera Pulveris* when first published in magazines hardly suggests that all felt they were expatiating in common—and yet both works are deeply dependent on an idea of the authority of literature.

Reading is not necessarily so passive nor as pacifying as Eagleton seems to imagine—and teaching people to read, to interpret, to, in a word, criticize not necessarily so mystifying as he suggests it was felt to be by the Victorians:

> The nineteenth century man of letters must suffer the blurring and troubling of this reasonably precise boundary. [That between literacy and illiteracy.] What is now most problematic

47

is not illiteracy which is after all a sort of absolute, determinable condition, but those who, while well able to read, are not quite able to 'read'—those who, capable of reading in a physiological and psychological but not culturally valorized sense, threaten to deconstruct the fixed opposition between 'influential persons' and 'multitude'. (*The Function of Criticism*, pp. 51–2)

Now it was precisely part of the debate about the twice-revised code that literacy was not felt to be a simple objective thing to define—or rather literacy is always a matter of cultural and political definition. There was a real problem in defining what it meant for a school-child to read 'fairly' or 'well'. The Commissioners demanded not only that a child read '*without conscious difficulty*' but that he or she should read '*in an intelligent manner*'—which meant, among other things, '*to read the Bible with intelligence*' (no small accomplishment!). They went further: a ten-year-old should be able to read the '*newspaper with sufficient ease to be a pleasure to himself and convey information to listeners*'. Again, this is no small accomplishment (and, interestingly, it gets us away from the idea of the reader as passive consumer, alone in a world of his own). These quotations (italicized in the original) come from Arnold's article on the twice-revised code (2,222). The fact that Arnold offers another definition of literacy further reinforces the point that literacy is not a mere physiological or psychological phenomenon.

Ruskin sees that diffusing masterpieces may have other consequences more problematic and potentially explosive than those intended. In 'Traffic', delivered in the Town Hall, Bradford in April 1864, he wrote thus:

What we *like* determines what we *are*, and is the sign of what we are; and to teach taste is inevitably to form character. As I was thinking over this, in walking up Fleet Street the other day, my eye caught the title of a book standing open in a bookseller's window. It was—'On the necessity of diffusion of taste among all classes.' 'Ah,' I thought to myself, 'my classifying friend, when you have diffused your taste, where will your classes be? The man who likes what you like, belongs to the same class with you, I think. Inevitably so. You may put him to other work if you choose; but, by the condition you have brought him into, he will dislike the work as much as you would yourself. You get hold of a scavenger or costermonger, who enjoyed the Newgate Calendar for literature, and "Pop goes the Weasel" for music. You think you can make him like Dante and Beethoven? I wish you joy of your lessons; but if you do, you have made a gentleman of him: he won't like to go back to his coster-mongering.' (XVIII, 436–37)

Ruskin could see the dilemma he got himself into here and it is considerably to his credit that he admitted and explored the contradictions in *Time and Tide*. And in those letters to a working man he had at least to flirt with the idea of a classless society, one in which the division of labour had to be transcended. It was a problem that was to remain with him—as *Fors* so eloquently indicates.

It is strange but true that almost all the books and essays with the function of criticism as their real or implied title take it for granted that *literature*, the written, is what is initially to be criticized. Ruskin's radical originality may well come from his starting-points: art and architecture—things to live with and look at, things to live in and look at.[3] That Ruskin frequently turns art and architecture into texts (even narratives) is true enough. In *The Stones of Venice* it is the idea of reading a building that he insists on—but it is the reading of a collabora-tive activity, not the interpretation of the work of a single consciousness. To 'read' buildings is to think about modes of production, when literature can too easily be conceived of as mere consciousness, criticism of life, reflection on rather than reflection of a social formation. Architecture is patently the product of several hands[4]—and patently involves the invest-ment of time and capital. The material base inevitably presents itself for consideration.

Painting equally declares the importance of its materiality— if only in the differences (say) between oils and water-colours. But more importantly a painting is a *unique* work. It is only a technical problem to get the bible into every household. It is rather more difficult to do the same with a Turner or a Tintoretto. One 'only' needs money and leisure to possess and enjoy one's own copy of Milton. But if one wants to see masterpieces made available to a wider audience, the public gallery (and public ownership) is the only answer with consequent social implications for ideas of ownership—as

Ruskin saw. Otherwise even to see certain paintings demands social position so that one can have access to private houses. It is Ruskin, then, who has the sensibility to entitle a course of lectures *The Political Economy of Art*—and who indicates the tensions involved in valuing works of art by entitling a later edition *'A Joy for Ever': (And Its Price in the Market)*.

I would suggest that Ruskin's sensitivity to the cultural clues provided by the newspaper is a product of his visual sense. There *is* something peculiarly odd about the collage of information that is the page of a newspaper—the movement from column to column should involve radically different responses. In November 1851, Ruskin wrote a letter which points to this awareness of the strange way in which a newspaper pictures the world:

> I was rather struck yesterday by three paragraphs in *Galignani*—in parallel columns—so that the eye ranged from one to the other. The first gave an account of a girl aged twenty-one, being found, after lying exposed all night, and having given birth to a dead child, on the banks of the canal near (Maidstone, I think—but some English county town); the second was the fashions for November, with an elaborate account of satin skirts; and the third, a burning to death of a child—or rather, a dying after burning—because the surgeon, without an order from the parish, would neither go to see it nor send it any medicine. (X, xl)

When Alexander says of this that 'in Victorian times newspaper stories had an almost magical way of arranging themselves in significantly paradoxical groups' (p. 81), one has to insist that similar discrepancies and contradictions can be found in any copy of any newspaper today—and that if we are not sensitive to those tensions, so much the worse for our ability to read critically.[5]

Ruskin's sensitivity to the conditions of production and distribution primarily, but not exclusively, of works of art ought to sensitize us to his concern to indicate that it is not only what is said, but where the statements were first made and how the writing was produced that gives the author his authority. 'Of Kings' Treasuries' was originally *spoken*—a fact to which Ruskin explicitly draws attention, though the very style of the lecture makes this clear enough. The decision to lecture (hopefully in all the great manufacturing centres) was a deliberate part of Ruskin's complex multi-pronged strategy towards his audiences (and a sign that he recognized that there were audiences). It springs from a recognition that there was no homogeneous public (or insofar as there was one, it was limited and limiting—witness the fate of *Unto This Last*)— and that what he had to say gathered force and point in book form from the readers' recognition that this had been spoken to a possibly hostile audience. 'Traffic' gains much of its authority from the fact that we know that it was delivered to the merchants of Bradford. 'War' was 'delivered at the Royal Military Academy, Woolwich'—and is a classic example of this tactic. Part of its force lies precisely in the fact that Ruskin has spoken directly to those whose trade is war—and to their mothers and sisters who enable war to take place. These are secular sermons—preached to the unconverted. The reader is almost overhearing a debate, or reports back from the battle-front. As Ruskin's letters show, the choice of the lecture was a deliberate and carefully thought out strategy—at once a way of reaching people who might not otherwise be reachable— and a way of seeing how what he said was received—instant feedback (XVI, xxi).[6]

Arnold, however, was speaking to an Oxford audience in terms that Oxford would appreciate. If it is objected that, after all, Arnold lacked a rich and generous father and was employed in a difficult and demanding profession, I would draw attention to the well documented fact that he could spend many an afternoon writing in the deep peace of his club (the Athenaeum as his style, perhaps, suggests) and to the invocation to Oxford and Oxford values which concludes the preface to *Essays in Criticism* (a passage so dark blue as to be nearly purple). More importantly there is the scandalous comment that appeared in, of all places, 'Equality' where he was addressing the Royal Institution:

> I have received a letter from Clerkenwell, in which the writer reproaches me for lecturing about equality at this which he calls 'the most aristocratic and exclusive place out.' I am here because your secretary invited me. But I am glad to treat the subject of equality before such an audience as this. . . . I speak to an audience with a high standard of civilization. If I say that

certain things in certain classes do not come up to a high
standard of civilization, I need not prove how and why they do
not; you will feel instinctively whether they do or no. . . .
Instead of calling this 'the most aristocratic and exclusive place
out,' I conceive of it as a *civilized* place; and in speaking about
civilization half one's labour is saved when one speaks about it
among those who are civilized. (8, 283, 4)

It is a breathtaking passage. Where should one begin? Perhaps
all one needs to do is note that he is there because he accepted
the secretary's invitation, accept that Bradford or Manchester
may have been too far to go—and ask whether Woolwich,
Clerkenwell or Camberwell were really out of reach. It is
easier to preach to the converted. When Arnold did finally
speak to a Working Man's College, the place was Ipswich, the
title was patronizing (did he imagine himself to be St. Paul or
Barnabas?), the message equally so, and the people he seems
to have wanted to impress were, to judge from his letters, not
his audience. When he reprinted it in *Irish Essays*, 'Ecce
Covertimur ad Gentes' was separated from 'A Speech at Eton'
by 'the Future of Liberalism'. It is a nice buffer and, no doubt,
deliberate. It is tempting to say that the first essay in the
volume would as far as the title goes have been more honest and
more suitable: 'The Incompatibles'. It may be complained
that this is unfair—but it is difficult to resist responding in
kind when faced by a writer who is unscrupulous and for all
the surface charm (and valuation of charm) himself quite
ruthless.

2

'You mean, then,' said Miss Merton, 'that a man of the highest
culture is a sort of emotional *bon vivant*?'

'That surely is hardly a fair way—' began Laurence.

'Excuse me, my dear Laurence,' broke in Mr. Luke, in his
most magnificent of manners, 'it is perfectly fair—it is admirably
fair. Emotional *bon vivant!*' he exclaimed. 'I thank Miss Merton
for teaching me that word! for it may remind us all,' Mr. Luke
continued, drawing out his words slowly, as if he liked the taste
of them, how near our view of the matter is to that of a certain
Galilean peasant—of whom Miss Merton has perhaps heard—
who described the highest culture by just the same metaphor,

as a hunger and thirst after righteousness. Our notion of it differs only from his, from the *Zeitgeist* having made it somewhat wider.'[7]

It is hardly surprising that Arnold was not amused by this description of his rhetorical style, but he really has himself largely to blame. Part of the problem with 'The Function of Criticism at the Present Time' is that it is very hard to come up with a definition of what Arnold is up to. (It is noticeable that commentary tends to bypass detailed analysis of the essay and its strategy; it is—apparently—so much something one has read that the critic of criticism or of Arnold is excused from having to describe what it says.) Eliot tried to reformulate the problem by saying that Arnold was a propagandist for criticism rather than a critic, but this then still leaves it open for an unkind reader to ask what kind of criticism is Arnold propagandizing for—and what methods does he use to propagandize? Do they stand up to criticism? It has frequently been pointed out that if we read on from 'The Function of Criticism' to *Culture and Anarchy* we see that we can read 'criticism' as meaning 'culture'—but this is merely to postpone the moment of definition, unless it is felt that 'culture' is adequately defined as being that which works against 'anarchy', that the title of his most famous work should read *Culture VERSUS Anarchy*. There is too much truth in that for comfort, perhaps, but it then leaves culture/criticism with an oddly limited and limiting rôle. The piece must stand or fall by its treatment of Elizabeth Wragg. If criticism's business is to know the best that has been known and thought in the world, if the rule for its course is *disinterestedness*, it is there that the reader should be able to see what Arnold means by those high-sounding if not self-explanatory terms. It might be thought that Adderley's and Roebuck's praise of their constituents (and, by implication, themselves) when detached from the contexts that gave them significance (if not much meaning) sufficiently declared their inanity—or, for a different kind of critic (Carlyle, say) revealed a dangerous weakness in this form of democratic representative government—but Arnold has a different target in view:

'A shocking child murder has just been committed at Nottingham. A girl named Wragg left the workhouse there on

Saturday morning with her young illegitimate child. The child was soon afterwards found dead on Mapperly Hills, having been strangled. Wragg is in custody.'

Nothing but that; but in juxtaposition with the absolute eulogies of Sir Charles Adderley and Mr. Roebuck, how eloquent, how suggestive are those few lines! 'Our old Anglo-Saxon breed, the best in the whole world!'—how much that is harsh and ill-favoured there is in this best! *Wragg!* If we are to talk of ideal perfection, of 'the best in the whole world,' has any one reflected what a touch of grossness in our race, what an original shortcoming in the more delicate spiritual perceptions, is shown by the natural growth amongst us of such hideous names,—Higginbottom, Stiggins, Bugg! In Ionia and Attica they were luckier in this respect than 'the best race in the world;' by the Ilissus there was no Wragg, poor thing! And 'our unrivalled happiness;'—what an element of grimness, bareness, and hideousness mixes with it and blurs it; the workhouse, the dismal Mapperly Hills,—how dismal those who have seen them will remember;—the gloom, the smoke, the cold, the strangled illegitimate child! 'I ask you whether, the world over or in past history, there is anything like it?' Perhaps not, one is inclined to answer; but at any rate, in that case, the world is [not] very much to be pitied. And the final touch,—short, bleak, and inhuman: *Wragg is in custody.* The sex lost in the confusion of our unrivalled happiness; or (shall I say?) the superfluous Christian name lopped off by the straightforward vigour of our old Anglo-Saxon breed! There is profit for the spirit in such contrasts as this; criticism serves the cause of perfection by establishing them. By eluding sterile conflict, by refusing to remain in the sphere where alone narrow and relative conceptions have any worth and validity, criticism may diminish its momentary importance, but only in this way has it a chance of gaining admittance for those wider and more perfect conceptions to which all its duty is really owed. Mr. Roebuck will have a poor opinion of an adversary who replies to his defiant songs of triumph only by murmuring under his breath, *Wragg is in custody* but in no other way will these songs of triumph be induced gradually to moderate themselves, to get rid of what in them in excessive and offensive, and to fall into a softer and truer key. (3, 273–74)

It is a neat right and left that Arnold achieves as he picks off the Tory and Liberal M.P.s—and the very ease with which the feat is accomplished economically suggests that Tory and

Liberal are not so very far apart. But that said is there anything else to say in defence of this famous passage—or should we say notorious? Even if Arnold's own vocabulary is deployed, does the passage stand up? Is Arnold here really attempting to see the object as in itself it really is? Is Arnold's argument adequate? Is this the free play of intelligence—or the tactics of the lower journalism?

It is certainly understandable that the inanely smug declamations of Adderley and Roebuck should get an irritated rebuke—but it is a tactic which can recoil on the critic. Fitzjames Stephen had a point:

> Criticism ought to show that Wragg should have been called (say) Fairfax; and that instead of saying 'Wragg is in custody,' the brutal journalist should have said, 'And so, on that cold November night, the door of Nottingham gaol was shut behind our sinful sister.' . . . To the general public this way of putting it may not seem to make much difference, but Mr. Arnold thinks otherwise. . . We do not envy the higher criticism if it has to go about 'murmuring Wragg is in custody', till all after-dinner speeches rise to the level of ideal beauty. (*Saturday Review*, 3 December 1864, p. 684)

Arnold would not have cared for the style that Stephen pretended to think that Arnold would have felt was appropriate for humane reporting. Nevertheless, Stephen however crudely and roughly makes a valid point. It *is* an odd moment to turn to an assertive aestheticism which only partially conceals a rather nasty class consciousness. Whether the ugliness of English names is really central to any point at issue is rather more than doubtful. (Is it even in good taste? It reads as though it was designed to raise either a smile or a curl of the lip from the original audience.) While the de-sexing, de-humanizing brutality of the report must be deplored, it must be questioned whether there was (except insofar as euphony is relevant) 'no Wragg beside the Ilissus'. Was there no Niobe (say), no Medea?

Here the problem of the shared knowledge of speaker and audience occurs in potentially explosive terms. Why the Ilissus? Byron referred to 'the dry ditch of the Ilissus'—having seen it. And Richard Jenkyns writes that the Ilissus stirred few romantic sentiments in the Athenians themselves; 'their poets never praised it, reserving their eulogies for the more ample river Cephisus.'[8] It looks as though the mention of this insignificant stream is intended to evoke very vaguely a whole set of values—'the grandeur that was Greece' perhaps. But Arnold seems to have forgotten that Clio is not the most unimportant of the Muses. The use of an imaginary past to criticize the self-congratulatory rhetoric of the present is either unscrupulous, unfortunate or a joke in very bad taste indeed. There *is* one piece of Greek literature which is famously set beside the Ilissus—and that is that major dialogue the *Phaedrus*. Since Arnold's reading for the Oriel fellowship included the *Phaedrus* and the *Republic*, one must presume that he knew the work well. The Phaedrus contains an explicit discussion of homo-erotic (if not homosexual) love which caused Jowett some trouble—as well as a celebration of Platonic love. Neither kind of relationship is likely to result in—issue.

We can agree that the climate of Greece is more pleasant than that of the Midlands. And who, in the 1860s, would not agree that factory smoke does not disfigure the Midland landscape? One admits that ancient Greece was not an industrial society. But further one cannot go in accepting Arnold's implied definition of the superiority of the Greek way of life. Arnold had read the *Republic*—where Socrates is quite clear:

> The proper officers will take the offspring of the good parents to the pen or fold, and there they will deposit them with certain nurses who dwell in a separate quarter; but the offspring of the inferior, or of the better when they chance to be deformed, will be put away in some mysterious, unknown place, as they should be. (V, 460, c, Jowett's translation)

And Aristotle may be less ruthless but is equally clear in his *Politics*:

> With regard to the choice between abandoning an infant or rearing it let it be lawful that no cripple child be reared. But since the ordinance of custom forbids the exposure of infants merely in order to reduce numbers, there must be a limit to the production of children. If contrary to these arrangements a copulation takes place and a child is conceived, abortion

56

should be procured before the embryo has acquired life and sensation . . . (Book VII, Ch. 16, J. A. Sinclair's translation)

It can hardly be objected that Plato and Aristotle are only referring to their Utopias. W. E. H. Lecky's learning may have been wide rather than deep—but on this issue at least he is reliable enough, and, writing at much the same time as Arnold he gives an account of what was generally known:

> If we pass to the next stage of human life, that of the new-born infant, we find ourselves in presence of that practice of infanticide which was one of the deepest stains of the ancient civilization. . . . Infanticide, as is well known, was almost universally admitted among the Greeks, being sanctioned, and in some cases enjoined, upon what we should now call 'the greatest happiness principle,' by the ideal legislations of Plato and Aristotle, and by the actual legislations of Lycurgus and Solon. Regarding the community as a whole, they clearly saw that it is in the highest degree for the interests of society that the increase of population should be very jealously restricted, and that the State should be as far as possible free from helpless and unproductive members; and they therefore concluded that the painless destruction of infant life, and especially of those infants who were so deformed or diseased that their lives, if prolonged, would probably have been a burden to themselves, was on the whole a benefit. The very sensual tone of Greek life rendered the modern notion of prolonged continence wholly alien to their thoughts, and the extremely low social and intellectual condition of Greek mothers, who exercised no appreciable influence over the habits of thought of the nation should also, I think, be taken into account, for it has always been observed that mothers are much more distinguished than fathers for their affection for infants that have not yet manifested the first dawning of reason. (*History of European Morals*, 2 Vols., Vol. 2, pp. 26, 27–8, London, 1869)

Lecky may overplay the ancient Greeks as modern utilitarians and underplay the private family element (the fact that, when a child was born, it was a matter for the *father's* decision whether it was to be reared or exposed, for example). But Arnold is hardly suggesting that it is the absence of paternal authority that matters in the case of Elizabeth Wragg any more than he is suggesting that exposure is preferable to strangulation or that she did the right thing from the Greek point of view. What can be seen is that Elizabeth Wragg and her child have been converted into a rhetorical stick to beat Roebuck's after-dinner speech—while at the same time a fictive, unhistorical, aestheticized ancient Greece is being deployed as an ideal (or, rather, idealized) standard. She was a stick he was quite willing to pick up again (in the preface to the first edition) to rap Wright over the knuckles:

> I will not even ask him,—what it almost irresistibly rises to my lips to ask him when I see he writes from Mapperly,—if he can tell me what has become of that poor girl, Wragg? She has been tried, I suppose: I know how merciful a view judges and juries are apt to take of these cases, so I cannot but hope she has got off. But what I should so like to ask is, whether the impression the poor thing made was, in general, satisfactory: did she come up to the right standard as a member of the 'best breed in the whole world?' were her life-experiences an edifying testimony to our 'unrivalled happiness?' did she find Mr. Roebuck's speech a comfort to her in her prison? But I must stop; or my kind monitor, the Guardian . . . will be putting a harsh construction upon my innocent thirst for knowledge, and again taxing me with the unpardonable crime of being amusing. (3, 536–37)

As the *Saturday Review* informed him, she was awaiting trial—and as Super tells us she got twenty years penal servitude. Is it priggish to suggest that this is scarcely a topic to be amusing about, to ask how F. R. Leavis could find Arnold's 'intelligence . . . informed by a mature and delicate sense of the humane values?' Another kind of defence has been mounted by Marcus:

> As writers [the great Victorian critics] were performing one of their quintessential functions: they were taking dead writing and transforming it back into living writing. Or we can say that they were transforming information into a present history whose structure they were simultaneously inventing. The imaginary line that runs from Dr. Alison's Irish widow in Edinburgh to Matthew Arnold's 'Wragg is in custody' may be considered as axial in the intellectual consciousness of the period. It is as close as nineteenth century English critical prose comes to writing or language as praxis.

As Spear says, 'Of Kings' Treasuries' would be a better example. Marcus admits (and well he might) that his conclusion would have been dismaying to Arnold.[9]

Arnold when he writes of Wragg and the Greeks can hardly be said to be attempting to see the object as in itself it really is. Whether the Greek name blinds him to the Greek thing and how far that blindness is unconscious or willed must be matters for speculation: what is clear is that it is indeed 'a very subtle and indirect action' which Arnold is 'thus prescribing for criticism'. Whether it is the 'only' or at all 'the proper work of criticism' seems to be something that needs to be radically questioned. It is open to Roebuck and Adderley to murmur or bawl back at Arnold that we at least condemn infanticide, to suggest that Arnold is hardly arguing—is he? that the poor woman should have been set free or recommending the totalitarianism of the *Republic* where the unwanted child becomes so mysteriously an unperson. The appeal to Greece is either immoral, irresponsible or ignorant. As Arnold himself says of Colenso

> It is unfortunately possible for a man in pursuit of truth to write a book which rests on a false conception. Even the practical consequences of a book are to genuine criticism no recommendation of it, if the book is, in the highest sense, blundering. (3, 278)

Exactly. The most that Arnold seems to aim at is to reform the rhetoric of a couple of M.P.s. The last part of the *Phaedrus* discusses the differences between rhetoric and dialectic. If Plato's definitions and valuations are accepted, Arnold must be defined (and condemned) as a rhetorician. Arnold, by starting from a quotation from *On Translating Homer*, has claimed for himself and for 'The Function of Criticism' the authority of the classicist. We have a choice; either Arnold is to be accused of *suppressio veri* or, at best, his beloved Joubert is to be quoted against him: 'Ignorance, which in matters of morals extenuates the crime, is itself, in intellectual matters, a crime of the first order' (3, 277).

The quotation comes as Arnold reminds us of the sins of Colenso; while claiming virtue for not reprinting his attack, he reminds us of its existence. Where, asks Arnold, shall we find language 'innocent' enough to enable us to tell the practical Englishman that the British Constitution is a colossal machine for the manufacture of Philistines? And he instances Cobbett (deceased 1835), Carlyle's *Latter-Day Pamphlets* (1850) and 'Mr. Ruskin, after his pugnacious political economy' (*Unto This Last* and *Munera Pulveris*, presumably, 1860 and 1862–63) as examples of those who have ruled themselves out of court—because their language was intended to result in action. Given these dates, it looks as though Ruskin is the principal target—though the second part of Arnold's title may be intended to recall and repudiate the first of the *Latter-Day Pamphlets*: 'The Present Time'. That ended in a fashion that must have been abhorrent to Arnold, claiming that there are things that should be *done* not spoken, 'that, till the doing of them is begun, cannot well be spoken'.

'We' (whoever constitutes 'we') must, according to Arnold, turn away from political practice for 'we have pretty well exhausted the benefits of seeing things in this connection.' So we are to 'try a more disinterested mode of seeing things'—and take to the life of the spirit. We must measure things by 'a high and perfect ideal' (an elementary law of criticism, apparently) (3, 284). On 29 October 1863, Arnold wrote to his mother:

> Partly nature, partly time and study have . . . by this time taught me thoroughly the precious truth that everything turns upon one's exercising the power of *persuasion*, of *charm*; that without this all fury, energy, reasoning power, acquirements, are thrown away and only render their owner more miserable. Even in one's ridicule one must preserve a sweetness and good humour.

One is glad to read a sentence or two further on that Lady de Rothschild has given him 'the prettiest little gold pencil in the world'. Still, is not there here a pernicious over-valuation of charm? And is not the same tone revealed again in a letter of 7 December 1864 where Arnold comments on Fitzjames Stephen's attack in the *Saturday Review* and ironically notes that he followed this up by sending Mrs. Stephen to pay a call on Mrs. Arnold (not an easy visit, one would imagine):

> my sinuous, easy, unpolemical mode of proceeding has been adopted by me, first, because I really think it the best way of

proceeding if one wants to get at, and keep with, truth; secondly, because I am convinced only by a literary form of this kind being given to them can ideas such as mine ever gain any access in a country such as ours.

The bland leading the bland into a land of perfection. . . . It sounds unexceptionable to ask 'what will nourish us in growth towards perfection?'—until Ruskin is heard: '*the demand for perfection is always a sign of a misunderstanding of the ends of art*', and remembers that that comes from 'The Nature of Gothic' with its examples of what the demand for 'perfection' has meant for the workman. Perhaps that should be set beside Ernst Fisher's Marxist emphasis in *The Necessity of Art*: '*imperfection is the greatness of man*'—if only as a way of stressing the mutual concern with a dynamic theory of history as opposed to Arnold's nostalgia and desire for stasis.

3

'My dear,' she whispered to Miss Merton, '. . . what a dreadful blowing-up Mr. Herbert gave us last night, didn't he? Now, that, you know, I think is all very well in a sermon, but in a lecture, where the things are supposed to be taken more or less literally, I think it is a little out of place.'

If Arnold disliked the tone of overt controversy, Ruskin attached to it a positive value:

It is to be remembered . . . that many of the subjects handled can be more conveniently handled controversially than directly; . . . and the crystalline vigour of a truth is often best seen in the course of its serene collision with a trembling and dissolving fallacy. (XXXIV, 470–1)

No doubt he also enjoyed a good fight—but Ruskin *had* to be controversial as he disliked so many *idées rescues*. (*Modern Painters*, after all, began as an attempt to defend Turner and modern art against the devaluation that came from an entrenched art establishment with an uncritical respect for the past, as a revolt against the uncritical acceptance of patriarchal authority.) For all the apparent authoritativeness of his authorial stance, he encouraged and desired other voices to join in the controversies he continued or initiated (if very often on his terms). The difficulty is to locate him politically. To suggest that he belongs to the family of Carlylean conservatives is too simple; few Tories of any school write like this to the *Telegraph* (in response to a request for subscriptions to rebuild Warwick Castle):

> Sir, I am at this hour endeavouring to find work and food for a boy of seventeen, one of eight people—two married couples, a woman and her daughter, and this boy and his sister,—who all sleep together in one room, some 18 ft. square, in the heart of London; and you call upon me for a subscription to help rebuild Warwick Castle.
>
> Sir, I am an old and thoroughbred Tory, and as such I say, if a noble family cannot rebuild their own castle, in God's name, let them live in the nearest ditch till they can. (XXXIV, 506–7)

For all Ruskin's insistence on hierarchy on one level of his discourse, on another there is a repeated insistence on the need to dissolve and destroy conventional class structures. Yet to see him as a kind of transforming link between Carlyle and Morris, while comforting for those constructing a 'tradition' (and indeed has its truth), is to ignore the contradictions that Ruskin so deeply explored (and lived)—and, too often, too easily to overvalue Morris. The tension expressed in *Fors* as he tries to come to terms with the Paris commune is perhaps as good an example as any of the tensions and contradictions that he lived through and did not try to resolve into any kind of spurious unity.

Ruskin was in no danger of falling into a Carlylean admiration for Plugson of Undershot; what comes through in *Fors* particularly is a brilliantly presented critique of capitalism—and the way in which it systematically steals from the workers. *Fors* is, of course, addressed to the workmen and labourers of England: Ruskin speaks, as it were, over the heads of the middle classes that were the object of Arnold's tender solicitude. At the same time he notes that he is rebuked for talking over the heads of his hoped-for audience—and responds that to talk down to them is to mystify them and such talk is intended to do just that:

> for my own part, I cannot at all understand why well-educated people should still so habitually speak of you as beneath their

level, and needing to be written down to, with condescending simplicity, as flat-headed creatures of another race, unredeemable by any Darwinism. (XXVII, 182)

As Ruskin goes on to show in his materialist fable of the turnips, he knows perfectly well why the educated have a vested interest in the 'stupidity' of the workers. And he suggests that if the labourers gave critical attention to the language used by and on them 'things might a little unsettle themselves'—a prospect that does not trouble him. When Arnold spoke at a Working-Man's College, he asked 'that workers support the idea of state middle-class schools so the working-class will have "a more civilized middle class—a class to rise into, if they *do* rise" '.[10] Ruskin's preface to the 1871 edition of *Sesame and Lilies* juxtaposed that text with *Fors* and confesses that *Sesame and Lilies* was chiefly addressed to the middle classes and their educational needs. It is not, however, a comforting message.

The point of departure for 'Of Kings' Treasuries' is very precisely an attack on a valuation of education which sees class position as central:

'The education befitting such and such a *station in life*'—this is the phrase, this the object, always . . . [A]n education 'which shall keep a good coat on my son's back;—which shall enable him to ring with confidence the visitors' bell at double-belled doors; which shall result ultimately in establishment of a double-belled door to his own house;—in a word, which shall lead to advancement in life. . . .' (XVIII, 54, 5)

That phrase 'advancement in life' is interrogated until it gives up its (conventional) meaning:

We want to get into good society, not that we may have it, but that we may be seen in it; and our notion of its goodness depends primarily on its conspicuousness. (XVIII, 56)

At this point, Ruskin involves his original audience in the drama by asking their opinion of this definition. It is a moment (however limited or limiting) for them to register their assent or dissent—a deliberate transgression of the rules of this kind of discourse. At the same time, that transgression problematizes the text that is before the reader who is not simply given Ruskin's language transcribed on to the page but also his report and interpretation of the reception of a part of that performance—as he tells us of an audience which does not know the proper thing to do 'being not sure that the lecturer is serious, and, partly, shy of expressing opinion' (XVIII, 57).

An irony of this piece, so delicately poised between the spoken and the written, starts from Ruskin's discussion of the differences between the 'spoken' and the 'written' as he attempts to distinguish between 'books of the hour' and 'books of all time'. The good book of the hour is equivalent to talk and printed only because its author cannot speak to thousands of people at once: the 'volume is mere *multiplication* of voice'. But a book is written, not to

> multiply the voice merely, but to perpetuate it. . . . That is his 'writing'; it is, in his small human way, and with whatever degree of true inspiration is in him, his inscription, or scripture. That is a 'Book.' (XVIII, 61)

This is indeed to privilege the written. Today's readers are, of course, sensitized to this issue by recent debates about phono-centrism and logo-centrism. But Ruskin himself problematizes the issue; the passage in red from the newspapers which makes his indictment of our inability to read the texts set before us is dependent for its force on being *read* rather than heard:

> I will print the paragraph in red. Be sure, the facts themselves are written in that colour, in a book which we shall all of us, literate or illiterate, have to read our page of, some day. (XVIII, 91)

This is to call attention to its status as writing. And in *Fors* (Letter 93, Christmas 1883), Ruskin gave another twist to the problems of reading when he said he had printed the passage thus 'to try if I could catch the eye at least, when I could not the ear or the heart'. And this is further problematized by the fact that the passage could not have been in the original since it was not published until Spring 1865. Ruskin misdates it as 1867 in the edition of 1871—but this only reinforces the teasing tension between the speakable and the writable—as the title page tells the reader that the lectures were 'delivered at Manchester in 1864'. The original performance is lost to us—and, even with the scrupulous research of Cook and Wedderburn, there is no way to recover it. The reader is left with a problem: what authority does this text claim over us—the spoken or the written?

Ruskin, after soothing his audience with a few bromides about the advantages of being able to be in the presence of the immortal great whenever we pick up a great book, pulls the mat from under our feet again. If these constitute 'high society', then 'advancement in life' must mean something very different. To have access to high society is in no sense dependent on class position: 'this court of the past differs from all living aristocracy in this:—it is open to labour and to merit, but to nothing else' (XVIII, 62). Real reading, for Ruskin, is in no sense a passive reception of great thoughts but a creative struggle with the text to discover its difficult, hidden meaning. This alertness that comes from the struggle to interpret carefully is crucial for an unexamined language is potentially mystifying. It is only too available to a class or interest to mask the truth from us. Ruskin points to the power of an unexamined language to, as it were, 'think' us unless we remain alert:

> There are masked words droning and skulking about us in Europe just now. . . . There never were creatures of prey so mischievous, never diplomatists so cunning, never poisoners so deadly, as these masked words; they are the unjust stewards of all men's ideas: whatever fancy or favourite instinct a man most cherishes, he gives to his favourite masked word to take care of for him; the word at last comes to have an infinite power over him,—you cannot get at him but by its ministry. (XVIII, 66)

It is here that we can see why etymology is so central to Ruskin (even if Arnold found that obsession absurd); to give a word a history and context is to discover more about its meanings, is to demystify it, to see how far it operates as unexamined, unrecognized metaphor, to see how far myth is a disease of language. It is at this point he selects a part of a text that he thinks his audience will know and offers an exemplary reading: Milton's *Lycidas*. That reading exists on at least two levels simultaneously. On the first we have the interpretation of what and why Milton wrote—and the unpacking of the meaning of 'blind mouths' is an example of Ruskin's critical intelligence. But at the same time there is an emphasis on the relevance of the issues to contemporary society. What *Lycidas* meant (to Milton) and what it means (to us) necessarily coexist, and there is a constant dialectical interplay between the two levels as the struggle to interpret is enacted in an attempt to show the strangeness of Milton—and his authority as author.

After this we are moved into a too quick, too sweeping indictment of virtually the whole culture; we despise literature, science, Art, and Nature—and telling instances are given in each case. We also despise compassion—and we are given an instance. Or rather, the whole thing might have been so quick as to be simplistic, if it were not for this instance—the famous passage printed in red which deals in matter-of-fact painful detail with the suffering and degradation of the exploited poor. It was in response to Ruskin's horror at this that the *Saturday Review* revealed its cruel coarseness—and the need for the kind of education in reading the signs of the times that Ruskin was trying to provide:

> Our Christianity only helps us to commit crimes, 'for we revel and luxuriate in our faith for the lewd sensation of it, dressing it up, like everything else, in fiction.' All this, and much more, is 'proved' by an extract from a newspaper describing the inquest upon a man who recently died of starvation rather than go into the workhouse. If a nation did not despise compassion, 'such a newspaper would be as impossible in a Christian country as a deliberate assassination permitted in the public streets.' 'If we were but unwholesomely un-Christian, it would be impossible.' . . . The inference is marvellous. A man chooses to die at home rather than live in the workhouse which is open to him. . . . We make our relief, it is said, insulting and painful. Precisely. A man is perfectly justified in marrying, as this poor wretch had done, in producing a large family . . . and then in demanding relief on his own terms. It must not be painful to him. Immense care must be taken not to hurt his feelings. Every temptation that can be thought of must be offered to induce him to consent to accept life at our hands. Every encouragement that can be devised must be thrust before the unthrifty and the improvident. They are to be told that the thrifty and the industrious and the provident shall be taxed abundantly so that they may enjoy warm rooms and fine food and good clothes, and every attention be paid to their delicate feelings. This is the bran-new

conception of Justice which is to renovate society, to breed diligent workers and contented citizens, and to make of our at present accursed country a land flowing with milk and honey. (15 July 1865, 83–4)

Here is proof enough that compassion is despised—not that that would be any comfort to Ruskin. It is an extraordinary failure to read the text put before the reader—or rather, it is a misreading. Ruskin had answered the question as to why the workhouse had been refused:

> Well, the poor seem to have a prejudice against the workhouse which the rich have not; for of course everyone who takes a pension from Government goes into the workhouse on a grand scale: only the workhouses for the rich do not involve the idea of work, and should be called play-houses. (XVIII, 94)

And so had the transcript of the case:

> Coroner: 'It seems to be deplorable that you did not go into the workhouse.' Witness: 'We wanted the comforts of our little home.' A juror asked what the comforts were, for he saw only a little straw in the corner of the room, the windows of which were broken. The witness began to cry, and said that they had a quilt and other little things. The deceased said he never would go into the workhouse. (XVIII, 92)

Our Mutual Friend appeared between May 1864 and November 1865 and offers remarkable parallel to Ruskin's outrage in the case of Betty Higden's fear of the workhouse:

> when we have got things to the pass that with an enormous treasure at disposal to relieve the poor, the best of the poor detest our mercies, hide their heads from us, and shame us by starving to death in the midst of us, it is a pass impossible of prosperity, impossible of continuance. It may not be so written in the Gospel according to Podsnappery; you may not 'find these words' for the text of a sermon, in the Returns of the Board of Trade; but they have been the truth since the foundations of the universe were laid, and they will be the truth until the foundations of the universe are shaken by the Builder. This boastful handiwork of ours, which fails in its terrors for the professional pauper, the sturdy breaker of windows and the rampant tearer of clothes, strikes with a cruel and a wicked stab at the stricken sufferer, and is a horror to the deserving and unfortunate. We must mend it, lords and gentlemen and

honourable boards, or in its own evil hour it will mar every one of us. (Book III, Ch. VIII)

For anyone who believes Bounderby or Podsnap to be unreal caricatures, a reading of the *Saturday Review* (high-class journalism, remember) provides a satisfactory cure.[11]

However, though Betty Higden's situation is deeply painful, she gets the death she wants and dies in the arms of Lizzie Hexam, who 'very softly raised the weather-stained grey head, and lifted her as high as Heaven'. However much Dickens warns the reader against social chaos, the reader gets a happy ending. What worries Ruskin is that one of the tragedies of the present state of affairs is that happy endings in fiction may blind us to the absence of them in life. It is one of the tragedies of the present state of affairs that the values of art and literature (and indeed human creativity in general) become deeply problematic. It is not only that religion may become a kind of aesthetic experience, a dramatic fiction, but that the enjoyment of fiction may take up the ethical energies that should inform political life. (And it is this concern that may go some way towards explaining Ruskin's invective against Dickens in *Fiction, Fair and Foul*.)

> The justice we do not execute, we mimic in the novel and on the stage; for the beauty we destroy in nature, we substitute the metamorphosis of the pantomime, and (the human nature of us imperatively requiring awe and sorrow of *some* kind) for the noble grief we should have borne with our fellows, and the pure tears we should have wept with them, we gloat over the pathos of the police court, and gather the night-dew of the grave. (XVIII, 97)

Ruskin is faced with a contradiction he cannot resolve; at least, as critic, he has pointed to the contradictions and placed them before his audience. Justice is to be found only in fiction: the police court is only a fiction of justice.

4

'I've been writing a little cat's paw bit about Wordsworth which, Joanie says, hits too hard. But Matthew Arnold has been sticking him up—out of all bounds' (XXXVII, 320). Their swords and paths were to cross many times before

Arnold's death, but the clash that reveals most clearly their different conceptions of the right functions of criticism comes in Ruskin's response in *Fiction, Fair and Foul* (1880, 1) to Arnold's preface to his selection of Wordsworth's poems (1879). Arnold leans yet again on his earlier work, silently lifting five lines from 'The Function of Criticism'. Here too is Roebuck again, here too another quotation from 'Equality'. And here are some of the claims for Wordsworth:

> taking the roll of our chief poetical names, besides Shakespeare and Milton, from the age of Elizabeth downwards, and going through it,—Spenser, Dryden, Pope, Gray, Goldsmith, Cowper, Burns, Coleridge, Scott, Campbell, Moore, Byron, Shelley, Keats (I mention only those who are dead),—I think it certain that Wordsworth's name deserves to stand, and will finally stand, above them all. (9, 40–1)

There is a slight taint of the exam-list here (with Shakespeare and Milton getting starred Firsts). And did not—say—Herbert and Blake (both known by Ruskin) not present themselves for examination? But let that pass. Arnold has a serious claim to press: 'Where, then, is Wordsworth's superiority? It is here: he deals with more of *life* than they do; he deals with *life*, as a whole, more powerfully' (9, 48). Though Arnold speaks centrally as judicial critic, separating the immortal wheat from the chaff, he also writes as a Wordsworthian:

> I can read with pleasure and edification *Peter Bell*, and the whole series of *Ecclesiastical Sonnets*, and the address to Mr. Wilkinson's spade, and even the *Thanksgiving Ode*:—everything of Wordsworth, I think, except *Vaudracour and Julia*. (9, 55)

Ruskin's response is two-fold—and, as he insists, it comes from a paid-up Wordsworthian (who placed a quotation from Wordsworth on the title-page of all five volumes of *Modern Painters*). First, he argues that (to use Arnold's terms) Wordsworth is simply not adequate, does not give us enough of *life* to be considered as great a poet as Scott or Burns or Byron; the value of Wordsworth's 'lacustrine seclusion' has been to arrive at 'many valuable principles of philosophy' as pure as the tarns of his mountains—and 'of corresponding depth'. Just in case we have missed the point, Ruskin adds a dead-pan footnote: 'I have been greatly disappointed, in taking soundings of our most majestic mountain pools, to find them, in no case, verge on the unfathomable.' What outrages Ruskin is Wordsworth's turning away from the significant history and experience of his epoch:

> So it was year by year, among the unthought-of hills. Little Duddon and child Rotha ran clear and glad; and laughed from ledge to pool, and opened from pool to mere, translucent through endless days of peace.
>
> But eastward, between her orchard plains, Loire locked her embracing dead in silent sands; dark with blood rolled Isar; glacial-pale, Beresina-Lethe, by whose shore the weary hearts forgot their people, and their father's house.
>
> Nor unsullied, Tiber; nor unswoln, Arno and Aufidius; and Euroclydon high on Helle's wave; meantime, let our happy piety glorify the garden rocks with snowdrop circlet, and breathe the spirit of Paradise, where life is wise and innocent.

Perhaps the prose enacts its criticism with a too brilliant compactness and multiple allusiveness. In any case, Ruskin becomes more direct:

> Only under Furness Fells, or by Bolton Priory, it seems we can still write Ecclesiastical Sonnets, stanzas on the force of Prayer, Odes to Duty, and complimentary addresses to the Deity upon His endurance for adoration. Far otherwise, over yonder, by Spezzia Bay, and Ravenna Pineta, and in ravines of Hartz. There, the softest voices speak the wildest words; and Keats discourses of Endymion, Shelley of Demogorgon, Goethe of Lucifer, and Burger of the Resurrection of Death unto Death—while even Puritan Scotland and Episcopal Anglia produce for us only these three minstrels [Burns, Scott, and Byron] of doubtful tone, who show but small respect for the 'unco guid', put but limited faith in gifted Gilfillan, and translate with unflinching frankness the *Morgante Maggiore*. (XXXIV, 322, 323–24)

There is more (much more). It is not simply that Wordsworth has not confronted world-history but that he has (taking 'Westminster Bridge' in evidence) refused to confront *the* modern fact—the city—and in that evasion he is (as Ruskin clearly enjoys telling us) less moral as well as less poetic than Byron!

Second, it is not only the producer of such art but the

consumers who come under the lash. The Wordsworthians (and by implication too many 'poetry-lovers') can treat poetry as a spiritual rest-room, well insulated from reality. Arnold's correspondence with Clough (and especially his criticism of Clough's poetry) bears regrettable and unkind witness as to how far he was tempted by such views. Here Ruskin is repudiating one kind of Romantic reading of poetry—which Williams has described in *Culture and Society*. Poetry, in this view, becomes

> a separate, ideal sphere. . . . Meanwhile, however, it is not only a promise but a refuge. . . . And this has become a very common way of regarding poetry, and art in general, with the obvious implied judgement of the rest of man's social activity.
>
> The basic objection to this way of regarding poetry is that it makes poetry a *substitute* for feeling. . . . Such a disposition has become characteristic, and both the practice and appreciation of art have suffered from art being thus treated as a saving clause in a bad treaty.[12]

Just how characteristic Arnold's theory and practice bears regrettable witness—as does his status as some kind of classic of cultural criticism.

One consequence of recognizing the force and extent of Ruskin's repudiation of this strand of Romanticism is to realize how inappropriate is such praise as Harold Bloom's—who calls Ruskin the 'linking and transitional figure between allegorical critics of the older Renaissance kind, and those of the newer variety, like Northrop Frye'.[13] Even if we go to something like *The Queen of the Air* (which is, indeed, an extreme and eccentric work though hardly 'provincial'), we find in the brilliant discussion of the natural symbolism of the serpent that the analysis of the mythical or achetypal elements is juxtaposed with the facts of social and political life:

> The serpent crest of the king's crown, or of the god's on the pillars of Egypt, is a mystery; but the serpent itself, gliding past the pillar's foot, is it less a mystery? Is there, indeed, no tongue, except the mute forked flash from its lips, in that running brook of horror on the ground?
>
> Why that horror? We all feel it, yet how imaginative it is, how disproportioned to the real strength of the creature! There is more poison in an ill-kept drain,—in a pool of dish-washings at

a cottage door,—than in the deadliest asp of Nile. Every back-yard which you look down into from the railway, as it carries you out by Vauxhall or Deptford, holds its coiled serpent: all the walls of those ghastly suburbs are enclosures of tank temples for serpent worship; yet you feel no horror in looking down into them, as you would if you saw the livid scales and lifted head.

At the same time that Ruskin seeks to interpret the symbol, to insist on its mystery, his eye is firmly on the social fact—and the natural fact for he breaks off to consider in a footnote the physiological problems of the 'swift forward motion of serpents' (XIX, 361–2, 3).

One key function of criticism for Ruskin is to insist on the connections between art and life. Poetry cannot be left as a separate, 'ideal' sphere, nor as an (inadequate) substitute for an (inadequate?) religion. Arnold was unwise to refer to that notorious spade; Ruskin felt impelled to ask whether admiration for such a poem by such a writer should not involve rather more than the graceful burning of incense in a shrine devoted to Poetry:

> My own experience . . . is that the amiable persons who call themselves 'Wordsworthian' . . . are seldom inclined to put into practice a single syllable of the advice tendered to them by their model poet.
>
> Now, as I happen myself to have used Wordsworth as a daily text-book from youth to age, . . . it was matter of some mortification to me, when, at Oxford, I tried to get the memory of Mr. Wilkinson's spade honoured by some practical spade-work at Ferry Hincksey, to find that no other tutor in Oxford could see the slightest good or meaning in what I was about. (XXXIV, 349)

It is not that Ruskin wants to demoli⹁h Wordsworth—for it is at this point that he, like Arnold, refers back to *his* keynote work of the mid 1860s, *Sesame and Lilies*, and quotes what he said of him there ('exquisite rightness'). It is that Ruskin's ideas on the functions of criticism are rather wider and deeper than Arnold's whether in the disturbed 1860s or the disturbing 1880s—raising as they do questions about mimesis and reform. Wordsworth, as Ruskin goes on to argue, quoting from an ecclesiastical sonnet, may well be an excellent poet for the private side of life; he is not reliable when it comes to history and politics. To return to Marcus's useful formulation; 'praxis' *is* a key term for an understanding of Ruskin's whole project: 'that form of truly human activity manifested in the life of the *polis*'.[15] Punch was right in its verdict on the roadmaking:

> Scholars of Ruskin, to him be true;
> The truth he has writ in *The Stones of Venice*
> May be taught by the Stones of Hincksey too.
>
> (6 June 1874)

NOTES

1. R. H. Super (ed.), *The Complete Prose Works of Matthew Arnold*, 11 Vols. (University of Michigan Press: Ann Arbor, 1961–77), Vol. 3, p. 284. E. T. Cook and A. Wedderburn (eds.), *The Works of John Ruskin*, XXXIX Vols. (George Allen: London, 1903–12), Vol. X, p. 202. The quotations come from 'The Function of Criticism at the Present Time' and 'The Nature of Gothic' (*The Sones of Venice*) All subsequent references will be placed parenthetically in the text.
2. For a very interesting and useful comparison of Arnold and Ruskin (to which I am greatly indebted) see E. Alexander, *Matthew Arnold, John Ruskin, and the Modern Temper* (Ohio State University Press: Columbus, 1973).
3. Ruskin, of course, valued right seeing extremely highly: 'the greatest thing a human soul ever does in this world is to *see* something, and tell what it *saw* in a plain way. Hundreds of people can talk for one who can think, but thousands can think for one who can see' (V, 333).
4. So, of course, is a printed book—but how many readers (or writers) can describe how a book is printed and bound?
5. Ruskin was later to compose these collages; there is a good example in 'Work' (*The Crown of Wild Olive*).
6. See for Ruskin's experiments with publishing an excellent article by Brian Maidment, 'Readers Fair and Foul', in J. Shattock and M. Wolff (eds.), *The Victorian Press: Samplings and Soundings* (Leicester University Press, 1982), pp. 29–58.
7. W. H. Mallock, *The New Republic* (Chatto & Windus: London, 1879), pp. 178–79. The epigraph to section III comes from p. 365. Mr. Luke is, of course, Arnold—and Mr. Herbert, Ruskin.
8. R. Jenkyns, *The Victorians and Ancient Greece* (Basil Blackwell: Oxford, 1980), p. 162
9. F. R. Leavis, 'Matthew Arnold as Critic', *Scrutiny* (Vol. VII, 1938–39), p. 323. I am grateful to this piece for quoting Bridges' acidly accurate description of Arnold: 'Mr. Kid-glove Cocksure'. Steven Marcus,

Engels, Manchester and the Working-Class (Weidenfeld and Nicholson: London, 1974), p. 108. Jeffrey L. Spear, *Dreams of an English Eden: Ruskin and his Tradition in Social Criticism* (Columbia University Press: New York, 1984), p. 254. This is one of the best recent books on Ruskin—and I am indebted to it.

10. Park Honan, *Matthew Arnold: A Life* (Weidenfeld and Nicholson: London, 1981), p. 383.

11. It is limited comfort to remember that the *Saturday* could write like this about a particularly nasty case of infanticide where an old woman seems to have set herself up as a domestic version of murder inc.: 'Now and then we get horrid glimpses of a foul current of life, running like a pestilential sewer beneath the smooth surface of society, which makes us doubt whether all our boasts about the superior morality of our domestic relations are not just a trifle premature' (5 August 1865, p. 162). Only now and then?

12. Raymond Williams, *Culture and Society* (Chatto and Windus: London, 1960), p. 67.

13. Harold Bloom, *The Ringers in the Tower* (Chicago, 1971), p. 174. Quoted by Patrick Parrinder in *Authors and Authority* (Routledge and Kegan Paul: London, 1977). I am indebted to this study—despite the disgracefully low valuation of 'Of Kings' Treasuries'.

14. Arnold really should have been more careful when suffering from aesthetic pain at the name 'Wragg'. He was working on 'Thyrsis' (that elegy for Clough that damned with faint praise) at the same time as he was meditating on the 'Functions of Criticism'. It is hard to forget J. M. Robertson's comment: 'An ugly Anglo-Saxon name, in the phrase "Wragg is in custody", gave him a text for a culture sermon; but mean names have free course in . . . "Thyrsis", where we read that "In the two Hinckseys nothing is the same", and are moved to add: "Except, of course, the despicable name" ' *Modern Humanists Reconsidered* (Watts and Co: London, 1927), p. 151.

15. Richard J. Bernstein, *Praxis and Action* (Duckworth and London, 1971, p. xi.

3

Matthew Arnold and the Colenso Controversy: The Bible in 'The Republic of Letters'[1]

by DAVID AMIGONI

1

Matthew Arnold's attack on the Bishop of Natal, John William Colenso, has often been read as an anomalous breach in the ranks of Liberal solidarity. For despite Arnold's elaborate insistences to the contrary, his contemporaries understood his position as a broadly 'liberal' one, whilst Bishop Colenso's notoriously turbulent career is evidence of an emphatically 'liberal' stance.[2] Given that there were grounds for sympathy between the pair, the controversy that raged when Arnold savaged Colenso for publishing his radical Old Testament criticism *The Pentateuch and the Book of Joshua Critically Examined* (1862) needs placing in context, and a context which goes beyond the infighting carried on between the pages of the periodical press. For, in one sense, Arnold's attack can be read as an episode in a wider conflict that was an expression of the need to organize education and culture in the 1860s and '70s.

Invariably recalled as one episode—Arnold's initial attack—the terrain covered by the controversy was in fact more extensive. Colenso's *Pentateuch*, an exhaustive work doubting

75

the Divine Authority of the Mosaic Narratives, appeared in seven volumes between 1862 and 1879. It was the first volume that Arnold reviewed and attacked in 'The Bishop and the Philosopher' (*Macmillan's Magazine*, January 1863), Colenso's work being dismissed by comparison with Benedict Spinoza's. Echoes of the controversy recur in 'The Function of Criticism at the Present Time' (1864) suggesting its importance in shaping Arnold's notion of the social practice of criticism.[3] However, it was not until Arnold's own work on the function of the Bible in a modern context appeared—*St. Paul and Protestantism* (1870), *Literature and Dogma* (1873) and *God and the Bible* (1875)—that attention focused again on the original storm. The versatile W. R. Greg in his *Creed of Christendom* (1873), for instance, suggested that the inspiration and aim of *Literature and Dogma* closely paralleled Colenso's work on the Pentateuch.[4] This recognition of affinity, contradicted by Arnold's need to aggressively dissociate himself from Colenso in the 1860s, has been a vague source of discomfort to later pro-Arnold scholars (such as Lionel Trilling and William Robbins) who have sought to demonstrate that Arnold was not 'saying the same thing' as Colenso. However, Terry Eagleton in his *Criticism and Ideology* has reopened an old wound by asserting that Arnold's refusal to support Colenso—'an authentic demythologiser'—is 'one of the more discreditable facts about Matthew Arnold'.[5] Accounts of the controversy read Arnold's position either as one of enlightened originality or intellectual dishonesty.

These polarities perpetuate moralistic judgements that have been run and re-run. They erase from the controversy its historical significance. Arnold and Colenso shared a common purpose, to reform attitudes to the Bible and Christianity. As such, they engaged with a prevalent nineteenth-century concern, which informed the texture of their perceptions, making their writings 'similar'; for they were operating within a common discursive context. This 'common context' was characterized by a programme of intellectual construction that sought to assimilate the wayward epistemological forms of supernatural theology to a dominant epistemic conception of 'naturalism'. Accordingly, a reformed epistemological totality, or an intellectual and moral hegemony, was the goal: Christian morality, stripped of its supernatural Revelation and reconciled to the invariable laws of 'nature'. In one sense, Arnold and Colenso are clearly involved in this eclectic activity; yet they are also representatives of the forces behind the tensions that contradicted its progress. For, in the later part of the nineteenth century, the nascent institutions of 'literature' and 'science' opposed each other over the organization of the educational curriculum. And it is in this sense that the 'difference' between Arnold and Colenso, and the nature of Arnold's attack, becomes meaningful, as the product of conflicting visions of a cultural ideal.

2

'The Bible, the whole Bible and nothing but the Bible!' Matthew Arnold found the slogan of the British and Foreign School Society to be practically 'absurd' (CPW, VI, p. 159).[6] Yet, in another sense, it goes some way towards reflecting a real phenomenon, for the Bible was a common reading experience amongst all classes in Victorian Society. The authorized King James version, 'The whole Bible', was known in precise detail by many, and thus represented a potent and formative introduction to literacy for large numbers. In 1865, Colenso observed that 'there never was a time when the Bible was more read than it is at the present day. . . .'[7] Behind this expansion, Colenso perceives a broader social process, principally the work of the Bible societies and the cheapness of printing. In this respect, the Bishop placed his finger on a genuine pulse. The British and Foreign Bible Society, founded in 1804, became pre-eminent in exploiting the new stereotyping process of printing developed during the early part of the nineteenth century. It guaranteed the production of cheap but accurately printed Bibles. Thus, in 1860 when paper at last became truly cheap, the Oxford Press printed one million copies of the Bible and Prayer Book (compared to 127,000 in 1780).[8] It was this, coupled with 'the advance of education' (Colenso), which prompted Benjamin Jowett's observation in his essay on 'The Interpretation of Scripture' (*Essays and Reviews*, 1860) that 'the printed page lies open to many'.[9]

Jowett's preoccupation with 'the printed page' and 'the

many' is also Matthew Arnold's concern in his opening broadside against Colenso, 'The Bishop and the Philosopher'. Arnold castigates the Bishop's *Pentateuch* on the grounds that the critical enterprise fails to 'instruct the few' and, more seriously, is incapable of providing edification for 'the many'. Behind this abstract notion of 'the many' as readers lie a number of assumptions, foremost amongst them being the recognition of the social impact of literacy; the acquisition of the skill of reading by the masses represented a new distribution of power in society. Yet the power structure of reading relations were far from one-sided; the very texture and style of Arnold's writings imply a bid to control opinion. Even if 'the many' had access to power as knowledge in the form of the mass-produced printed page, control of their collective judgement might also be secured through associated mediating channels. In short, the 'meaning' of the Bible could be arbitrated by the critical institutions, embodied in commentaries and works of exegesis, that imposed on its pages a particular doctrinal meaning. Such a communicative network had the potential to shape and mould moral and intellectual opinion.

However, 'the many' was not a homogenous block. It was its very heterogeneity that mobilized 'the power of print' in an effort to homogenize it. Those who read the Bible were inevitably to apply a variety of different 'glosses' to the Record of Revelation. Christian society in Britain was diffuse and multi-denominational; 'the many' could be represented as a sort of sectarian patchwork. In constitution, it ranged from a significant proportion of the middle class, who chose to worship in dissent of the Anglican church, to rationalist 'free thinkers' amongst the educated working class, who were moving towards a rejection of Christianity. To the former group, Arnold addressed *St. Paul and Protestantism*, and to the latter the introduction to *God and the Bible* where the danger is identified as 'a kind of revolutionary Deism hostile to all which is old, traditional, established, and secure' (*CPW*, VII, p. 144). In implicitly asserting a need for balance, which would be ruptured by the dissolution of Judeo-Christian ethics, Arnold focuses on the cohesive force of a commonly held ethnical code in the establishment of consensus amongst 'the many', a component central to Gramsci's thesis of 'hegemony'. Gramsci theorized the means by which antagonistic social groups might be assimilated through the medium of an 'organised culture' as institutionalized in and inseparable from an educational system, for 'every relationship of hegemony is necessarily an educational relationship.' Moreover, at the base of this bid for 'moral and intellectual leadership' would be a legitimating ideology with correspondingly assimilative aspirations: an ideology 'totalitarian' in structure, that is to say one which 'determines a reform in the whole of philosophy'.[10] This model, positing a relationship between education, culture and epistemological reform, becomes an illuminating analytic tool for exploring the dynamics of the Arnold/Colenso controversy.

There is no question that a perception of Christianity as a binding social force in need of philosophical reform is manifest in Matthew Arnold's assertion that

> at the present moment two things about the Christian religion must be clear to anyone with eyes in his head. One is that men cannot do without it; the other is that they cannot do with it as it is. (*CPW*, VII, p. 378)

This amounts to the confrontation of the crucial problem experienced by those whose assent to the moral force of Christianity was checked by intellectual misgivings. A reform of philosophy was thus imperative; the quasi-positivist epistemology, stressing a 'law governed' universal order, and fast becoming the dominant intellectual mode, was in direct contradiction to the epistemological assumptions behind the Biblical accounts of Creation and Revelation. Arnold and Colenso were struck by this dilemma, and set out to resolve it. Yet, the formal solutions they offered to smooth over the contradiction were not wholly personal responses. Instead, they were the outcome of a pre-existing discursive context: an attempted 'reform of philosophy' that sought to incorporate Christianity and the Bible within a new hegemonic intellectual force.

The nineteenth-century universe had become a law governed affair. The 'Reign of Law' was nature itself, so consequently all human law governed activity, mental and physical, could be bracketed together in the Domain of Nature. In much the same manner the 'laws of Nature' became the measurements of textual accuracy and representational validity. Thus, the ascendancy of 'Naturalism' in this form marked a watershed for the perception of the Bible as the Inspired Record of Revelation, for as E. S. Shaffer has remarked, 'the text was liberated from the letter of Divine Inspiration and became a system of human significances'.[11] Situating the Biblical text in the space of 'Naturalism' and interpreting it as 'a system of human significances' was the strategic aim of David Strauss's *Life of Jesus Critically Examined* (1835). Strauss's 'mythical point of view' which exploded the old doctrine of literal inspiration identified the unhistorical character of myth as evident

> When the narration is irreconcilable with the known and universal laws which govern the course of events. Now, according to these laws, agreeing with all just philosophical conceptions and all credible experience, the absolute cause never disturbs the chain of secondary causes by single arbitrary acts of interposition. . . .[12]

Strauss's notion of the 'unhistorical', or the negative aspect of myth, undermined narrated accounts of scriptural miracles which presented discordances in the invariable relationships between phenomena and thus denied the supremacy of 'Nature'. However, his related concept of the 'fictive' component of myth, present in the Gospel narratives as 'the product of the particular mental tendency of a certain community' at once rescued an 'untruthful' narrative from the charge of crude deception, and provided Strauss with a route out of a conceptual corner. For whereas there was understood to be a unity between exterior order and its interior reception by the modern mind, an obvious hiatus existed in the case of the ancient mind and its perception of the natural world. Strauss stated the problem, and its potential for resolution, accordingly:

> Wherever a religion, resting upon written records, prolongs and extends the sphere of its dominion, accompanying its votaries through the varied and progressive stages of mental cultivation, a discrepancy between the representations of those ancient records, referred to as sacred, and the notions of more advanced periods of mental development will inevitably sooner or later arise.[13]

Thus, when religion passes from an early to a later phase of civilization, a conflict will emerge between the records of an earlier level of perception and a later and higher plane of understanding which has 'developed'. Mankind's ability to grasp and understand the primacy of the domain of 'Nature' is in this sense inseparably linked to 'development', or progressive stages of mental improvement. This relationship between 'Nature' and 'Development' evolved paradigmatic status and became general intellectual currency; it was structurally central to both Arnold's and Colenso's assumptions in their respective Biblical criticisms.

For this model depicting mental progression culminating in the unclouded perception of the pure relationships of nature was made to perform a similar operation on the language of the Bible and the Theological edifice born out of it. In the same way that Comtean teleology displayed the Positivist era as temporally and dynamically liberated from the historically distinct régimes of Theology and Metaphysics, so Strauss's 'Higher Criticism' and its offshoots understood their own position of historical privilege in terms of the ability to 'cut away' Theological and Metaphysical accretions from the Biblical text, revealing an essential religious substance; Ludwig Feuerbach was not alone in seeking 'The Essence of Christianity', or an inalienable central meaning that was 'deeply laid in the very truth itself' (Colenso). To cement hegemony in its intellectual and moral aspect involved the need to pinpoint the substance of truth in Biblical words that had an alarming tendency to offer more than one meaning. As Benjamin Jowett remarked:

> If words have more than one meaning, they may have any meaning. Instead of being a rule of life or faith scripture becomes the ever changing aspect of religious opinions.[14]

In the same way that there was but one Domain of 'Nature', the progress of mental 'development' attempted to abolish plurality by assimilating all conflicting aspects of religious practice and doctrine to an uncontested 'essence' inherent in the text of scripture.

The mechanism through which this ideal would be ultimately grasped was conceived in terms of an inexorable

81

'intellectual division of labour'. In the same way as the latter represented an advance towards cognitive perfection in the positivist telos, so the development and diversification of intellectual discourses when applied to Christianity would progressively reveal a harmonious vision of moral and intellectual truth. The mechanism is classically deployed in the conclusion to Arnold's *Literature and Dogma*:

> And yet, as man makes progress, we shall surely come to doing this. For the clearer our conceptions in science and art become, the more will they assimilate themselves to the conceptions of duty in conduct, will become practically stringent like rules of conduct and will invite the same sort of language in dealing with them. (*CPW*, VI, p. 410)

The organizing strategies that compose this 'Essay Towards a better Apprehension of the Bible'—mental progress and an intellectual division of labour between the 'sciences' and 'arts' assimilating the intellectual to the moral through a commonly received language articulating a central, self-validating truth—are by now familiar. Expressed in this form, they are the distinctive ingredients of the epistemological reform bound up with hegemonic ambition. To a greater or lesser degree, Arnold and Colenso shared this ambition; furthermore, they employed the assumptions and strategies described here in seeking to realize it.

That such unity of purpose was, in the final analysis, flawed is clearly evident though in Arnold's attack on Colenso. The eclecticism of epistemological reform was thus ensnared in an internal contradiction. In 1870, J. C. Shairp recognized this. Shairp's thesis, *Culture and Religion in some of their Relations* was itself a contribution to the continuing 'religion and society' debate which had earlier embraced the first phase of the Arnold/Colenso controversy; Arnold wrote *Literature and Dogma* specifically in response to Shairp's thesis. However, Shairp's polemic is important because it contains a perceptive insight into the logic motivating Arnold's violent divergence from Bishop Colenso. For whereas Arnold envisaged the division of intellectual labour between 'arts' and 'sciences' as an antecedent to a contradiction-free cultural hegemony embracing a morally and intellectually streamlined religion, Shairp saw the intensified differentiation between the intellectual practices known as the 'arts' and the 'sciences' as increasingly antagonistic and competitive. Arnold constructed a fiction of harmony, whereas Shairp, in writing of the 'scientific theory of culture' and its adversary the 'Literary Theory of Culture', recognized conflict.[15] Paradoxically, though Arnold displays a blindness to this contest, he was palpably involved in its processes. For its structure was integrally bound to the ongoing debate concerning the organization of the curriculum that accompanied demands for national educational measures in the 1860s and beyond. Thus, neither Arnold (as an H.M. Inspector of Schools) or Colenso (as author of standard arithmetic textbooks that had been widely absorbed by the existing mathematical curriculum) were innocent bystanders in educational matters. Moreover, Arnold, as former Oxford Professor of Poetry, and Colenso, scientistic Second Wrangler from Cambridge, possessed opposed intellectual genealogies that led them into conflicting ideological and institutional camps when intellectual life began to fragment around the 1870s.[16] Accordingly, their respective visions of organized culture were at odds, as is ultimately clear from the differing rôles that each assigns to the Bible as an organ of educational authority.

3

For the root of this ideological rupture can be dug out of the Biblical criticism that Colenso and Arnold produced. Indeed, its basis can be expressed epigrammatically; in disposing of the Bible, Colenso managed to retain God, whilst in getting rid of God, Arnold succeeded in holding on to the Bible. The relationship that both struggle to establish between 'God and the Bible' is peculiarly revealing, in that it says a great deal about each's understanding of the representational properties possessed by language; at its most fundamental, the capacity of the Bible to represent the Revealed Word of God is being scrutinized. Colenso followed the theology of F. D. Maurice, for whom a personal God was the foundation of religious faith. Likewise, Colenso's God was a personal patriarchal form— the Universally Loving Father inviting the reciprocal love of

the Great Human Family.[17] Colenso's problem is to find Him
between the pages of what he ultimately deems to be a
linguistically discredited text. On the other hand, Arnold's
God is a metaphor; the Hebraic anthropomorphic God is but
the poetic manifestation of phenomena variously translated by
Arnold into a 'stream of tendency by which things fulfil the
law of their being' or 'the not ourselves that makes for
righteousness'. If this can be viewed as ironic—given that it
was Colenso who was found to be heretical by the Anglican
church—then it can also be seen as reflective of their attitudes
to the authoritative value of the Bible or the power of the
'Text'; Colenso's God is supremely 'a-textual', while Arnold's
God is powerful primarily at a poetic representation in the
Biblical Text. However, before probing this ideological
division more deeply, it is necessary to look at the deployment
of certain assumptions and argumentative strategies which
bind Arnold and Colenso in brotherhood to a common
discursive inheritance, and which makes this point of divisive-
ness all the more significant.

Both Arnold and Colenso display a sensitivity to the diverse
composition of 'the many' and the potential for using Biblical
criticism as a medium for engaging a particular point of view,
with the aim of welding it into a wider moral and intellectual
consensus. Colenso's episcopal function was almost subordinate to his practical rôle as a Missionary in British Colonial
South Africa, educating the uninitiated into the Christian
Pale. Arnold, as Lay H.M. Inspector of Schools with special
responsibility for the voluntary schools of Protestant Dissenters,
was inclined to feel that he was dealing with the zealously
over-initiated, as he made clear to Gladstone in 1869:

> For fifteen years I have seen the Protestant Dissenters close
> from inspecting their schools; and more and more observed how
> their real need is not more voluntarism and separation for their
> religious organizations, but a larger existence and more sense of
> public responsibility.[18]

In this context, Arnold's *St. Paul and Protestantism* can be seen
as a component in a broader social vision; in undermining the
moral and thus organizational legitimacy of separatism, it
foregrounds certain broad spiritual tenets as the basis for

assimilating Dissent to a 'National Church' or institutional consensus. This could apply equally to Colenso's 'Heathen', whom he sought to include beneath a broad, central span of belief, bereft of theological nuance. In both cases, the complexities of theology, metaphysics and morality were erased in an attempt to establish a socially cohesive set of beliefs. In the case of Arnold, the strategy is inseparably bound to the very tone and style of his prose; heterogenous 'points of view'—the Dissenter, the working-class 'free Thinker'—are courted by a consciously cultivated author/reader relationship, only to be bound together by a tone of reasoned reassurance, pressing for unconditional assent.

If Colenso was less obviously conscious of building such a relationship, his first venture into scriptural interpretation still suggests an awareness of the need to make the vehicle for his views accessible; Peter Hinchliff has described the Bishop's *St. Paul's Epistle to the Romans: Newly Translated and Explained from a Missionary Point of View* (1861) as writing displaying 'an easy readable style, less dated than a good many Victorian works of theology'.[19] Significantly, and like Arnold, Colenso also chose a Pauline text to work on as the starting-point for his attitude 'reformation'. Moreover, the concept of 'point of view' stands prominently in the title, acknowledging the heterogeneity of social composition and the function of criticism in drawing the disparate into a consensus. Like Arnold, Colenso sees different points of view as objects to be accommodated, rather than wholly negated;

> The teaching of the Great Apostle to the Gentiles is here applied to some questions, which daily arise in Missionary labours among the Heathen, more directly than is usual with those commentators, who have not been engaged personally in such work, but have written from a very different point of view in the midst of a state of advanced civilisation and settled Christianity.[20]

Both Arnold and Jowett trouble to remark on the legitimate relationship between missionary work and the interpretation of scripture. In *Literature and Dogma* Arnold points up the poverty of the missionary message obscured by theological abstraction (*CPW*, VI, p. 382) and Jowett issues a remedy:

> The missionary should . . . be able to separate the accidents
> from the essence of religion; he should be conscious that the
> power of the Gospel resides not in the particulars of Theology,
> but in the Christian life. . . .[21]

A remedy indeed that Colenso can be seen to adopt, for *Romans*
seeks to reconcile the 'point of view' or cultural difference of
the 'Heathen' to a particular 'essence' of Christianity expressed
in terms of 'conduct' as opposed to Doctrine. By way
of parallel, the watchwords of *St. Paul and Protestantism*—
'Righteousness' and the 'Sweet Reasonableness' of Jesus—
merging with the persistent assertion in *Literature and Dogma*
that 'conduct is three fourths of life', indicate that Arnold's
strategy for binding diverse 'points of view' together is through
an appeal to the primacy of religious practice over and above
abstruse Doctrine. This mutual apprehension becomes important, given the accepted 'tradition' in which the text they
engaged had historically existed. For the Pauline Epistle had
come to be the scriptural cornerstone of the exclusivist tenets
of individualistic Protestantism, providing raw material for the
theological structures of Justification by Faith Alone and
Predestination. These implied, as Colenso perceived, a severe
restriction on the volume of God's love for the faithless
'Heathen'. Similarly, Arnold saw the sense of independent
self-identification amongst factions of the English middle class,
itself generated by Protestant Dogma, as inimical to the
establishment of hegemony. The aim then is to usurp control
of the text, overthrowing the old meaning, and installing and
legitimating a new one. Consequently, a vision of moral and
intellectual consensus and the act of critical exegesis begin
perceptibly to intertwine.

Expressed then in the twists and turns of practical interpretation, Arnold's and Colenso's treatments of St. Paul work
to suppress some meanings and foreground others. Arnold's
choice of a polemical form through which to project his
interpretation can manage selectivity with ease, though
Colenso's use of the more conventional commentary containing the entire Epistle requires more deft acts of reading, and
the reconciliation of the entire text to his universalist contention. To this end, Colenso's method is to superimpose his

own strategy of an appeal to 'point of view' on to his perception of the historical conditions in which the Epistle was circulated. In Colenso's view, St. Paul's Roman audience were Christian believers who had primarily accepted Christ as a Messianic presence. Thus, their acceptance was 'tainted' with vestiges of Judaic exclusivism. According to Colenso's interpretation, Paul's letter uses the language of exclusivism initially to engage the 'point of view' of his readers, though only in order to turn this language in on itself, to draw out its Universalist potential:

> It is impossible not to notice the rhetorical ingenuity of his proceeding, how gradually and insensibly he leads on his Jewish readers, repeating twice the summary of the doctrine he wished to teach them, in different terms, so as to set it plainly before their eyes, but then passing on, before they can see all at once the full depth of its meaning. . . . [Yet] they will feel that something more lies in his words than they had as yet distinctly realized.[22]

In this sense, the Pauline text rehearses the strategies and persuasive function that Colenso's commentary performs in a different historical epoch.

Breaking down the legitimacy of a language that becomes a manifesto for religious exclusivism is Arnold's concern in *St. Paul and Protestantism*. In order to suppress readings of the text that support doctrines inspiring sectarianism, Arnold promotes the idea of two distinct types of Pauline writing. Arnold argues that Paul 'orientalises' and 'Judaises' throughout (*CPW*, VI, pp. 21–2). Race and writing coalesce in 'Judaising' to produce a misdirected appeal to the Jewish understanding of scripture in order to 'prove' a universally applicable Christian idea. This comes close to Colenso's perception of Paul's use of a language tinged with familiarity, employed to persuade. For both, however, these inescapable features of the text are significantly subordinate to the legitimate reading that they seek to project. In addition, Arnold claims, the right message is further obscured by the Western mistranslation of Paul's inevitable 'orientalising'. In rendering literally 'a vivid figure of rhetoric', or 'language thrown out at an object of consciousness not fully grasped, with inspired emotion' (*CPW*, VI, p. 189), Western

Theology misrepresents the true experience of early Christianity. In treating an 'approximate' use of language as 'scientific' in its bearings, or logically precise in its relations to a corresponding set of concepts, the institution of Western Theology gravely misapprehends the 'essence' of religion. The need then is to rediscover it by restoring it to the Domain of 'Nature' as progressively revealed through mental 'Development'.

In Arnold's *Literature and Dogma*, the celebrated antithesis between Theism (Revealed religion) and Deism (Natural theology) is abolished. The difference between them is 'not one of kind but only of degree': however, Arnold adds that 'the real antithesis, to natural and revealed alike, is invented, artificial' (*CPW*, VI, pp. 194–95). Out of the collapsing Deism/Theism opposition, the trimmed precepts of Christianity are assimilated to the Domain of 'Nature'. The remaining antagonism becomes centred upon the difference between 'Natural' and 'Artificial', the latter being represented by the institutional edifice of Western Theology, and the 'Doctrinal Accretions' which its false processes of 'abstruse reasoning' have generated. In the same manner, Colenso implicitly holds Revelation to be a component of the Domain of 'Nature' in his *Commentary on Romans*. Reflecting on the source of evil and sin, Colenso concludes that Paul's Epistle

> Point[s] to the laws of the moral world, as sure and stable as those of the physical, which make the darkening of the mind, and the hardening of the heart, the natural and necessary consequence of continuance in known evil. It must be so.

The concept of 'Nature' ambiguously slips around in Colenso's commentary; but the main thrust of its use is clear. In the end, as Peter Hinchliff points out, Colenso 'virtually teaches a dualism of God and Nature'.[23]

The assumption that allows Arnold to preach the great 'Natural truth of Christianity' is also based on bracketing God and 'Nature'. God, as 'the stream of tendency by which things fulfil the law of their being' is, after all 'Nature'. It is this vision of an invariable mechanism that enables Arnold, through a strategic rhetorical appeal to notions of 'Nature', 'Science', 'Verifiability' and 'Experience', to construct a conceptual totality. In *St. Paul and Protestantism*, Arnold contends that the 'worth of a religious teacher is, after all, just the scientific value of his teaching, its correspondence with important facts and the light it throws on them' (*CPW*, VI, p. 8). Facts are 'scientifically' accurate not in a deductively rigorous sense, but insofar as they are 'verifiable': that is, they agree with the judgement of a cultivated faculty that infallibly registers certain truth values. Dismissing 'abstruse reasoning' from this function, Arnold assigns 'experience' to the vacant rôle. Consequently 'experience' rejects all that is *a priori*, theoretical and thus 'artificial' and perceives 'Nature' to be true. Arnold thus travels full circle back to his notion of natural order, 'the Eternal, not ourselves, that makes for Righteousness'. In following this path to his Deity, Arnold can show no compunction in assigning the God of the Bible and Christianity to the Domain of 'Nature', and as a consequence Christ is sent the same way; for Arnold claims in *St. Paul and Protestantism* that 'the Jesus of the Bible follows the universal moral order' rather than displaying an originally creative rôle in revealing it (*CPW*, VI, p. 42). This casts an ambiguous shadow over the saving grace afforded to Christianity by 'Nature'. Likewise, Colenso, in discrediting the traditional wisdom of a Penta-teuchal narrative written by Moses, flatly contradicts Christ's apparently inspired pronouncement on Mosaic authorship issued in the Gospels. A Christ immersed in the natural 'conditions of humanity' can thus be plain wrong. Colenso's salvaging strategy is to argue that the Incarnation in a natural human form involved accepting the state 'which makes our growth in all ordinary knowledge gradual and limited'.[24] Having virtually neutralized the force of Christ's presence through equating him with 'Nature', Colenso averts his awkward dilemma by bringing into play the concept of slowly evolving mental growth. Similarly, Arnold reaches a point where he needs to make Christ's teaching stand out from 'Nature' while still suppressing inferences of the supernatural, and is led to coin the term 'non-natural' in his description of Jesus, which is

> Like the grace of Raphael, or the grand style of Phidias, eminently natural; but it is above common low pitched nature. It is a line of nature not yet mastered or followed out. (*CPW*, VI, pp. 255)

As the closing metaphor strikingly suggests, Arnold also rescues the damagingly expansive concept of 'Nature' by recourse to the concept of 'Development'.

Thus, a notion of 'Development' is situated at the heart of Arnold's and Colenso's interpretative systems; however, it is a heart that pounds with a double beat. On the one hand, 'Development' stands for the harmful process by which cumulative artifice in the form of 'doctrinal accretions' build on and obscure a 'Natural' truth; on the other hand, 'Development' signifies a progressive form of mental growth that sears through cancerous accretions to restore 'Natural' truth, and unites it with moral practice and the higher critical disciplines. However, crucially for Arnold, the two senses are not wholly irreconcilable, and the relationship he constructs between them allows him to claim privilege for literary discourse as the basis for a new critical practice. Arnold's original encounter with the idea of 'Development' seems to have come from reading J. H. Newman's *Development of Christian Doctrine* (1845). Picking up Newman's contention that 'the whole Bible is written on the principle of development' (*CPW*, VI, p. 88), Arnold transforms it into a leading principle for defining the relationship between textual meaning, moral truth and the disfiguring power of theological doctrine.[25] Yet, he does so by standing Newman's thesis on its head; whereas Newman conceives of Revelation as a vastly complex, multi-faceted idea, present but never wholly apprehended, Arnold represents the Christian Revelation as 'a small body of ethical truths' (De Laura). Newman's 'Development' means infinite complexity, Arnold's restrictive simplicity, or the progressive but selective stockpiling of 'verifiable' meanings extracted from the Biblical text. Arnold places the legitimating ideal of verification in constant tension with his notion of 'Aberglaube' (Extra Belief), defined in *Literature and Dogma* as the evolution of 'belief beyond what is certain and verifiable' (*CPW*, VI, p. 212). Whereas 'experience' verifies and thus foregrounds a central 'nuclei' of religious meaning, 'Aberglaube', as superfluous beliefs developed through time, is the non-verifiable remainder, which negatively defines 'essence' through being its opposite. Hence, an understanding of 'Aberglaube' isolates a pure interior from a crustacea of exterior 'accretions'.

Its application is nowhere better illustrated than in Chapter VI of *God and the Bible* (*CPW*, VII), 'The Fourth Gospel From Within', where Arnold separates the Logos idea, introduced by an Evangelist narrator of metaphysical bent ('Aberglaube') from Christ's teaching pertaining to 'righteousness', which manifests itself as a verifiable 'nuclei', through a plenitude of meaning not present in the Logos.

Significantly, a striking parallel can here be drawn with Colenso, who in writing of the Logos in John makes the same observation, using identical discriminative categories, so that the narrator is 'Employing Platonic formulae to translate the language of the Old Hebrew Scriptures. We have no reason to suppose these traditional Dogmas.'[26] For an unspecified notion of 'Aberglaube' pervades Colenso's *Pentateuch and the Book of Joshua Critically Examined* as it does his comments on the New Testament. While Part One only exposes the contradictions in the narratives comprising the Pentateuch, Part Five of the work (1864), and the later *Lectures on the Pentateuch and the Moabite Stone* (1873) have advanced to argue that the contradictions are the result of multiple narratives, textual interpolations and compound authorship. Colenso's driving concern is that these inconsistent narratorial accumulations have generated moral ambiguities, which have themselves become untenable doctrine. The solution is to purge them away, to reveal the spurious moral basis of doctrinal convention. The aim is for the Bible to be purified of that which has given rise to 'the gross accretions of human dogmatic teaching', leaving intact those moral truths which are 'true in themselves by whomsoever spoken or written' (Colenso). While Arnold in *God and the Bible* seeks from the Fourth Gospel a validating 'primitive theme' (*CPW*, VII, p. 314), Colenso looks to the unearthing of 'a primitive truth', a small body of moral precepts emerging again in 'the simpler forms in which they first appeared, though with a great advance in clearness and certainty'.[27]

Colenso's projection of a set of ultimately simple moral rules, progressively 'developed' to a point of sharpness and clarity, strikingly echoes Arnold's conclusion to *Literature and Dogma*. Indeed, 'the March of Mind' is the clinching mechanism in both instances. The new revelation of an old truth is effected for Arnold by the Time Spirit, or 'Zeit Geist', and for Colenso by the force of 'modern science'. When Arnold follows Newman in asserting that 'the whole Bible is written on the principle of development', the concept is in fact applied as an evolutionary process of relativistic adjustment, imposed on the text by the 'irresistible breath of the Zeit Geist' (*CPW*, VI, p. 113). Arnold's 'Time Spirit' is a versatile tool, carving out an ideological totality and welding intellectual and moral discourses together into a hegemonic force capable of 'bring[ing] a reluctant Christianity into line with the larger movement of the Western mind'.[28] While preserving a 'Kernel' of moral truths, the '*Zeit Geist*' invades the territory of defunct metaphysics, translating its language into concepts reconcilable with the advancing intellectual forms of philosophy and criticism. Yet for Colenso the very same process consti-tutes a sure foundation for intellectual and moral security in that 'our wisdom will be to translate the language of the devout men of older ages into that of our own.'[29] Thus, as translator of the anachronistic, and discriminator between conflicting claims of knowledge, Colenso's 'modern science' performs the same function as Arnold's 'Zeit Geist', gen-erating an intellectual division of labour that ends in the manifestation of a small number of moral rules regulating conduct.

In this sense their respective panaceas lead Arnold and Colenso to conclusions that bear comparison in their assess-ments of the scope claimed for Biblical authority. For the 'Zeit Geist' tells Arnold that the formal scientific pretensions of Western Theology are incompatible with the fluid, un-rigorous language of the Bible from which they are illegitimately drawn. But this itself makes Arnold's public justification for his attack on Colenso—that the Bishop naïvely read the Bible as science ('The Function of Criticism at the Present Time'— (*CPW*, III, pp. 276–77))—appear rather shallow, given that Colenso's own position touched Arnold's even here. For Colenso, the authority vested in the language of Scripture is

> Not in matters of science and history, but in those words of Eternal life which come to us with a power not of this world, and find us out in our inner being with messages from God to the soul.[30]

An assertion which renders Arnold's strident critical mockery of the Bishop difficult to uphold. Both Arnold and Colenso re-read, or reinterpret the Bible with the aid of a basically similar vocabulary constructed from a common discursive context. What is more to the point—in that Arnold's attack on the Bishop requires real meaning—is that Arnold reads, or interprets, Colenso himself as 'science'; or rather as a representative of the emerging institution of physical science which defined itself through a rationalistic ideology and conceived itself as the focal point of educational reform. Thus, in the embattled context of the 1860s and '70s, when the scope and nature of all levels of education were being hotly debated, Arnold's response must be seen primarily as that of public spokesman for the nascent institution of 'literature'. As such, Colenso is beheld as an enemy of 'literature's' claim to a privileged position in the curriculum, enmity signified by the rationalist tendency to downgrade the educational authority of the Bible because of its apparent 'unreliable' use of language. It is in this sense that the authoritative right to interpret Biblical language became an issue generating conflict, and Arnold's Biblical Criticism should accordingly be read as a bid to enshrine 'literary' cultural practices at the centre of the curriculum: an attempt to claim the Bible for 'The Republic of Letters'.

4

The study of language for its own sake came low down in the list of learning priorities set by the nineteenth-century educational establishment. In Robert Lowe's view, 'as we live in a universe of things and not words, the knowledge of things is more important to us than the knowledge of words.'[31] Indeed, it was Robert Lowe's unashamedly utilitarian Revised Code (1861) that set in motion a debate that sought alternative educational strategies and ideals; this debate intensified in the late 1860s when demands for national elementary education looked like becoming a legislative reality. However, the reformers found themselves essentially divided; broadly speaking, they fell into two camps—in J. C. Sharp's terms either advocates of the 'scientific' or 'literary' theories of culture. Appropriately the ideological base line of both theories can be found within Lowe's terms of epistemological reference; science looked to the empirical study of 'things', literature to a textual universe of 'words'. Such an ideological rift propels Arnold's assault on Colenso. Its complete character may ultimately be seen in the contrast between their practical attempts to reorganize the curriculum and education. But initially, it can be traced from their irreconcilable notions of the form and value of Biblical language itself.

Colenso's notion of the authoritative value of the Bible as a unified reading experience is beset by ambivalence. In Part V of *The Pentateuch*, the Bishop states that it is not possible to 'pick and choose' among the contents of the Bible, absorbing ethics here and rejecting a miracle there. Yet, elsewhere, there are clear and contradictory exhortations to select, and if found wanting, reject. In striving to transcend this contradiction, and thus justify the elimination of whole portions of text, Colenso sets up a dialectical opposition, a conflict, 'which in the lapse of time is continually renewed again and again. It is . . . the battle of the spirit against the letter.'[32] The letter is an accretion, or the word that fails to correspond to a 'thing'; the spirit of the word of God is the living remainder. Yet, Colenso effectively envisages the latter as independent and distinct of all speech and writing as it is nowhere evident in the actual language of the Bible, for 'it is not necessary to have a right form of words respecting things for which words are inadequate.' This profound mistrust of the outward form of language leads Colenso to sever completely any remaining relationship between God and the language of the Bible and theology. Thus, when the Anglican church deems an anthropomorphism in the creed to be metaphoric, Colenso argues that the lesson should be applied more widely;

> If we are taught to understand metaphorically one clause of the creed, why shall we not be allowed, when the necessities of our modern knowledge of facts requires it, to use the same liberty with others?[33]

Consequently, when 'words' do not correspond to a real 'thing', the term can be downgraded to metaphor, a form which ceases to have a real meaning. Metaphor becomes the means by which redundant 'accretions' are put out to grass. Having been so linguistically discredited, the Bible becomes effectively meaningless in matters of fact, and, most drastically, educationally redundant in large areas of the curriculum.

Like Colenso, Arnold assumes that the language of the Bible is referentially out of line with 'the object of consciousness' it is seeking to represent. Yet this discrepancy between language and knowledge as sensory experience is manipulated by Arnold to champion the source of 'Aberglaube', or language which is 'fluid, passing and literary'. Identifying this form of language as 'literary' is crucial, for it is the means by which Arnold seeks to construct a relationship between Biblical language and the specialized educational experience which interprets it. In line with this the theologian is held to suffer from a narrow acquaintance with 'the way in which men have thought and spoken', which leads them to treat literary language as though it were 'rigid and fixed'. By contrast, a broad training in 'letters' enables one to read in the text 'where [to] rest . . . with weight, and where . . . to pass lightly' (*CPW*, VI, p. 152), and in so doing reveals the authoritative value of Biblical language; for

> this language is approximative merely, while men imagine it to be adequate; it is thrown out at certain realities which they very imperfectly comprehend. It is materialised poetry, which they give as science; and there can be no worse science than materialised poetry. But poetry is essentially concrete; and the moment one perceives that the religious language of the human race is in truth poetry which it mistakes for science, one cannot make it an objection to this language that it is concrete. (*CPW*, VI, p. 396)

Arnold here argues that the hiatus between the 'words' of the Bible and the 'things' of common experience is legitimately the privileged territory of 'poetry' and, as such, interpreting the Bible correctly ultimately involves annexing it to the province of 'literature'. For to see through the disfiguring linguistic refraction of 'Aberglaube' and to realize the concrete presence of 'poetry' as the true form of religious language, is to entrust the act of Biblical exegesis to the jurisdiction of the critic of literature. If for Colenso metaphor reduces the Bible to a dead letter, in Arnold's eyes the form revives the text as a meaningful centre of authority, significantly justifying the primacy of literary cultural practice as an agent of intellectual reform. Arnold's 'literature', and its Biblical handmaiden, thus gravitate towards the centre of the curriculum.

These implicitly conflicting assessments of the Bible as an organ of educational authority were realized palpably in Arnold's and Colenso's conflicting visions of an ideal curricular content, evident in vigorously contrasting school textbooks that each published. Colenso's name had passed into public currency as the author of 'Colenso's Arithmetic' many years prior to the storm surrounding his *Pentateuch*, which can be taken as evidence of a practical step towards the goal of textbook standardization called for by Arnold in his Inspector's *Reports on Elementary Schools*.[34] However, if the strategy to promote educational uniformity was an agreed one, the content and values to be disseminated remained contested; the institutional factions representing the values of 'words' and 'things' were at odds, and Arnold and Colenso dealt blows for them respectively. Accordingly, Colenso's *First Lessons in Science: Designed for the Use of Children* (1861) offers itself, quite consciously, as an educational antidote to the reading of uninformative 'literature'. Moreover, the Bible comes in for Colenso's customarily equivocal treatment when he declares that 'the Bible was not given to us to make us wise in matters of [modern science]' and

> If we had not the Bible to teach us . . . yet the contemplation of the works of God shows us an order in his universe—a steady sequence of cause and effect.[35]

As this suggests, Colenso's leanings towards the ideology of the institution of science means that the Bible is effectively marginalized, having no authority in the study of a universe of 'things' which is a discrete and dominant area of knowledge in the curriculum.

By complete contrast, Arnold's *A Bible Reading for Schools (Isaiah XL–LXVI)* (1872) pushes the Bible to the very centre of the curriculum, though in a rôle essentially crafted for it by Arnold; 'And why is the attempt made? It is made because of my conviction of the immense importance in education of what is called "Letters" ' (*CPW*, VII, p. 499). Writing at this time, it is significant that Arnold uses the old concept of 'letters' in essentially a new context. 'Letters' had previously signified the widest possible sphere of literacy and critical activity; however, here Arnold defines 'letters' as a discrete educational practice, or the specialized intellectual code of a new and self-conscious institution of 'literature'.[36] In this way, Arnold's assertion of the authoritative value of Biblical language is inseparable from his educational aim of building literature into the leading force for organizing education and culture. For the Bible as 'literature' becomes a unique textual centre of moral and intellectual authority in Arnoldian ideology, by means of its capacity to mediate values through the privileged discourse of 'poetry'. And, as Arnold makes clear in his famous essay on 'The Study of Poetry' (1880), a hegemony of 'poetry' recognizes no boundaries in its mission to renovate culture;

> More and more mankind will discover that we have to turn to poetry to interpret life for us, to console us, to sustain us. Without poetry, our science will appear incomplete; and most of what now passes with us for religion and philosophy will be replaced by poetry. (*CPW*, IX, pp. 161–62)

A 'poetic' vision; and one, to reiterate the words of Gramsci, which 'determines a reform of the whole of philosophy'.

Thus, re-reading the Bible as the Divine Revelation of 'literature' brings Arnold one step closer to proclaiming the impending ascendancy of 'The Republic of Letters'.

NOTES

1. I should like to thank firstly Dr. Charles Swann for his initial help in directing this piece towards publication, and secondly Caroline Baggaley for typing the manuscript.
2. By far the most balanced account of Colenso's whole career—rather than just one small episode of it—can be found in Peter Hinchliff's *John William Colenso, Bishop of Natal* (Nelson, London, 1964).
3. Cf. Sidney Coulling, *Matthew Arnold and His Critics* (Ohio University Press, Athens, 1974), pp. 100–36.

4. W. R. Greg, *The Creed of Christendom: Its Foundations Contrasted with its Superstructure*, Vol. 1 (London, 1877), Fifth edition, pp. xviii–xxv.
5. Terry Eagleton, *Criticism and Ideology* (Verso, London, 1976), p. 109.
6. All references to Arnold's principal works will be to the *Complete Prose Works*, ed. R. H. Super (Ann Arbor, Michigan), and will appear as an inset in the text.
7. J. W. Colenso, *Natal Sermons (First Series)* (Trubner, London, 1866), p. 12.
8. Owen Chadwick, *The Victorian Church*, Pt. II, Second edition (A. & C. Black, London, 1972), pp. 56–7.
9. Benjamin Jowett, *On the Interpretation of Scripture and Other Essays* (Routledge, London), p. 32. (No date)
10. Antonio Gramsci, *Selections from the Prison Notebooks*, edited and translated by Quintin Hoare and Geoffrey Nowell Smith (Lawrence and Wishart, London, 1971), p. 350, p. 57, p. 366.
11. E. S. Shaffer, *Kubla Khan and the Fall of Jerusalem* (Cambridge University Press, 1975), p. 10.
12. D. F. Strauss, *The Life of Jesus Critically Examined* (1835; Swan Sonneschien, London, 1906), p. 88.
13. Ibid., p. 87, p. 39.
14. Jowett, op. cit., p. 31.
15. J. C. Shairp, *Culture and Religion in Some of Their Relations* (Edmonston and Douglas, Edinburgh, 1870), pp. 26–48: pp. 49–72.
16. Cf. T. W. Heyck, *The Transformation of Intellectual Life in Victorian England* (Croom Helm, London, 1982).
17. Peter Hinchliff, op. cit., p. 20.
18. W. H. G. Armytage, 'M. Arnold and W. E. Gladstone: Some New Letters', *U.T.Q.* XVIII (April, 1949), p. 222 (cf. *CPW*, VI, p. 417).
19. Hinchliff, op. cit., p. 80.
20. Colenso, *St. Paul's Epistle to the Romans* (Macmillan, Cambridge, 1861), p. v.
21. Jowett, op. cit., p. 171.
22. Colenso, *Romans*, p. 40.
23. Ibid., p. 50, Hinchliff, op. cit., p. 81.
24. Colenso, *The Pentateuch and the Book of Joshua Critically Examined*, Part 1 (Longman, London, 1862), p. xxxi.
25. Cf. David De Laura, *Hebrew and Hellene in Victorian England* (University of Texas Press, Austin and London), p. 83.
26. Colenso, *Natal Sermons (First Series)*, p. 103.
27. Colenso, ibid., p. 13 and *Lectures on the Pentateuch and the Moabite Stone* (Longman, London, 1873), p. 10.
28. De Laura, op. cit., p. 86.
29. Colenso, *Natal Sermons (First Series)*, p. 84.
30. Colenso, ibid., p. 10.
31. Peter Gordon and Denis Lawton, *Curriculum Change in the Nineteenth and Twentieth Centuries* (Hodder and Stoughton, London, 1978), p. 57, quoting from D. W. Sylvester, *Robert Lowe and Education* (Cambridge University Press, 1974).

32. Colenso, *The Pentateuch and the Book of Joshua Critically Examined*, Part V (1865), p. 311 (cf. Hinchliff, op. cit., p. 99); *Natal Sermons (First Series)*, p. 5.

33. Colenso, *Natal Sermons (First Series)*, p. 106, ibid., p. 84.

34. Arnold, *Reports on Elementary Schools*, 1852–1882 (HMSO, London, 1910), p. 23.

35. Colenso, *First Lessons in Science* (1861; Ridgeway, London, 1887), p. 29, p. 193.

36. For a discussion of the changing conception of 'Letters' and the men who practised them, cf. Heyck, op. cit.

4

The Sick King in Bokhara: Arnold and the Sublime of Suffering

by JOHN WOOLFORD

1

> Years went on, and his friends became conspicuous authors or statesmen; but Joubert remained in the shade. His constitution was of such fragility that how he lived so long, or accomplished so much as he did, is a wonder: his soul had, for its basis of operations, hardly any body at all: both from his stomach and from his chest he seems to have had constant suffering, though he lived by rule, and was as abstemious as a Hindoo. Often, after overwork in thinking, reading, or talking, he remained for days together in a state of utter prostration,—condemned to absolute silence and inaction; too happy if the agitation of his mind would become quiet also, and let him have the repose in which he stood in so much need. With this weakness of health, these repeated suspensions of energy, he was incapable of the prolonged contention of spirit necessary for the creation of great works.[1]

This description of Joubert seems to typify certain recurring features of Arnold's perception of other writers of his own period. He favoured shy and reclusive merit. Like Joubert, Maurice de Guerin 'remained in the shade', and 'died in the year 1839, at the age of 28 without having published anything';[2] Etienne de Senancour earned 'little celebrity in

France, his own country; and out of France ... is almost unknown';[3] Edward Quinillan evoked the comment:

> I saw him sensitive in frame,
>   I knew his spirits low;
> And wished him health, success and fame—
>   I do not wish it now.[4]

The third line indicates how closely, for Arnold, obscurity, as the obverse of 'success and fame', was tied to illness, the obverse of 'health'; and the other figures I have mentioned were also diseased. Illness was the cause of early death for Guerin and Quinillan, and the constant affliction of the longer lives of Joubert, Senancour, and Heine, the subject of one of Arnold's most moving descriptions:

> In 1847 his health, which till then had always been perfectly good, gave way. He had a kind of paralytic stroke. His malady proved to be a softening of the spinal marrow: it was incurable; it made rapid progress. In May 1848, not a year after his first attack, he went out of doors for the last time; but his disease took more than eight years to kill him. For nearly eight years he lay helpless on a couch, with the use of his limbs gone, wasted almost to the proportions of a child, wasted so that a woman could carry him about; the sight of one eye lost, that of the other greatly dimmed, and requiring, that it might be exercised, to have the palsied eyelid lifted and held up by the finger; all this, and, besides this, suffering, at short intervals, paroxysms of nervous agony. I have said he was not pre-eminently brave; but in the astonishing force of spirit with which he retained his activity of mind, even his gaiety, amid all his suffering, and went on composing with undiminished fire to the last, he was truly brave.[5]

The controlled crescendo of this passage, moving from the staccato opening sentences into longer ones, haunted by the stabbing repetitions of 'eight years' and 'wasted', and the carefully placed 'palsied', and the false pause before 'all this', and the subsequent addition of anguish to anguish, marks an unusual intensity of feeling, or at least an unusual rhetorical interest in incurable disease.

Of course, Heine was not, like the others, a little-known writer; yet in Arnold's sense he ought to have been. In calling him 'not pre-eminently brave', Arnold recalls the qualification with which he began the essay, and which, though never fully explicated, colours it throughout: that Heine lacked *courage*, the 'natural force', the 'inborn force and fire' pre-eminent in Byron; and that, lacking these qualities, he appears by comparison the diminutive figure which his illness actually made of him. This sense of being crushed by a prestigious predecessor applies to other cases as well. Guerin comes under the malign and blighting influence of his Jesuit teacher Lammenais, who

> never appreciated Guerin; his combative, rigid, despotic nature, of which the characteristic was energy, had no affinity with Guerin's elusive, undulating, impalpable nature, of which the characteristic was delicacy.[6]

These words might with equal aptness be applied to the relation between Quinillan, the minor poet, and his father-in-law Wordsworth, at whose contribution to Quinillan's decline Arnold glances in his 'Stanzas'.[7] In an obliquer fashion, Arnold regards Senancour too as threatened by the proximity of the mighty dyad of Wordsworth and Goethe, who, in company with Byron, are wheeled on time and again in Arnold's work to represent the giants before the flood, by comparison to whom modern writers appear paltry, shrill and insincere.

Various possible explanations of this complex of preoccupations in Arnold's work seem possible; here, I shall consider three. Figures like Guerin, Heine, Joubert, Senancour, Quinillan—at this point, Arnold's friend Clough might be added to the list—may be seen as representative fragments of Arnold's diagnosis of his own culture as diseased and deficient; as portraits, or even occult self-portraits, of the writer struggling to create in the wake of the giant flood of Romanticism; or as modifications of the Romantic sublime of suffering. Needless to say, these possibilities are intimately interconnected and in no way mutually exclusive.

2

> . . . this strange disease of modern life
> With its sick hurry, its divided aims. . . .[8]

Arnold's diagnosis of his culture as inherently *ill* is famous, though hardly original. Elizabethan concepts of the 'body politic' mediated by, among others, Shakespeare in his history plays, had grounded the political process in metaphors of bodily health and sickness. Carlyle, following Hegel, expanded the metaphor within the context of a historical story built in phases or periods, an idea which his essay, *Characteristics* definitively characterized for his Victorian disciples, including Arnold. Arnold's social polemic, as it developed during and after the 1860s, was based, indeed, upon criteria not very similar to Carlyle's, but relied on Carlyle's argument that English society of the nineteenth century was diseased and in need of cure. Like Carlyle, Arnold casts Goethe in the rôle of the physician who

> took the suffering human race,
> And read each wound, each weakness clear;
> And struck his finger on the place,
> And said: *Thou ailest here, and here!*[9]

Wordsworth he saw as a 'healing power', the medicine, so to speak, prescribed by Goethe, Byron as a Titanic transformation of disease, the 'bleeding heart', into a 'pageant', a gigantic, near-tragic exhibition of power. But these various triumphs all depend upon living at the right time. Arnold qualifies his praise of Goethe in 'In Memory of the Author of "Obermann"' with the comment,

> For though his manhood bore the blast
> Of a tremendous time,
> Yet in a tranquil world was passed
> His tenderer youthful prime.
>
> But we, brought forth and reared in hours
> Of change, alarm, surprise—
> What shelter to grow ripe is ours?
> What leisure to grow wise?[10]

Wordsworth's 'sweet calm', similarly, results from his cultivation of an artificial 'shelter' and 'leisure': sequestered in Nature, his 'eyes avert their ken/ From half of human fate' (53–4). Senancour, who serves for Arnold as the Romantic who anticipates the central character of Arnold's own period, appears by comparison gripped by a disease he can neither escape, diagnose nor cure:

> A fever in these pages burns
> Beneath the calm they feign;
> A wounded human spirit turns,
> Here on its bed of pain.[11]

In 'Obermann', Arnold is prepared to rank Senancour with Goethe and Wordsworth; his more usual response, however, is to superimpose a moral indictment of his age upon his Hegelian sense of it *as* an age, with a distinctive 'spirit'. Byron, the Romantic poet he felt closest to his own period's anguish (hence his omission from 'Obermann', where Senancour is credited with some of his characteristics), provokes the most agonizing contrasts:

> And Byron! let us dare admire,
> If not thy fierce and turbid song,
> Yet that, in anguish, doubt, desire,
> Thy fiery courage still was strong.
>
> The sun that on thy tossing pain
> Did with such cold derision shine,
> He crushed thee not with his disdain—
> He had his glow, and thou hadst thine.
>
> Our bane, disguise it as we may,
> Is weakness, is a faltering course.
> Oh that past times could give our day,
> Joined to its clearness, of their force![12]

'Courage', the title of this poem, will recall Arnold's critique of Heine; the elder Romantics epitomize 'courage', the will and power to be great; their successors evince 'weakness', they fold under the strain and exhibit pathos where only heroic strength will serve. As Arnold remarked in an MS note to *Tristram and Iseult'*,

> The misery of the present age is not in the intensity of men's suffering—but in their incapacity to suffer, enjoy, feel at all, wholly and profoundly; in having their susceptibility eternally agacee by a continual dance of ever-changing objects.[13]

Here the 'sick hurry' repeats itself within the individual mind as a shallowness which corresponds to and promotes the 'weakness' afflicting Victorian man.

The Sick King in Bokhara: Arnold and the Sublime of Suffering

Such comparisons—and they are very widespread in Arnold's work—lead naturally to my second hypothesis: that the 'illness' of Arnold's period is directly *caused* by the elder Romantics, whose greatness inflicts an irreparable 'anxiety of influence' upon their successors. It is certainly not difficult to rephrase Arnold's statements about Wordsworth, Byron and Goethe into confessions of such anxiety, or to interpret his own stylistic irresoluteness, his proclivity for pastiche of Romantic modes, as consequential evidence. The Freudian raw material which, for Bloom, would underlie and promote influence-anxiety is richly prominent in Arnold's life, overwhelmed as he was, like his partial surrogate Clough, by Thomas Arnold's cult of conscience and duty. The Sohrab-Rustum story, with its father-son conflict and ironic victory to the father, or 'A Picture at Newstead', where the father stands mourning the idiocy he has himself inflicted on his son, are only the most obvious dramatizations of Arnold's sense of filial bondage. An even more extraordinary portrait of the resulting neurosis of inadequacy is found in his poem upon the death of an even closer surrogate than Clough, his brother Tom. Like so many of Arnold's figures, Tom died young, and died of a painful illness. Arnold waxes peevish on the feebleness of Tom and his wife, 'two jaded English', who, like the rest, 'never once possess [their] soul/ Before [they] die'. It is an affront to their burial-places, India and the Mediterranean, that representatives of such an inadequate culture should usurp the place which rightfully belongs to 'Some sage to whom the world was dead', or 'Some grey crusading knight austere', or

> Some youthful troubadour, whose tongue
>   Filled Europe once with his love-pain,
> Who here outworn had sunk, and sung
>   His dying strain;
>
> Some girl, who here from castle-bower,
>   With furtive step and cheeks of flame,
> 'Twixt myrtle-hedges all in flower
>   By moonlight came
>
> To meet her private-lover's ship;
>   And from the wave-kissed marble stair
> Beckoned him on, with quivering lip
>   And floating hair.[14]

Allot[15] complains that 'the Byronic romanticism of this [the last] vignette was outmoded even in 1859', but that seems to me to be the point: Arnold's list of heroic types is a sequence of Romantic vignettes whose very simplicity, crudity even, evinces a strength uncompromised by doubt or irony. The 'floating hair' of Arnold's girl adds to this strength the nuance that it might include that of the inspired poet of 'Kubla Khan', whose power has leaked away in the ignominious time to which Tom and his wife belong, rendering them unworthy tenants of the ground their bodies usurp:

> But you—a grave for knight and sage,
>   Romantic, solitary, still,
> O spent ones of a work-day age!
>   Befits you ill.[16]

The only thing that saves this distinctly unamiable passage is its evident applicability to Arnold himself, its illustration of his own panic before the formidable adequacy of the 'Romantic' and 'solitary'.

But if, as I argue, Arnold's anxiety arises from the contrast between his own writing and that of the Romantics, what of his own contrast, most famously drawn in the 1853 *Preface*, between the writing of his own period and that of *classical* times? If there is a contradiction here, it arises from the very intensity of Arnold's anxiety about the Romantics, resulting in their displacement by the safer, less adjacent authority of the classics. But even in Arnold's own thought there is no necessity to suppose a real contradiction. As he makes clear in *On the Modern Spirit in Literature*, and indeed, though obscurely, in *1853*, the characteristics of 'modernity' can be found flourishing in all historical epochs, including superficially 'classical' ones; conversely, the 'classical' virtues may and do appear in so-called 'Romantic' writers. So much (with reservations) Arnold himself concedes. What he is less ready to concede is that the quality for which he admires both Sophocles and Wordsworth, the quality which he christened with the ambiguous name 'the grand style', is not 'the calm, the cheerfulness, the disinterested objectivity', but an 'action' which is 'greater', 'personages' who are 'nobler', 'situations' which are 'more intense': in other words, the *sublime*, whether of classical or Romantic art.[17] His uppermost sense is of the contrast between weakness and strength, and strength, the Longinian or Burkean Sublime, belongs—in different ways and degrees—to Sophocles, to Dante, to Shakespeare, to Milton, to Wordsworth, Byron and Goethe. It does not belong to any Victorian writer, and that, for Arnold, is the real contrast: between an enfeebled and emaciated present, a Heine, a Guerin, a Thyrsis writhing on his 'bed of pain', and the loftier anguish of their predecessors.

The third possibility I wish to consider is that the very 'weakness' of which Arnold complains, and the illness and obscurity which result from it, are precisely extensions of the sublimity which they appear, and appear to him, to compromise. In order to explain what I mean by this, I must describe what I call 'the sublime of suffering' in Romantic art.

3

Burke's theory of the sublime joins together the ideas of suffering, solitude and infinity with that of power. Having argued that negative experiences like '*pain, sickness,* and *death*' (p. 57), and the so-called negative emotions, such as grief, are sources of pleasure to the mind contemplating or experiencing them, he introduces his principal subject in these terms:

> Whatever is fitted in any sort to excite the ideas of pain, and danger, that is to say, whatever is in any sort terrible, or is conversant about terrible objects, or operates in a manner analogous to terror, is a source of the *sublime*.[18]

He explains that the reason behind this apparently perverse delight in suffering is its proximity to an idea of *power*:

> I know of nothing sublime which is not some modification of power. . . . pain is always inflicted by a power in some way superior, because we never submit to pain willingly. So that strength, violence, pain and terror, are ideas that rush in upon the mind together.[19]

The pleasure derives, however, not from submission to power, but from identification with it:

> Now whatever either on good or upon bad grounds tends to raise a man in his own opinion, produces a sort of swelling and

triumph that is extremely grateful to the human mind; and this swelling is never more perceived, nor operates with more force, than when without danger we are conversant with terrible objects, the mind always claiming to itself some part of the dignity and importance of the things which it contemplates.[20]

Logically, this 'swelling' becomes greatest when the object contemplated is omnipotence, or 'infinity': 'hardly any thing can strike the mind with its greatness, which does not make some sort of approach towards infinity.'[21] And this is not only because infinity is the most gigantic thing we can conceive, but also because it is the *obscurest*, the most intellectually inaccessible. Burke remarks, 'To make any thing very terrible, obscurity seems in general to be necessary.'[22] Therefore it is precisely the fact that 'there is nothing of which we really understand so little' which makes 'The ideas of eternity, and infinity, . . . among the most affecting we have'.[23]

Commentators have not failed to note the importance of the Burkean sublime in Romantic thought, yet I am not sure it has been given its full weight. It figures, for Wordsworth, Coleridge, Byron, Shelley, and De Quincey, less as a repertoire of effects than as a definition of the poetic imagination itself as a dark, demonic power born of pain. Such a definition emerges plainly from two passages, one by Wordsworth, the other by Byron (for Arnold, the two greatest, and, more importantly, the definitive English Romantics). The first is a speech from *The Borderers*, Wordsworth's abortive early drama, a speech which reappears as the epigraph to a crucial poem in his development, 'The White Doe of Rylstone':

> Action is transitory—a step, a blow,
> The motion of a muscle—this way or that—
> 'Tis done; and in the after-vacancy
> We wonder at ourselves like men betrayed:
> Suffering is permanent, obscure and dark,
> And has the nature of infinity.

This passage gathers together most of Burke's criteria for the sublime. Suffering is 'dark', it is 'obscure'; most importantly, and also, in a sense, consequently, it 'has the nature of infinity'. Only the antithesis to 'action' is not directly borrowed from Burke, but that too is implicit in Burke's

distinction between the *solitude* necessary for the sublime, and
the essentially *social* character which the 'beautiful' derives
from its basis in sexual attraction. Action is social; suffering, as
it is inherently internal, isolates the sufferer and may end by
denying the social altogether.

The latter point is reinforced in another major statement of
the sublime, the final speech in Byron's *Manfred*. Manfred
addresses it to the spirits who have arrived to conduct him to
Hell:

> Thou hast no power upon me, *that* I feel;
> Thou never shalt possess me, *that* I know:
> What I have done is done; I bear within
> A torture which could nothing gain from thine.
> The mind which is immortal makes itself
> Requital for its good and evil thoughts,
> Is its own origin of ill and end,
> And its own place and time.[24]

Manfred states here what is in effect an absolute independence
of what he calls 'the fleeting things without', an absolute
solitude, a solitude produced by 'torture' and productive of an
entire self-creation. The cause of Manfred's suffering is never
made explicit, remaining, as Wordsworth would say, 'obscure',
and that obscurity both prevents it from competing with the
sublime mind's self-origination and adds a dimension to the
'immortal' stature of that mind by equating it, in Burke's
terms, with the mystery of infinitude.

Only suffering, then, brings about 'the repetition in the
finite mind of the infinite I AM', as the human mind produces
what Burke calls 'the artificial infinite' by 'claiming to itself
some part of the dignity and importance of the things'—Burke
calls them 'terrible objects'—'which it contemplates'. Hence,
for example, the Romantic fascination with storm and tempest;
agents of destruction, they become, in the mind's identification with them, premises of creation. Shelley's west wind is
'destroyer and preserver both' not because its ferocity prefaces
spring as well as concluding summer, but because its power
stings the contemplating mind into a rivalry—'Be thou me,
impetuous one'—which is the precondition of creative effort.
Burke argues that 'a state of rest or inaction' will produce

'melancholy, dejection, despair, and often self-murder' unless counterbalanced by 'exercise or labour'; but 'labour' is not the antithesis of suffering, but a creative form of it: 'labour is a surmounting of difficulties, an exertion of the contracting power of the muscles; and as such resembles pain.' It is creative labour, as a counterpart to suffering rather than its anodyne, that involves the Romantic imagination in the toil of poetic creation.

Arnold's relation to the Romantic sublime of suffering is a highly complex one. In 'A Summer Night', he presents a portrait of what Allott calls 'the Romantic poet-outlaw' in a spectacular apotheosis of storm, suffering and effort:

> And then the tempest strikes him; and between
> The lightning-bursts is seen
> Only a driving wreck,
> And the pale master on his spar-strewn deck
> With anguished face and flying hair
> Grasping the rudder hard,
> Still bent to some port he knows not where,
> Still standing for some false impossible shore.[25]

Allott is right to note[26] the debt to *Adonais* 488–92, but in the 'pale master' Arnold has added to Shelley's picture a purely Byronic image of resistance and defiance. There is an even more striking resemblance to a passage Arnold probably never read, the 'analogy' sequence in the 1804 *Prelude*, where Wordsworth, to illustrate the nature of the poetic imagination, adduces a series of calamitous images of storm and shipwreck: of Dampier, confronted by

> the sea
> Roaring and whitening at the night's approach,
> And danger coming on[27]

—danger, which for 'Sir Humphrey Gilbert, that bold voyager', takes the similar shape of a 'furious storm' in which 'The ship and he a moment afterwards' were 'Engulphed and seen no more' (*WP*, 498). Wordsworth comments that

> Kindred power
> Was present for the suffering and distress
> In those who read the story at their ease,[28]

and his phrasing links writer, reader and subject in a common apotheosis of the sublime of suffering in calamitous death. But

Wordsworth broke off and abandoned this draft, perhaps in alarm at the demonic character imputed to the imagination by such analogies; Arnold's revulsion, despite what Allott calls 'some involuntary admiration', arises from embarrassment at the ritual strength evinced by his Romantic mariner, whom he calls a 'madman'. The alternative is to abandon resistance, and adopt what Wordsworth himself calls a 'wise passiveness'. But in the 1853 *Preface* Arnold rejects this in turn:

> What then are the situations, from the representation of which, though accurate, no poetical enjoyment can be derived? They are those in which the suffering finds no vent in action; in which a continuous state of mental distress is prolonged, unrelieved by incident, hope, or resistance; in which there is everything to be endured, and nothing to be done. In such situations there is inevitably something morbid, in the description of them something monotonous.[29]

The echo of Wordsworth's terms, with their echo, in turn, of Burke's, indicates that this statement repudiates the sublime of suffering, despite the apparent contrast between the convulsed effort of Arnold's 'poet-outlaw' and the absence of 'incident, hope, or resistance' which he cites in the *Preface*. But the contrast is more apparent than real. In 'A Summer Night' the 'morbid' and 'monotonous' suffering mentioned in the Preface appears as the dreary tribulations of ordinary Victorian men, living 'in the sun's hot eye' 'in a brazen prison', who 'languidly/ Their lives to some unmeaning taskwork give'.[30] As this state protracts itself 'year after year',

> Gloom settles slowly down over their breast;
> And while they try to stem
> The waves of mournful thought by which they are pressed,
> Death in their prison reaches them.[31]

A comparison of the language of this passage with that describing the shipwreck of the 'poet-outlaw' shows that the two conditions are tied more closely together than they seem; both suffer 'gloom' and experience the oppression of 'waves'; the difference is merely that for the Romantic 'madman' these are externalized into spectacular and sublime apparitions, while for the wretched 'slave' they are purely internal. This covert bond specifies the real nature of the relation between the Romantic and the modern for Arnold. Both suffer, and suffer analogous anguish. But the Romantic experiences, or transforms his suffering into an encounter with the spectacular in nature and an emulation of the infinite in metaphysics. The modern has not the comfort of this extravagance. A world deserted by visible or metaphysical grandeur turns his suffering into a Carlylean dyspepsia or an Arnoldian depression: into *illness*, considered as an internalization of external meaninglessness and frustration. Burke mentions 'sickness' as one manifestation of sublime pain, but the idea is undeveloped, preference being given to 'pain' and 'death'; Arnold, after his cameo of the 'poet-outlaw' in 'A Summer Night', turns to the present as a spectacle of imprisonment, gloom, and triviality which contrasts with, but also continues, sublime pain. The covert kinship of the two conditions is what causes Empedocles to reject not simply the 'hot prison of the present' but also its apparent obverse, the solitude of sublime creativity:

> And lie thou there,
> My laurel bough!
> I am weary of thee.
> I am weary of the solitude
> Where he who bears thee must abide.[32]

'The Strayed Reveller' indicates the indissoluble link between such solitude, sublime pain, and the diurnal ennui of 'most men'. The gods do not suffer. They

> are happy.
> They turn on all sides
> Their shining eyes,
> And see below them
> The earth and men.
> . . . . .
> These things, Ulysses,
> The wise bards also
> Behold and sing.
> But oh, what labour!
> O prince, what pain![33]

Sharing the infinite perspective of the gods, poets participate, as the gods do not, in the sufferings they perceive:

112

> such a price
> The Gods exact for song:
> To become what we sing.[34]

When, therefore, in 'A Summer Night' or 'A Southern Night', Arnold directly contemplates the 'brazen prison', he too suffers the pain of 'sick hurry' without the marginal solace of companionship with those who suffer.

This leads me to a curious feature of the poem which lent me the title of this essay, 'The Sick King in Bokhara', which is that in it everyone *but* the poet appears sick. The poem's first sickness is that of the 'Moollah' who, in a fever, curses the friends and relatives who have drunk the water he was saving for himself. For him, such an act represents the greater sickness of mortal sin, and he demands that the king ordain his trial and punishment, death by stoning. Twice the king refuses him; the third time he allows punishment, but orders that the man should be allowed to escape if he wishes; he does not, dies; the king falls sick. The poem opens at this point, with the Vizier, who has missed the story through being 'sick/ These many days', hearing it in the king's presence from the poet Hussein, after which the king, despite the Vizier's objections, gives the Moollah a splendid burial.

The varieties of sickness here reflect Arnold's reading of his time and of himself. The Moollah is a glorious anachronism, sublimely sick of a moral disease which however he himself, like Manfred, can cure by willing his own destruction. His sickness reveals, and is a mode of, power, not its negative; the king's sickness reflects his discovery of his own weakness: wishing to pardon the Moollah, and thus enforce his own clemency, he finds himself conquered by the Moollah's will to self-punishment, and encounters the boundaries, the finitude of his power. His sickness, then, reflects his weakness, and his posthumous glorification of the Moollah is a forlorn tribute to sublimity he cannot emulate. The fact that he buries the Moollah *in his own grave* completes the portrait of usurpation. The Vizier's sickness is more straightforwardly a mechanism to get the story told, but it also spreads the sickness of the two central figures into a more widespread social malaise, and proleptically punishes/expresses his flinty refusal of charity to the man he calls a 'dead dog'.

The only person in the poem who is not literally ill is the poet Hussein, yet he, as the thoroughfare through which the story proceeds, is, in the terms of 'The Strayed Reveller', the greatest, and perhaps the only true sufferer. The poet is isolated from his kind and apparently shielded from their diurnal anguish, but in reality perceives and feels the entire panorama of human suffering. Empedocles' rejection of his solitude presages Arnold's rejection of 'Empedocles on Etna', which in turn represents the rejection of poetry itself, since Arnold could neither free himself from the Romantic conception of poetry as the product of the sublime of suffering, nor reconcile himself to paying the price exacted.

But Arnold's attitude was hardly as simple, and his gesture hardly as complete, as such an account implies. His interest in illness sees him bring the sublime of suffering from the mountain-tops to the sickbed, and reduce it to the merely painful and ignominious; yet that reduction simultaneously retrieves an occult reaffirmation of that sublime, and allowed Arnold to continue, for a while, to create.

4

'Men spent by sickness, or obscure decay'.[35] Considering the case of Maurice de Guerin, Arnold glimpses the possibility of reading illness as a privilege, not a privation:

> In him, as in Keats, . . . the temperament, the talent itself, is deeply influenced by their mysterious malady; the temperament is *devouring*; it uses vital power too hard and too fast, paying the penalty in long hours of unutterable exhaustion and in premature death.[36]

The argument is very close to that of 'Early Death and Fame', the short poem which was all that remained in *1867* of a long poem published in *Fraser's Magazine* in 1855, 'Haworth Churchyard'. 'Haworth Churchyard' was Arnold's elegy for Charlotte Brontë, recently dead of consumption, and for Harriet Martineau, apparently on the point of death when the poem appeared (it was her recovery which presumably caused Arnold to withold the poem from all collections until after her death in 1876). As in the case of Guerin, Arnold was clearly fascinated by the conjunction of early death and literary talent in the Brontë family (all four siblings are mentioned), and 'Early Death and Fame' suggests in general terms the ferocious appetite for life which the premature approach of its end engenders:

> Fuller for him be the hours!
> Give him emotion, though pain!
> Let him live, let him feel: *I have lived*.
> Heap up his moments with life!
> Triple his pulses with pain![37]

Charlotte Brontë's celebrity causes him to add 'fame' to the heap of benefits which the early-dying can accumulate; in the case of Guerin, a more characteristic Arnold alter-ego, this is lacking, but its absence is seen as an occult benefit rather than—or as well as—a privation.

> So he lived like a man possessed; with his eye not on his own career, not on the public, not on fame, but on the Isis whose veil he had uplifted. He published nothing: 'There is more power and beauty,' he writes, 'in the well-kept secret of one's self and one's thoughts, than in the display of a whole heaven that one may have inside one.'[38]

Here the illness which threatens the life with closure gives rise, within the logic of Arnold's reasoning, to *secresy*, a voluntary rather than enforced obscurity which contributes directly to the 'power and beauty' (note the Burkean resonance of the terms) of the abbreviated life. Arnold's admiration for the heroic effort of secret creation shades off, however, into an interest in the weakness it accompanies and expresses. He concludes his translation of a particularly weary and dispirited passage from Guerin with the remark: 'Such is this temperament in the frequent hours when the sense of its own weakness and isolation crushes it to the ground.'[39] The phrase 'weakness and isolation' distinguishes Guerin's state from the sublime of suffering, in which isolation produces and is produced by *power*; the contrast with a more directly Romantic contemporary, Browning, reinforces the point:

> *Valens:* [*advancing*]   The lady is alone!
> *Berthold:* Alone, and thus? So weak and yet so bold?
> *Valens:* I said she was alone—

Berthold: —and weak, I said.
Valens: When is man strong until he feels alone?[240]

Weakness, in wholesale contrast to the 'courage' of Byron, is linked to obscurity in Arnold's thought, and that even in the case of Arnold's strongest modern, Senancour. His work, in contrast to Byron's, is pervaded by 'languor', he has surrendered to 'despair', and the result is a work which is 'fraught too deep with pain' to attract 'the world around'.[41] But that very despair, the weakness it expresses, and the obscurity it engenders, are themselves manifestations of the sublime of suffering. Arnold refuses, in retrospect, to demand 'health, success and fame' for Quinillan not for the reasons he gives— that fame as a poet would have made him less amiable as a man—but because the Arnoldian sublime adopts and transforms qualities which seem the reverse of sublime, qualities such as weakness, obscurity, illness, and even mediocrity. Hence in the palinode to 'A Southern Night' Arnold praises his brother and sister-in-law for qualities—gentleness, grace, charm—which are the direct product of the ordinariness which the main body of the poem mocks and deplores; as in the Guerin essay, such qualities are the cherished and fragile obverse of a ruder Romantic strength.

But the logic of Arnold's position goes beyond the discovery and praise of a Burkean 'beauty' in the lives of the obscure. It involves a kind of self-annihilation, the cultivation of weakness and obscurity *in his own work*. Arnold hears Senancour call out '*Strive not! Die also thou!*',[42] and the fact that these words are in turn not Senancour's but Homer's diagnoses the weakness of the modern as a capitulation to predecessors, a collapse before the illustrious forefathers. In the Preface to *1854*, Arnold remarks that one reason for choosing great—i.e. classical— subjects is that they possess 'an immortal strength':

> the most gifted poet, then, may well be glad to supplement with it that mortal weakness, which, in presence of the vast spectacle of life and the world, he must forever feel to be his individual portion.[43]

To confess such 'weakness' while bowing down to the superior power of earlier writers is what Arnold seems here to advocate, but there is another answer. A *refusal to write—*

literary death, to which Arnold's *1853* and *1854* visibly sentenced him—can, in its very feebleness and inadequacy, represent a decisive innovation and an exhibition of paradoxical strength.

It will be sufficiently obvious that I have it in mind to argue that Arnold stopped writing poetry in obedience to the logic of his reversed sublime. As Gottfried notes, it is a cliché of Arnold criticism to note 'Arnold's failure as a poet to satisfy his own classical standards'[44] and to suggest that he frustrated his own talent with his theories; I add that the process was in some sense a deliberate achievement, a dismantling of talent as the ultimate display of talent. And I think that Arnold's work, and his treatment of his work, evidences this. I will not enlarge here on the stylistic features that might be adduced: the halting, stark-naked diction, the sparse and banal metaphors, the coat-of-many-Romantic-colours bleached out by enervated pessimism. I am interested in the drift towards *fragmentation* that besets his works both initially and through the process of revision. The parts of Arnold's poems split apart and drift away not only in the part-metaphorical sense that he 'cannot make it cohere', but in the literal sense that the revisionary process often takes, in his case, the form of a series of predatory raids upon the body of the finished work, in the course of which it is mutilated, if not slain outright.

Everything about the story of 'Empedocles on Etna' is significant, and nothing more so than its dismemberment, in *1853* and *1855*, into a few brief passages—mainly the lyrics of Callicles—after the suppression of the whole poem in *1853* on a policy explained in the famous Preface. Those lyrics were always, in some sense, disjoined, and the poem actually thematizes the disjunction, as Empedocles, hearing the songs, comments on his own mental alienation from 'the freshness of the early world' they represent. The one passage in *1855* in which Empedocles speaks—ll. 276–300, renamed 'The Philosopher and the Stars'—adheres to the same pattern: Empedocles is momentarily seduced into mythologizing the stars into a history of disillusionment like his own. In 'Empedocles', Empedocles goes on to deny the identification; without that palinode, 'The Philosopher and the Stars', like the lyrics of Callicles without Empedocles' commentary, settles into a simpler and less demanding shape. Taken together, then, these passages 'complete' the poem by obeying its logic of separation; they also, like the Preface, *dramatize* Arnold's self-extinction by refusing to allow it to become complete or remain private. A similar pattern arises in the case of 'The Youth of Man', another victim of the surgery of *1853*. Of the 118 lines of the *1852* poem only two short fragments, one of nine lines entitled 'Richmond Hill', the other of seven lines entitled 'Power of Youth', survived in 1853 (though the whole poem was restored in *1855*); here again, the result is that a poem which the 1853 Arnold presumably thought morbid is replaced by two of its own lyric passages which, out of context, suggest a more hopeful outlook. (The other more mournful and discouraged poems of *1852*, such as 'Despondency', 'The Buried Life' and 'Youth's Agitations', were simply suppressed, 'Despondency' never to be reprinted.)

Arnold's stated policy was to banish the morbid and ineffectual, but the resulting simplifications produce more album-leaves than epic actions, and the overall effect of the omission or fragmentation of all the serious poems of *1853* was of Arnold *turning himself into a minor poet*. 'Courage', significant both in title and in content to Arnold's sense of the drama of the sublime, disappeared as well, as thought to suggest that for Arnold that drama was at an end. His devastation of his own work points, however, not to the inception of a heroic future but an aftermath of poetic silence, which in turn, advertised and even flaunted as it is in *1853*, becomes the gesture of the reversed sublime. In *1853* Arnold turned his contention with the Romantics into a psychomachia, a self-inflation which the simultaneous part-extinction of his own talent only threw into sharper relief.

This gesture was repeated in the case of 'Haworth Churchyard' which, though suppressed, as I noted above, between 1855 and 1877, contributed a fragment of itself under the title 'Early Death and Fame' to the intervening collections. In this case, the body was never reassembled, since 'Early Death and Fame' was kept separate from 'Haworth Churchyard' in *1877*, and this fact itself has significance, both in that the mutilation is, as it were, preserved by it, and in that the fragment's demand for 'life' and 'fame' for the early-dying is kept away

118

from Charlotte Brontë, modulating her into something close to the obscured strength, the reversed-sublime, of Arnold's other 'heroes'. Arnold simultaneously stripped from the poem other passages affirming the vigour and achievement of Brontë and Martineau, and one which contrasts them with himself: 'I beheld; the obscure/ Saw the famous.'[45] The removal of these lines seems to me almost whimsically double. For Arnold, famous in 1877, to paint out the original picture of his 'obscure' self at once denies and enhances the 'obscurity', as his deletions elsewhere had brought the Brontës closer to the counter-sublime of 'obscure decay'. In his revision and finally his cancellation of his own poetry, Arnold accuses it of the sickness of modernity and punishes it by mutilation and terminal illness, surrendering himself, as in another way Tennyson did, to the anonymity and mediocrity of the times; yet these gestures amount to and anticipate Beckett's plenary negation of creativity. 'Helpless to write' because 'there is nothing to write and nothing to write about',[46] the Beckett who 'exits weeping' from his dialogues with Georges Duthuit extracts never-diminishing returns from failure and silence, as Arnold did.

NOTES

1. *The Complete Prose Works of Matthew Arnold*, edited by R. H. Super, Vol. III (1962), p. 186.
2. Ibid., p. 12.
3. Kenneth Allott (ed.), *The Poems of Matthew Arnold* (London, 1965), p. 129.
4. Matthew Arnold, 'Stanzas in Memory of Edward Quinillan', ll. 1–4.
5. *The Complete Prose Works of Matthew Arnold*, op. cit., p. 117.
6. Ibid., p. 23.
7. Kenneth Allott (ed.), *The Poems of Matthew Arnold*, op. cit., p. 244.
8. Matthew Arnold, *The Scholar Gipsy*, ll. 204–5.
9. Matthew Arnold, *Memorial Verses*, ll. 19–22.
10. Matthew Arnold, 'In memory of the Author of "Obermann"', ll. 65–72.
11. Ibid., ll. 21–4.
12. Matthew Arnold, 'Courage', ll. 17–28.
13. Quoted in Kenneth Allott (ed.), *The Poems of Matthew Arnold*, op. cit., p. 220.

14. Matthew Arnold, 'A Southern Night', ll. 97–108.
15. Kenneth Allott, op. cit., p. 461.
16. Matthew Arnold, 'A Southern Night', ll. 113–16.
17. Kenneth Allott, op. cit., pp. 591, 594.
18. Edmund Burke, *A Philosophical Enquiry into the Origin of Our Ideas of the Sublime and the Beautiful* (1757; reprinted Menston 1970), p. 58.
19. Burke, ibid., pp. 111–12.
20. Ibid., pp. 83–4.
21. Ibid., p. 108.
22. Ibid., p. 100.
23. Ibid., p. 105.
24. Byron, *Manfred*, III, iv, ll. 385–92.
25. Matthew Arnold, 'A Summer Night', ll. 62–9.
26. Kenneth Allott, op. cit., p. 269.
27. Wordsworth, *The Prelude* (1799, 1805, 1850), edited by Jonathan Wordsworth (M. H. Abram, Stephen Gill, New York, 1979), p. 499.
28. Ibid.
29. Kenneth Allott, op. cit., p. 592.
30. Matthew Arnold, 'A Summer Night', ll. 37–40.
31. Ibid., ll. 46–9.
32. Matthew Arnold, 'Empedocles on Etna', Act II, ll. 196–200.
33. Matthew Arnold, 'The Strayed Reveller', ll. 130–34, 206–11.
34. Ibid., ll. 232–34.
35. Matthew Arnold, 'Baldur Dead', l. 325.
36. *The Complete Prose Works of Matthew Arnold*, op. cit., p. 32.
37. Matthew Arnold, 'Early Death and Fame', ll. 15–19.
38. *The Complete Prose Works of Matthew Arnold*, op. cit., p. 34.
39. Ibid., p. 33.
40. Robert Browning, 'Columbe's Birthday', III, ll. 228–31.
41. Kenneth Allott, op. cit., p. 171.
42. Matthew Arnold, 'In memory of the Author of "Obermann" ', l. 92.
43. Kenneth Allott, op. cit., p. 609.
44. L. Gottfried, *Matthew Arnold and the Romantics* (1963), p. 20.
45. Kenneth Allott, op. cit., p. 391.
46. 'Three Dialogues by Samuel Beckett and Georges Duthuit', in *Samuel Beckett*, edited by Martin Esslin (New Jersey, 1965), p. 19.

5

'A Religion of Sorrow': Arnold's Relation to Comedy

by WILLIAM KAUFMAN

In a discussion on French theatre, Matthew Arnold offered a description of tragedy and comedy which in no small measure contributed to the erroneous impression often held by undergraduates that he was one of the least humorous figures in English literature:

> Only by breasting in full the storm and cloud of life, breasting it and passing through it and above it, can the dramatist who feels the weight of mortal things liberate himself from the pressure, and rise, as all seek to rise, to content and joy. Tragedy breasts the pressure of life. Comedy eludes it, half liberates itself from it by irony.[1]

Any discussion of Arnold's relation to comedy, if dependent wholly upon his expressed theories and sentiments, might tend to corroborate the impression of his grimness; it may be argued that the bulk of his prose is more critical than complimentary, and his poetry more steeped in melancholy than joy. Comedians, it is well known, were a bane to him. Yet any writer discussing Arnold's antipathy towards comedy owes it to Arnold's reputation to remind his readers that Arnold was indeed a humorous man, not only personally, but in much of his writing—one need only read Arnold's

121

'Friendship's Garland', his letters, or Park Honan's biography, to find evidence of this. His talent for wit and irony was first-rate and apparent in innumerable passages of his criticism. Anyone about to pounce on Arnold for his humourlessness would do well to remember Max Beerbohm's caricature in *The Poet's Corner*, showing a dandified Arnold lolling against a mantelpiece, sporting a mischievous smile, in front of his little niece, who asks, 'Why, Uncle Matthew, Oh why, will not you be always wholly serious?' It is necessary to recall that Arnold fell victim to the good intentions of his Victorian family and friends who wished to protect his reputation as a serious man of letters. Thus while G. W. E. Russell could refer to Arnold's 'playfulness' and 'inexhaustible fun' in the preface to Arnold's collected letters, he would elsewhere complain that 'every trace of humour' had been deleted by his family before giving him the letters to edit, resulting in a 'curious obscuration' denying Arnold's 'most characteristic traits'.[2] A. T. Quiller-Couch, while on one hand admitting Arnold's playfulness, seemed likewise intent on countering the impression of it:

> For the mass of his countrymen he came somehow to personify a number of things which their minds vaguely associated with kid gloves, and by his ironical way of playing with the misconception he did more than a little to confirm it. But in truth Arnold was a serious man who saw life as a serious business, and chiefly relied, for making the best of it, upon serene common sense.[3]

Thus it would be good to remember, when examining Arnold's theories of comedy as a means of evasion often connected with a juvenile or under-developed intelligence, that the examination is of a man whose society had forced him to restrain his own powerfully playful instincts, a man utterly sensitive to the wretched conditions of his society, and devoted to improving them.

Many illuminating fragments of Arnold's life and work that pertain to his deepening antagonism towards comedy can be seen in the context of his childhood and youth, when, as the son of the headmaster of Rugby—himself highly accomplished at an early age—Matthew Arnold grew up under the over-bearing shadow of awesome public responsibility. Before his death at the age of 40, Dr. Thomas Arnold had gained national renown for his persistent crusading for industrial, educational, religious, and social reform. From him Matthew Arnold developed early a sense of, and respect for, authority, not only in religious and cultural matters, but as reflected in his later heroes in whom he saw the virtue of tenacity—Cromwell, Wellington, Napoleon, and U. S. Grant. The moral fervour with which Arnold championed a strong, benevolent, though strict cultural authority stems from the example of his father, as witnessed in his poem, 'Rugby Chapel'; and the same fervour in his father was conditioned, if not overwhelmingly, by the comic sense noted later by Matthew's brother, Tom: 'My father was not witty, nor—though he could appreciate humour—was he humorous: but the comic and grotesque side of life attracted him strongly.'[4] After Dr. Arnold's death, his wife, Mary, looked anxiously for his traits in their children, persistently attempting to check Matthew's juvenile laziness and frivolity. She worried often about his sobriety; as Honan notes, her 'fretful attitude' about Matthew's idleness and waywardness became 'a major factor in his life'. Matthew was infected early by her pathos and melancholy, the themes of which appear in her extensive journals as well as her son's later poetry.[5] Under such influential and relentless guidance, there was little chance that the Arnold children could easily get away with the mischievous anarchy that inspires not only childhood, but the bulk of comedy as well.

Still, anarchy and mischief were integral parts of Matthew Arnold's youthful nature, however much he condemned it in society. As a youth he was as defiantly playful as his father had evidently been—and he was frequently reminded that his father had *outgrown* it. Matthew was nonetheless playful, violently so; he loved guns, shot at birds, gave his brother bloody noses, and once pretended to be drowned in Lake Windermere. His antics were in part a form of rebellion, fuelled by the fact of his brothers and sisters being constantly upheld as good examples, while Matthew was chided for his 'obstinacy'; thus does Honan see a relationship between the playful aggression of the child and the often deadly sobriety of the man as witnessed in print: 'Matthew's strenuous exertion in maturity, his lethally effective critical manner, and his deep, fierce pride are connected to early and repeated sensations of being outstripped.'[6]

His juvenile gaiety was reflected in a poem written at the age of 14—'The First Sight of Italy'—whose joyfully irresponsible sentiments could hardly be attributed to the poetry of the mature Matthew Arnold. He writes as a teenager of 'joy in the sparkling eye/ Of the maidens dancing merrily' and visions 'In the depths of the sea/ Where the Whale and the Dolphin are rolling in glee'. His irresponsibility continued well into the next decade, when as a Balliol scholar at Oxford he became more renowned for his pranks than his academic achievements; his tutors complained about his antics, his laziness, his lack of reading, and his extra-long holidays. His clothes, minor feats, and laughter had him marked as a slightly crazed dandy, and he was known for his appreciation of gin, whisky, wine, champagne, and ale, as well as his aversion to teetotallers. According to his sister, he was superficial enough to meticulously perfume his sideburns with *Eau de Mille Fleurs*, eau de Cologne, 'and twenty eaux beside'. His Oxford friend, Manley Hawker, had frequent cause to remark, 'Matt utters as many absurdities as ever, with as grave a face.'[7] This same Hawker noted one of Arnold's milder practical jokes after a visit from Oxford:

> We arrived here on Friday evening, after sundry displays of the most consummate coolness on the part of our friend Matt, who pleasantly induced a belief into the passengers of the coach that I was a poor mad gentleman, and that he was my keeper.[8]

Arnold also precipitated the streaking fad by over a century when he ran naked around the hallowed quadrangles of Oxford, replying on the spot to a reprimanding cardinal, 'Is it possible that you see anything indelicate in the human form divine?' His jokes were not limited during the Oxford years to antics and utterances; he also put his stamp of humour on paper, burlesquing Shakespeare, Milton, and Wordsworth in his *Fox How Magazine*, as well as mocking and parodying Cardinal Newman's *Tracts for the Times*, written by Dr. Thomas Arnold's most outspoken critic and intellectual adversary, who Matthew grew to respect. Still, it was, perhaps, no surprise to Matthew when he received a second-class degree—a veritable scandal for a Balliol scholar—however branded he was as 'a shallow, lazy, silly man with a great name, who had thrown every chance to the winds and sunk to mediocrity'. Arnold's reaction was typical for those days; he responded with a drinking and gambling spree.[9]

This high-spirited, gleeful dandy, so willing to laugh and provoke laughter, was also on the verge of turning out his first mature poetry. In the decade between 1843 and 1853 Arnold produced not only his prize-winning poem, 'Cromwell', but also three collections of poetry: *'The Strayed Reveller' and Other Poems* (1849), *'Empedocles on Etna' and Other Poems* (1852), and *Poems by Matthew Arnold* (1853). These, along with certain desk notes written in the same decade, show that Arnold's youthful, gay, irresponsibility bears a direct relation to his theories of poetic inspiration and creativity, formulated before he had thrown himself into the self-supporting drudgery of Victorian England, whose ennui, trauma, and despair he would later reflect famously. Lionel Trilling has noted the relationship between Arnold's poetry and his high-spirited arrogance and irresponsibility:

> If we are to understand the relation of Arnold's poetry to his life we must understand the relation of his cockiness to his philosophy; for when the dandyism was at work, Arnold produced poetry, but when the dandyism failed, poetry failed too.[10]

Arnold revealed his belief in these years that his chosen vocation, poetry, depended precisely upon such joyful disengagement and unfettered irresponsibility as that which he had yet shown in his youth. But he was the son of Dr. Thomas Arnold, a forthright man of action, becoming increasingly aware of his own and his age's distress. After his Balliol disappointment, he responsibly buckled himself down to winning an Oriel fellowship at Oxford, thereby redeeming himself in the eyes of his family, and soon supporting himself through the humourless drudgery of teaching-school in Victorian England.

Thus did Matthew Arnold begin the soul-search that

125

showed him how 'fragmented' he was; here was a born poet, in his own words breathed on in the 'helpless cradle' by Pan, seeing a detachment from the world's stagnating, stultifying hubbub as the only course to true poetic vision—yet realizing concurrently that the state of his society could only be improved by determined, responsible action and hard, thankless work. Hence the division of 'Cromwell', written by a 21-year-old jokester, showing the lurking recognition that irresponsibility and detachment can only be symptoms of youth. He tries to reconcile a double-vision, that of an old soldier reflecting on his profligate youth and steady maturation. The opening synopsis betrays Arnold's awareness of his own ill-spent youth, as well as his hopes for himself: 'The germs of his future character probably formed during his life of inaction'; thus 'Youth stain'd with follies' gives way to 'A life—that wrote its purpose with a sword/ Moulding itself in action, not in word!' There is a note of desperation in Arnold's plea that his life of inaction might yet produce some good for himself and his society: 'Say not such dreams are idle: for the man/ Still toils to perfect what the child began.'[11] During his dreadful school-teaching tenure he produced more poems showing the despair of a man whose creativity was threatened by the unavoidable absorption into the worldly routine: 'The Strayed Reveller', portraying the poet desperate in his life of inaction when the need for action and social participation is so painfully obvious; or 'To a Gipsy Child by the Sea Shore', reflecting Arnold's horror that a child, in whose untarnished youth the hope of poetry rests, should wear such a visible mask of time-worn, worldly grief before his time. Again, 'The Scholar Gipsy' reveals Arnold's fear of what his growing sense of social commitment would do to his muse:

> But fly our paths, our feverish contact fly!
>   For strong the infection of our mental strife,
>   Which, though it gives no bliss, yet spoils for rest;
>   And we should win thee from thy own fair life,
>   Like us distracted, and like us unblest.
>   Soon, soon they cheer would die,
>   Thy hopes grow timorous, and unfix'd thy powers,
>   And thy clear aims be cross and shifting made:
>   And then thy glad perennial youth would fade,
>   Fade, and grow old at last, and die like ours.[12]

Arnold's deepening social awareness, and its concurrent melancholy, resulted in the perplexed reception of his first volume of poems by his family and friends. His sister could not believe that they were written by a man whose spirits were otherwise so 'gloriously gay'; and his friend James Anthony Froude complained, 'I wish M. didn't so utterly want *humour.*'[13]

Arnold's friends and family could not have been fully aware of the crisis raging within the outwardly gay, ironical, dry-witted joker; hence their surprise at the melancholy of his poems. For even though he had chosen poetry as his vocation, his deepening sense of morality and social commitment, undoubtedly fired by the memory of his father, bound his lyricism and quelled his exuberance. Even a poem as early as 'Cromwell' revealed what Honan calls a conflict between 'creative retreat on one hand and responsible moral action on the other'. Arnold himself was to harp frequently on that same string, stressing the incompatibility between the muse and social participation, in Trilling's words, 'the antagonism between the creative imagination and the critical intellect'; thus does the conflict recur in 'Sohrab and Rustum', depicting the slaying of an exuberant son by his mighty father, written two years after Arnold finally forsook the poet's retreat out of necessity, beginning thirty-five years of committed over-work as an inspector of schools. He became one of the first eminent Victorian writers to support himself fully by non-literary work, and one of the first to so utilize the new railroads as to expose himself daily to the wretchedness and squalor of British lower-class life.[14] Sometimes working eighteen hours a day, travelling the length and breadth of Britain as well as the continent, comforting when he could over-worked teachers and underfed schoolchildren, and knocking his head against the brick wall of official bureaucracy on behalf of educational reform, Arnold found his severely critical intellect overtaking the free-wheeling muse of poetry, however he tried to protect his muse. Always and unquestionably outwardly cheerful, he nevertheless revealed both the inward corrosion of his gaiety and the reasons for it in such poems as 'A Summer Night', written during his first year of inspectorship; he finds himself threatened with

127

imprisonment in the same cage as the mass of Victorian humanity:

> For most men in a brazen prison live,
> Where in the sun's hot eye,
> With heads bent o'er their toil, they languidly
> Their lives to some unmeaning taskwork give,
> Dreaming of naught beyond their prison wall,
> And as, year after year,
> Fresh products of their barren labour fall
> From their tired hands, and rest
> Never yet comes more near,
> Gloom settles slowly down over their breast.
> And while they try to stem
> The waves of mournful thought by which they are prest,
> Death in their prison reaches them
> Unfreed, having seen nothing, still unblest.[15]

He had always felt that the poetic imagination depended on a childlike intuition and fancy, yet he writes while in the thick of inspecting, 'My respect for reason as the rock of refuge to this poor exaggerated surexcited humanity increases and increases.' Citing Locke as a philosophical mentor during the necessary process of maturation, Arnold insists that 'we *must* [forsake] the aimless and unsettled but also liberal and open state of our youth.' Gradually the relentless analytic school inspector and critic usurped the fancy of the poet, and, in 'Empedocles on Etna', he predicts the death of the poetic imagination, as the poet chooses suicide in the face of a wholly rational, materialistic world.[16] His last thin volume of poetry presents his ultimate poetic despair and desiccation, containing 'Dover Beach', 'Though the Muse be gone away', 'The Last Word', and numerous impressions on growing old. He was only 45 when it was published.

Thus did Matthew Arnold gradually mature into a mortal enemy of evasion, artistic or otherwise. The committed social reformer and critic thrust himself headlong into attacking the ills of his nation and age, devoting the remainder of his life's free time to writing voluminous essays and criticisms with astonishing determination, and gaining world renown for it.

'A Religion of Sorrow': Arnold's Relation to Comedy

His last volume of poetry was published in 1867, and for the next twenty years, until his death, he wrote little verse, save for a few notable poems like 'Westminster Abbey' (1882). He had found that his poetry had depended on evasion, on escape from the mire of worldly involvement, and this was irreconcilable with his moral fervour and social commitment.

It is with this understanding that one must approach Arnold's antagonism towards comedy. Evasion was an anathema to him; and rather than admit that comedy often pretends to draw attention away from its subject while in fact highlighting it, Arnold saw comedy only as a means of detachment from the pain and troubles of life. Comedy enforced a separation of the mind and the emotions, divorced or deflected attention from one's own condition and that of the world. Arnold wrote in an early desk note that the 'disease of the present age is divorce from oneself', blaming it upon the sorts of distraction and befuddlements not unlike those produced in the spirit of comedy: the 'misery of the present age' is caused by human susceptibility

> eternally *agacée* by a continual dance of ever-changing objects . . . in their having one moment the commencement of a feeling, at the next moment the commencement of an imagination, and the eternal tumult of the world mingling, breaking in upon, hurrying away all.[17]

In other words, Arnold meant 'anarchy', in the sense that it was a response divorced from reason and bound by no discipline. Whether it was intellectual, social, or artistic anarchy, Arnold saw it as an enemy to the improvement, advancement, and refinement of culture. Anarchy was to him the wilful divorce from accepted convention and an evasion of responsibility; and he knew too well that comedy could amount to the most anarchic of artistic responses. He would almost certainly have been appalled, for instance, by many modern comedians who followed in the traditions of his own contemporaries; thus can be felt the Arnoldian spirit in a pronouncement made decades later by Charlie Chaplin, himself terrified by the thought of anarchy in the 1930s:

> The Marx Brothers are frightening. Thurber, Stewart, Joe Cook, Benchley—yes, all of them. They say, 'All right, this is

how we live and we'll live that way'. They go in for being crazy.
It's a soul-destroying thing. They say, 'All right, you're insane,
we'll appeal to your insanity'. They make insanity the convention. They make humor a premise. Acquiescence in everything
disintegrating. Knocking everything down. Annihilating everything. There's no *conduct* in their humor.[18]

If social improvement depended on the adherence to a rigid,
tested, and proved cultural standard, Arnold argued, how
could even the slightest eccentricities be tolerated? Thus did
he condemn Whitman for his poetic eccentricities, and *The
Times* for its orthographical eccentricities:

> Some people will say these are little things; they are not; they
> are of bad example. They tend to spread the baneful notion that
> there is no such thing as a high, correct standard in intellectual
> matters; that every one may as well take his own way; they are
> at variance with the severe discipline necessary for all real
> culture; they confirm us in habits of wilfulness and eccentricity,
> which hurt our minds, and damage our credit with serious
> people.[19]

With such rigid allowances as Arnold's, what chance would
such joyful eccentrics and cultural anarchists as Chaucer,
Burns, Molière, Heine, and Mark Twain have when brought
to his attention? About the same chance as Voltaire, who came
under Arnold's attack via his quoting of the French critic
Joubert. Arnold quotes Joubert on Voltaire in order to extol
the 'soundness and completeness' of Joubert's critical judgement, with his chosen quote reinforcing his own detestation of
the atmosphere which allows and promotes a wit like Voltaire's:

> Voltaire is sometimes afflicted, sometimes strongly moved; but
> serious he never is. His very graces have an effrontery about
> them. He had correctness of judgement, liveliness of imagina-
> tion, nimble wits, quick taste, and a moral sense in ruins. He is
> the most debauched of spirits, and the worst of him is that one
> gets debauched along with him. If he had been a wise man, and
> had had the self-discipline of wisdom, beyond a doubt half his
> wit would have been gone; it needed an atmosphere of *licence* in
> order to play freely. Those people who read him every day,
> create for themselves, by an invincible law, the necessity of liking
> him. But those people who, having given up reading him, gaze
> steadily down upon the influence which his spirit has shed

abroad, find themselves in simple justice and duty compelled to detest him.[20]

Arnold was well aware of the comedy's seductive power, despairing that entire nations such as France and the United States had been infected by it. Too much laughter was a dangerous anaesthetic, craftily drawing attention away from the spiritual and social malaise of life, falsely convincing humanity of its own well-being. As early as 1849, he warned of the seduction of the false gaiety inspired by 'The New Sirens' of his age:

> Mad delight, and frozen calms—
> Mirth to-day and vine-bound tresses,
> And to-morrow—folded palms—
> Is this all? This balanc'd measure?
> Could life run no easier way?
> Happy at the noon of pleasure,
> Passive, at the midnight of dismay?[21]

Arnold conceivably had personal grounds for being so suspicious of comedy and laughter as shields to pain, responsibility, and commitment; as it has been shown, through his jokes and pranks and laziness at Balliol, he had suffered a blow to his academic success. Fully aware of the distance his own gaiety caused—from his own troubles and responsibility towards himself and his friends—he employed humour and joking to keep himself aloof from worldly entanglements that would otherwise have harmed his poetry, or so he said when he found his college friends growing too intellectually and philosophically critical. They repeatedly complained bitterly that his mockery and irony kept them at bay, so that he had to deliver such apologies as those that went to J. D. Coleridge:

> Your last letter is penetrated with that unfortunate error as to my want of interest in my friends. It is an old subject. . . . I laugh too much and they make one's laughter mean too much. However, the result is that when one wishes to be serious, one cannot but fear a half suspicion on one's friends' parts that one is laughing, and, so, the difficulty gets worse and worse.[22]

In print as well, Arnold found that his attempts at levity had often backfired. In his essay 'On Translating Homer', delivered as a lecture when he was Oxford's Professor of

Poetry, he had employed wit and irony to give an element of detachment and relief to his criticism; the *Saturday Review* condemned him for his 'low buffoonery'. Arnold responded with a defence of his 'vivacity' in the preface to *Essays in Criticism*, wherein he said that without such liveliness, 'we shall all yawn in one another's faces with the dismallest, the most unimpeachable gravity.' He was slapped on the wrist again for the likes of this, which pervades *Essays in Criticism*; the *Guardian* began its review with the question: 'What is the unsatisfactory element in Mr. Arnold as a writer? Why, with his great gifts, is he of little or no weight as a teacher?' The answer might have come from the mature Arnold himself: 'Misplaced jokes are dangerous things, and rash personalities are out of place, whether we are joking or in earnest.'

Arnold was not only stung when his own levity backfired; he was seriously stung when levity was aimed at him. As Honan notes, he could mock but could not stand being mocked: 'No sooner did he become sexually interested in a woman, than he complained of her mockery or inattention.' Thus he wept over his fiancée's 'mockery', and complained of Mary Claude, the probable 'Marguerite' of his poems, with her 'French mockery', 'power of ridicule', 'wit', 'abuse', and 'spleen'.[23] Similar complaints find their way into 'The Buried Life', where jesting is characteristically paired with pain and mockery in Arnold's mind:

> Light flows our war of mocking words, and yet,
> Behold with tears my eyes are wet.
> I feel a nameless sadness o'er me roll.
> Yes, yes, we know that we can jest,
> We know, we know that we can smile;
> But there's a something in this breast
> To which thy light words bring no rest,
> And thy gay smiles no anodyne.[24]

Likewise, Arnold responded to his friends' laughter with a poem that on first glance shows more than a trace of self-pity; 'To My Friends, Who Ridiculed a Tender Leave-Taking' is Arnold's reply to his friends who laughed over Mary Claude's having stood him up at a Swiss hotel:

> Laugh, my Friends, and without blame
> Lightly quit what lightly came:

Rich tomorrow as to-day
Spend as madly as you may.
I, with little land to stir,
Am the exacter labourer.[25]

Arnold associates his friends' laughter with frivolous youth—
although he himself is only 27—recalling such sentiments in
himself:

But my Youth reminds me—'Thou
Hast liv'd light as these live now:
As these are, thou too were such:
Much hast had, hast squander'd much'.
Fortune's now less frequent heir,
Ah! I husband what's grown rare.

Insisting that such levity betrayed a lack of the sensibility to
feel, Arnold capped his criticism with the ultimate insult that
his friends were 'more American than English'.[26]

Yet, however much the first glance suggests, the accusation
of self-pity will not suffice. As his most fervent writings reveal,
Arnold imagined the sentiments of tragedy as the most
beneficial for mankind, the state of mind which allowed the
fullest depth of feeling. Hence his denigration of comedy,
which he felt evaded feeling, and hence his championing of
tragedy as the supreme artistic expression:

In presence of the most tragic circumstances, represented in a
work of Art, the feeling of enjoyment, as is well known, may still
subsist: the representation of the most utter calamity, of the
liveliest anguish, is not sufficient to destroy it: the more tragic
the situation, the deeper becomes the enjoyment, and the
situation is more tragic in proportion as it becomes more
terrible.[27]

He thus turns Wordsworth on his head, marking sorrow rather
than happiness as the worthy measure of human dignity and
sensibility. With this intent do so many of his writings and
indeed his very reputation sustain the sentiments of 'Fragment
of Chorus of *A Dejaneira*':

O frivolous mind of man,
Light ignorance, and hurrying, unsure thoughts,
Though man bewails you not,
How I bewail you![28]

133

The noblest of aims, he says in 'Resignation', is not to amuse, but 'to set free'—this is tragedy's accomplishment: freedom through the confrontation with the terrible rather than the evasion of it. Arnold finds no higher example than Obermann, as his poem of that name reveals, for the 'air of languor, cold, and death' which makes its pages burn with a tragic fever, in which 'A wounded human spirit turns/ Here, on its bed of pain.' Wordsworth's clear, free vision of joy was well enough for a man whose 'tender, youthful prime' was passed in tranquillity; but Arnold's age has 'a worse course to steer':

> Too fast we live, and too much are tried,
> Too harass'd, to attain
> Wordsworth's sweet calm, or Goethe's wide
> And luminous view to gain.[29]

And so he turns to Obermann, the 'sadder Sage':

> To thee: we feel thy spell.
> The hopeless tangle of our age—
> Thou too hast scann'd it well.

Men like Arnold, who have conscientiously watched their world, cannot but feel misery and revile evasion—'Can neither, when we will, enjoy;/ Nor, when we will, resign.' They must live in the world; and Arnold looks to the tragic Obermann for strength, comfort, and partnership in his suffering: 'but thou—

> Thou melancholy Shade!
> Wilt not, if thou canst see me now,
> Condemn me, nor upbraid.

Arnold knows he is *right* in his tragic appreciation of the world, quoting Sainte-Beuve in implying a moral dimension to the appreciation of both tragedy and comedy:

> the first consideration for us is not whether we are amused and pleased by a work of art or mind, nor is it whether we are touched by it. What we seek above all to learn is, whether *we were right* in being amused with it, and in applauding it, and being moved by it.

For Arnold it is in fact a matter of honour; a man 'is bound to honour and obey the right' and is 'disgraced by cleaving to the wrong'.[30]

What is the wrong? In this context, it is the antithesis of tragedy and its appreciation; it is the 'religion of pleasure' as conceived and described by Heinrich Heine, whom Arnold quotes in preface to blasting him:

> The fairer and happier generations, offspring of unfettered unions, that will rise up and bloom in the atmosphere of a religion of pleasure, will smile sadly when they think of their poor ancestors, whose life was passed in melancholy abstinence from the joys of this beautiful earth, and who faded away into spectres, from the mortal compression which they put upon the warm and glowing emotions of sense. Yes, with assurance I say it, our descendants will be fairer and happier than we are; for I am a believer in progress, and I hold God to be a kind being who has intended man to be happy.[31]

There is more than just sexual licence implied in Heine's 'religion of pleasure'; it is the sort of licence Arnold condemned in his treatment of Voltaire, the licence that allowed his wit to 'play freely'—the artistic, intellectual, and social licence of France, which Arnold often condemned and Heine always extolled. The thought of this light, frivolous, cheerful 'pagan' life, the sort abounding in the comic idylls of Theocritus, fatigues and revolts Arnold, oppresses and confines him 'with a desire for an utter change, for clouds, storms, effusions, and relief'. Its natural end is the retribution of Herculaneum and Pompeii—joy caught dancing unawares.[32] To Arnold, the most 'brilliant champion' of the religion of pleasure is Heine, and for this reason he was one of the first of a long line of comedians to come under the scathing of Arnold's critical pen.

As a young man, Arnold was 'disgusted' by Heine, or so he told his mother.[33] Yet as he showed later in his two major writings on Heine—the essay 'Heinrich Heine' and the poem 'Heine's Grave'—he grew to admire Heine for his enlightenment and detestation of Philistinism; he respected Heine for the form of his poetry, honoured him for his social commitment, and was moved by Heine's courage in the face of a lingering death and tragic end. For all this, however, Arnold's final pronouncement on Heine was that the end was inevitable—the predictable, Vesuvian end to a devotee of pure pleasure and grand comedy.

Heine himself declared that a sword, rather than a laurel wreath, should be placed on his coffin, for he considered himself a poet secondly, and a social activist primarily. In 'Heinrich Heine', Arnold concurs, echoing Heine's declaration that he was a 'soldier in the Liberation War of Humanity'. For this reason alone does Arnold in fact declare Heine 'the most important German successor and continuator of Goethe', a fact which Carlyle was remiss in noting twenty years before.[34] Ever devoted to the impression, if not the reality, of critical even-handedness, Arnold praised Heine's breadth of vision and desire to infect his native Germany with the beneficent cultural and political influences of elsewhere, notably France. He elevated Heine as a 'child of light', the enemy of provincialism and Philistinism:

> The enthusiast for the idea, for reason, values reason, the idea, in and for themselves; he values them, irrespectively of the practical conveniences which their triumph may obtain for him; and the man who regards the possession of these practical conveniences as something sufficient in itself, something which compensates for the absence or surrender of the idea, of reason, is, in his eyes, a Philistine.

Arnold noted that Heine brought to a reluctant, intellectually glutted and sluggish Germany a fresh, intense modernism, rejecting 'stock classicism and stock romanticism', bringing his nation into the timely point of view of the nineteenth century; for this did Heine strike Arnold as 'so remarkable'— for his 'wonderful clearness, lightness, and width of range'. Arnold's praise extended to Heine's 'incomparable' poetical mastery, employed with 'the most exquisite lightness and ease', and evident in such of Heine's works as the *Reisebilder* and *Romancero*.

Yet all this praise is a characteristic prelude to a severe dose of punctuating criticism, revolving particularly around Heine's employment of wit and, the old Arnoldian terror, mockery. 'Dissolvents of the old European system of dominant ideas and facts we must all be', says Arnold; but 'what we have to study is that we may not be acrid dissolvents of it.' Rather than praise Heine for his 'divine sarcasm', as Nietzsche did, Arnold prefers to hold up the example of Goethe's 'Olympian politeness' as an important element lacking in Heine. Of Goethe's politeness, Arnold wrote: 'Nothing could be more really subversive of the foundations on which the old European order rested.' In contrast, Heine was left with a blemished name; 'With his crying faults', Arnold asks, numbering among them his 'incessant mocking', 'how could it be otherwise?' Again, Heine's end was inevitable, for he was 'profoundly *dis*respectable; and not even the merit of not being a Philistine can make up for a man's being that'. Suggesting that even Heine must have predicted the reasons for his demise, Arnold quotes the poet's own words in a gesture of accusation:

> Alas! the mockery of God is heavy upon me! The great author of the universe, the Aristophanes of Heaven, has determined to make the petty earthly author, the so called Aristophanes of Germany, feel to his heart's core what pitiful needle-pricks his cleverest sarcasms have been, compared with the thunderbolts which his divine humour can launch against feeble mortals!

But there is a perceptible touch of triumphant mockery in Arnold's own pronouncement: 'what a manifest failure is the last word of the religion of pleasure!' Even in his later poem, 'Heine's Grave', though Arnold seeks to rescue the dead poet from the 'mocking laughter' of 'bitter spirits', and would rather speak at his grave not in pity and censure, but awe, the implication remains that Heine was the inevitable victim of a 'divine humour' much more terrible than his own. In the essay, Arnold is willing to grant the comic poet a feeble escape clause, but even then proclaims it an unfair advantage:

> One man in many millions, a Heine, may console himself, and keep himself erect in suffering, by a colossal irony of this sort, by covering himself and the universe with the red fire of this sinister mockery; but the many millions cannot,—cannot if they would.

Instead, Arnold offers *his* alternative, a solution steeped in the spirit of tragedy which he champions. Implicit in his preference is his ever-present denunciation of comedy as an art form:

137

That is where the sentiment of a religion of sorrow has such a vast advantage over the sentiment of a religion of pleasure; in its power to be a general, popular, religious sentiment, a stay for the mass of mankind, whose lives are full of hardship.

With this sentiment upheld by such a firm adherent to the 'religion of sorrow', in his eyes Heinrich Heine could be only an unfortunate fallen angel.

Heine's was not the only poetic spirit marred by a tendency towards the comic. As it has been shown, Arnold was not too kind to Voltaire because of his wit; likewise, Molière was flawed, 'hampered and lamed' by comedy, which escapes 'the test of seriousness'—again, a test of tragedy, 'breasting in full the storm and cloud of life, breasting it and passing through it and above it'. Molière's *Misanthrope* and *Tartuffe* are marred by artificiality, since by its light and evasive nature, the 'artificial can pass in comedy more easily'. Precisely for Molière's employment of comedy in verse—his great error—does Arnold believe that 'this true and great poet is actually most satisfactory in his prose.'[35] That Molière could indeed have been a serious man is no matter; his fault was the fault of France: a misguided elevation of wit and a lack of 'higher seriousness' in poetry.

This is the key phrase at the core of Arnold's 'The Study of Poetry', wherein any poet condemned is so condemned for his lack of 'higher seriousness'—it reveals itself in the very construction of the poetry, he says, proportional in superiority to that of diction and movement. Yet, as Lionel Trilling has noted, the construction seems not the essence of a poem's quality as much as its 'grimness or sadness or melancholy or resignation'. Arnold is particular about which poets possessed such qualities, in both respects: Homer, Dante, Shakespeare, who may be forgiven for his lapses into comedy and 'buffoonery', and Milton. Chaucer, however, not only used the ten-syllable couplet—admittedly permissible for 'story-telling not of the epic pitch and often admirable for a few lines even in poetry of a very high pitch'—but his major fault was even greater. Granted that he is 'the father of our splendid English poetry', Chaucer is nonetheless 'not one of the great classics' because he lacks seriousness—'high and excellent seriousness'. However large his view of life, however free, shrewd, or benign his criticism, Chaucer lacks what Homer, Dante, Shakespeare, and Villon at his best moments possess: the accent and virtue of seriousness.[36]

What mars Chaucer likewise mars Burns, who also 'comes short of the high seriousness of the great classics' in his manner and matter. He has the fleeting grace of 'a profound and passionate melancholy', but he is flawed by his overly joyful irony. Rather than reflecting 'Thou Power Supreme, whose mighty scheme/ These woes of mind fulfil', Arnold complains, Burns's criticism of life is far more *'Whistle owre the lave o't!'* Burns is plainly too happy, far happier than life really permits of any conscientious man, too easily the reveller and the scot-free Scot. Yet it is not the 'Scotch' quality Arnold objects to when quoting Burns on the joys of drink; it is his evasiveness:

> There is a great deal of that sort of thing in Burns, and it is unsatisfactory, not because it is bacchanalian poetry, but because it has not that accent of sincerity, which bacchanalian poetry, to do it justice, very often has. There is something in it of bravado, something which makes us feel that we have not the man speaking to us with his real voice; something, therefore, poetically unsound.

So preoccupied with 'the high seriousness which comes from absolute sincerity', Arnold could never admit the tragic implications of a man dancing so boldly in the face of overwhelming cosmic odds; he demanded that it be seen at face value.

In the end, 'The Study of Poetry' reveals more than Arnold's abhorrence of comedy as an art form; it also reveals his sense of the demise of poetry, flattened by the steamrollers of prose and reason. The verse of Dryden is admirable only 'for the purposes of the inaugurator of an age of prose and reason', the verse of Pope admirable only 'for the purposes of the high priest of an age of prose and reason'. The commanding quality of this age, Arnold fears, is a severe shortage of 'high seriousness'. No wonder, he says, there is a lack of 'powerful

139

poetic application'. 'The Study of Poetry' is a revelation of dread, an elegy for the tragic glory of Byron, Shelley, and Obermann. In 'Stanzas from the Grande Chartreuse', Arnold bewailed the breaking of their tragic spell at the hands of 'the eternal trifler'. He, Arnold feels, has become the demonic voice of the new age of prose, reason, and Philistinism—the voice of Mephistopheles, or at least, Tartuffe, smiling, flattering, deceitful, and seductive. A man of Arnold's persuasion had reason to shudder, for in his eyes the far-reaching and overpowering bastion of Philistinism was America, and during his last years the shining star in the American firmament was a comedian called Mark Twain.

The trouble between Arnold and Mark Twain began in 1882 and did not end until four years after Arnold's death. Arnold met Sam Clemens only twice, on two consecutive days, and if contemporary reports are to be believed, they hit it off well personally. Yet the decade of antagonism in print, sparked off by a mere handful of Arnold's critical offerings, ended in a demonstration of how impossible it was to escape the wrath of Mark Twain's pen—in his own words, 'a pen warmed up in hell'. Not even Arnold's death could cool it down.

In 1882, Arnold wrote and published what today seems a generally measured criticism of American society called 'A Word About America'. He had not yet visited America, and admitted it; he did not hold England up as an example for the Americans to follow, but on the contrary wished American democracy well, hoping that it might serve as an example by which 'the want of equality' in England might be eradicated. 'Nothing would please me better', he wrote,

> than to find the difficulty solved in America, to find democracy a success there, with a type of equality producing such good results, that when one preaches equality, one should illustrate its advantages not from the example of the French, but . . . from the example of the people of the United States.[37]

However, as in most of Arnold's criticism, there was a 'but'; in this instance it was his arch-enemy, the Philistine.

Now, anybody who had read the first series of *Essays in Criticism*, especially the Heine essay, would have known that Arnold had never excused England from the crime of Philistinism, but rather designated England 'the very headquarters of Goliath'. Yet, while admitting that there were in America 'lovers of the humane life, lovers of perfection' emerging from all classes and pointing towards a better future, Arnold argued after Renan that

> the United States have created a considerable popular instruction without any serious higher instruction, and will long have to expiate this fault by their intellectual mediocrity, their vulgarity of manners, their superficial spirit, their lack of general intelligence.

He quoted another French critic in his belief that the 'literature exactly expressing a people of this type, and no higher'—the type being 'the Philistine of the more gay and light type'—was the 'Quinionian humour of Mr. Mark Twain'.

Arnold abhorred Quinion, the 'rowdy Philistine' of *David Copperfield*, just as he abhorred Murdstone, the 'bitter, serious Philistine' of the same novel. He hoped, he said, to find an American example that might deliver England from Murdstone and Quinion—'But now it seems doubtful whether America is not suffering from the predominance of Murdstone and Quinion herself—of Quinion at any rate.' It was true; *Innocents Abroad*, *Roughing It*, and Mark Twain's comic lectures were taking America by storm, all of which were delivered from a deliberately Philistine point of view, upon which most of their comedy rode. By his probably limited knowledge of such works did Arnold form his impression; there is no indication, and little chance, that he later read *Huckleberry Finn*, and as Trilling suggests, it probably would not have appeased Arnold much.*

There is also no indication as to whether Clemens ever read Arnold's essay. At any rate, Arnold was in America the next year on a lecture tour. He tried to visit William Dean Howells

---

* Trilling also notes in a definite understatement: 'What he would have thought of Oxford's conferring of the Litt. D. degree on Mark Twain in 1907 makes amusing conjecture' (*Matthew Arnold*, p. 393n).

in Boston, but was told that Howells was in Hartford, visiting Mark Twain. Evidently, Arnold was shocked: 'Oh, but he doesn't like *that* sort of thing, does he?' he asked, receiving in reply a testimony to one of the firmest friendships in American literary history: 'He likes Mr. Clemens very much, and he thinks him one of the greatest men he ever knew.' A short time later, Arnold was honoured at a reception in Hartford; he greeted Howells, and then gestured at an eagle-eyed guest with a mane of whitening red hair. 'Who—who in the world is that?' he asked. 'Oh', Howells replied, 'that is Mark Twain', later reporting that, after introducing the two men, the fascinated Arnold was at Clemens's side for the rest of the night.[38]

The next evening, Arnold was a dinner guest at the home of Mr. and Mrs. Clemens. In *Mark Twain: A Biography*, A. Bigelow Paine describes the end of the gathering, also attended by Clemens's friends, the Reverends Joseph Twichell and Edwin Parker:

> Dr. Parker and Arnold left together, and, walking quietly homeward, discussed the remarkable creature whose presence they had just left. Clemens had been at his best that night—at his humorous best. He had kept a perpetual gale of laughter going, with a string of comment and anecdote of a kind which Twichell once declared the world had never before seen and would never see again. Arnold seemed dazed by it, unable to come out from under its influence. He repeated some of the things Mark Twain had said, thoughtfully, as if trying to analyze their magic. Then he asked solemnly:
> 'And is he *never* serious?'
> And Dr. Parker as solemnly answered:
> 'Mr. Arnold, he is the most serious man in the world.'

Arnold left no corroborating mention of either meeting in his letters or journals, although Twichell's diary reports that Arnold and his family made 'a most favorable impression' at the dinner, with Arnold evidently 'a gentler, more sympathetic person than his writings would lead some people to expect'.[39]

From such an inauspicious and even benign personal first encounter, one would hardly expect the fury relentlessly delivered at Arnold from the pen of Mark Twain only a few years later, and for so many years following. What set Clemens off was not so much related to his rôle as a humorist as much as that as a businessman. In 1886 he published the memoirs of Ulysses S. Grant, for whom he felt the utmost respect as a soldier and writer. Grant was one of his heroes; and when the January and February 1887 issues of *Murray's* magazine appeared, Clemens was incensed by Arnold's review of Grant's memoirs.

His wrath was unbelievable, considering the fact that Arnold's review contained a few paragraphs of criticism against thirty-five pages of undeniable praise. The incident sheds light on how a particularly volatile artist could respond with such increasing violence towards Arnold's criticisms, so that *anything* he would say about humour would be taken as a personal insult. Overall, Arnold praised Grant for his 'sagacity and justice', his tenacity, his modesty, his 'concern for the public good', and his moderation. His praise was not merely even-handed lip service as a prelude to general condemnation; his last sentence carried the tone of the entire review, as he asked America for 'more Lees, Lincolns, Shermans, and Grants'. Of the *Memoirs*, he wrote:

> I found a language straightforward, nervous, firm, possessing in general the high merit of saying clearly in the fewest possible words what had to be said, and saying it, frequently, with shrewd and unexpected turns of expression.

Yet he indeed provided qualification, while Clemens evidently would settle for nothing less than unqualified praise for his dead hero and literary protégé. The sole paragraph that offended him shows, on examination, more compliment than criticism:

> I found a language all astray in its use of *will* and *shall*, *should* and *would*, an English employing the verb *to conscript* and the participle *conscripting*, and speaking in a despatch to the Secretary of War of having badly *whipped* the enemy; an English without charm and without high breeding. But at the same time I found a man of sterling good-sense as well as of the firmest resolution, a man, withal, humane, simple, modest; from all restless self-consciousness and desire for display perfectly free; never boastful where he himself was concerned, and where his nation was concerned seldom boastful, boastful only in circumstances where nothing but high genius or high training, I suppose, can save an American from being boastful.[40]

143

Clemens hit the roof. In a speech to the Army and Navy Club of Connecticut in April 1887, he complained that 'a great and honored author, Matthew Arnold, has been finding fault with General Grant's English.' He then accused Arnold of providing more grammatical mistakes to the page in his review than Arnold had found in Grant's book. Placing Arnold in a '*lofty*' fellowship of the English language's most 'slovenly' writers, Clemens quoted a paragraph of Arnold's review, sneering, 'To read that passage a couple of times would make a man dizzy; to read it four times would make him drunk.'[41]

Clemens was still smouldering a year later when Arnold's essay, 'Civilization in the United States', appeared in *Nineteenth Century* magazine. In this follow-up to 'A Word About America', written after the experience of his visit, Arnold felt compelled to deliver more criticism than in the first essay. While re-establishing his respect for American political institutions and the apparent lack of class division as found in England, Arnold upbraided American society for its irreverence:

> Goethe says somewhere that 'the thrill of awe is the best thing humanity has'. . . . But, if there be a discipline in which the Americans are wanting, it is the discipline of awe and respect.

Citing Lincoln as an example of a man without distinction, he continued:

> In truth everything is against distinction in America, and against the sense of elevation to be gained through admiring and respecting it. The glorification of 'the average man', who is quite a religion with statesmen and publicists there, is against it

—and, not the least important: 'The addiction to "the funny man", who is a national misfortune there, is against it.' As if this were not enough to make America's premier 'funny man' throw down the gauntlet, Arnold set out to attack the American newspapers for their 'absence of truth and soberness' and their 'poverty in serious interest'—the newspapers being the medium that had given birth to Mark Twain, and which held his highest esteem.[42]

On 15 April 1888, Arnold died—but that did not appease Clemens. That summer he accepted an honorary M.A. degree from Yale, which he said had 'forcibly and timely' exonerated all humorists after 'the late Matthew Arnold's sharp rebuke to the guild of American "funny men" in his latest literary delicacy'.[43] Clemens continued to hurl epithets of outrage and insult at Arnold's ghost for the next four years, filling hundreds of notebook and manuscript pages with contempt for Arnold and his '*superficial polish*', planning and abandoning spiteful, rebuking publishing ventures against Arnold's memory, and even condemning him by name in his novel, *The American Claimant*, wherein Mark Twain's reactionary, patriotic boasting seems only to confirm one of Arnold's few objections in the Grant essay. Moreover, as many critics and Mark Twain's own notebooks suggest, his reaction against Arnold fuelled the Anglophobia that lies at the heart of *A Connecticut Yankee at King Arthur's Court.*

Thus did the unwitting Matthew Arnold play a part in inspiring the production of America's first major literary comedian. It is almost certain that he did not pay Mark Twain a fraction of the attention which Mark Twain paid him, although, had Clemens read more of Arnold than those few paragraphs of criticism that incensed him, he might have softened his response. He might have even found a kindred spirit in 'Friendship's Garland', the anomalous fragment of criticism that shows Arnold's own striking ability as a comedian; it is indeed, in R. H. Super's words, 'some of the wittiest writing of a very witty era'.[44] Begun in 1866, when Mark Twain was an unknown Confederate deserter in California, and continued after a three-year interruption, this series of letters to the *Pall Mall Gazette* presents Arnold reduced to an outright dunderhead, playing the foil to the blustery Prussian, Baron Arminius Von Thunder-ten-Tronckh. 'Friendship's Garland' must be read to be appreciated, yet as a vehicle for delivering an intense social critique in the guise of humour, the often hilarious first-person discomfiture of Arnold's self-portrait might have been an effective model for the similar, if not better executed, technique of Mark Twain.

Still, it must be admitted that 'Friendship's Garland' is a remarkable exception to the rule of Arnold's writing; for although he frequently employed strong doses of irony in his writings, it was seldom with such a dramatically comic voice and setting. As it has been shown, Arnold's fervent social commitment more often threw him into a profound inner melancholy which he rarely revealed except in print—a melancholy that he himself believed the rest of the world considered 'a pass'd mode, an outworn theme'. Nonetheless, as his treatment of comedy revealed, the new mode, that of the 'eternal trifler', was to be resisted, however quixotically. 'Stanzas from the Grande Chartreuse' declares, along with the bulk of his writing, that life is serious business, and that the 'religion of sorrow' must be upheld until history indeed proclaims it an outworn theme:

> There may, perhaps, yet dawn an age,
> More fortunate, alas! than we,
> Which without hardness will be sage,
> And gay without frivolity.
> Sons of the world, oh, haste those years;
> But, till they rise, allow our tears![45]

NOTES

1. Matthew Arnold, 'The French Play in London', *English Literature and Irish Politics*, ed. R. H. Super (Ann Arbor, 1973), pp. 64–85 (p. 72).
2. Park Honan, *Matthew Arnold: A Life* (London, 1981), pp. viii, ix.
3. A. T. Quiller-Couch, introduction, *The Poems of Matthew Arnold* (Oxford, 1909), p. iv.
4. Honan, pp. 13, 26, 41.
5. Honan, pp. 6, 32, 45, 71.
6. Honan, pp. 3–14.
7. Honan, pp. 51–68.
8. Lionel Trilling, *Matthew Arnold* (London, 1974), pp. 19–20.
9. Honan, pp. 51–9, 79.
10. Trilling, p. 22.
11. Arnold, *Poems*, pp. 27–33.
12. Arnold, *Poems*, pp. 230–37.
13. Honan, p. 179.
14. Trilling, p. 115; Honan, p. 241.
15. Arnold, *Poems*, pp. 166–68.
16. Honan, p. 279.
17. Honan, p. 126.
18. Max Eastman, *Enjoyment of Laughter* (London, 1970), p. 108.

19. Arnold, 'Literary Influence of Academies', *Essays in Criticism* (London, 1911), pp. 42–79 (p. 58).
20. Arnold, 'Joubert', *Essays in Criticism*, pp. 265–306 (pp. 297–98).
21. Arnold, *Poems*, pp. 66–73.
22. Honan, p. 72.
23. Honan, pp. 154, 211.
24. Arnold, *Poems*, pp. 168–71.
25. Arnold, *Poems*, pp. 63–4.
26. Honan, p. 152.
27. Arnold, preface, *Poems*, p. 2.
28. Arnold, *Poems*, p. 405.
29. Arnold, *Poems*, pp. 174–79.
30. Arnold, 'Literary Influence of Academies', *Essays in Criticism*, p. 48.
31. Arnold, 'Pagan and Medieval Religious Sentiment', *Essays in Criticism*, pp. 194–222 (p. 216).
32. Arnold, 'Pagan and Medieval Religious Sentiment', *Essays in Criticism*, pp. 209–10.
33. Honan, *Matthew Arnold: A Life*, p. 158.
34. Arnold, 'Heinrich Heine', *Essays in Criticism*, pp. 156–93 *passim*.
35. Arnold, 'The French Play in London', *English Literature and Irish Politics*, pp. 64–85.
36. Arnold, 'The Study of Poetry', *English Literature and Irish Politics*, pp. 161–88 (pp. 176–77); also 'Maurice de Guerin', *Essays in Criticism*, p. 84.
37. Arnold, 'A Word About America', *Philistinism in England and America*, ed. R. H. Super (Ann Arbor, 1974), pp. 1–23 (pp. 4–5).
38. William Dean Howells, *My Mark Twain* (New York, 1910), pp. 28–9.
39. Howard G. Baetzhold, *Mark Twain and John Bull* (Bloomington, 1970), pp. 97–8; 338, note 53.
40. Arnold, 'General Grant', *The Last Word*, ed. R. H. Super (Ann Arbor, 1977), pp. 144–79 (pp. 145–46).
41. Albert Bigelow Paine, *Mark Twain: A Biography* (London, 1912), II, p. 1651.
42. Arnold, 'Civilization in the United States', *The Last Word*, pp. 350–69 (pp. 360–63).
43. Baetzhold, p. 119.
44. Arnold, *Culture and Anarchy*, ed. R. H. Super (Ann Arbor, 1965), Critical notes, p. 359.
45. Arnold, *Poems*, pp. 270–75.

6

Matthew Arnold's Fight for Ireland

by OWEN DUDLEY EDWARDS

1

The sea is calm to-night.
The tide is full, the moon lies fair
Upon the straits;—on the French coast the light
Gleams and is gone; the cliffs of England stand,
Glimmering and vast, out in the tranquil bay.
Come to the window, sweet is the night-air!
Only, from the long line of spray
Where the sea meets the moon-blanch'd land,
Listen! you hear the grating roar
Of pebbles which the waves draw back, and fling,
At their return, up the high strand,
Begin, and cease, and then again begin,
With tremulous cadence slow, and bring
The eternal note of sadness in.

('Dover Beach')

The United Kingdom of Great Britain and Ireland existed from 1801 to 1922. It came into being for strategic reasons, immediately, to increase British security during the Napoleonic wars. Before that time Ireland was a separate kingdom, under the same monarch, since Henry VIII's time (the English kings had been, by Papal decree, lords of Ireland since Henry II). Ireland had been reduced to a caste situation by several land confiscations, rebellions and wars, the Roman Catholics being

148

largest and lowest, the Presbyterians next, and the Church of Ireland, Protestant episcopalian and the state established church, being the only religion whose votaries enjoyed full civil and religious rights. Some Catholic emancipation had been achieved by the Union, and the mass Catholic movement under Daniel O'Connell's leadership won the repeal of most remaining civil disabilities in 1829. The Presbyterians had won a similar victory shortly before. The Government gave a little money to the seminary of St. Patrick's College, Maynooth, which was increased to sounds of great controversy in 1845, but opposition to state endowment of Catholic education from extremist Irish Catholics (who feared that it might corrupt their religious and, in some cases, national identities) and extremist Protestants (who feared the growing strength of Rome) resulted in the Irish education system remaining very weak, and no satisfactory university education for Irish Catholics was established in the nineteenth century.

The rôle of the British creative writer in this situation was curious. He or she was the subject of a state which constitutionally presumed the equality of all as regards place of birth or residence within the United Kingdom. Class differences and, especially in Ireland, caste differences, remained. Matthew Arnold on analysis concluded that the United Kingdom was one of the most unequal societies in the civilized world.[1] But the Union was supposed to have made Irishman and Englishman equal. In practice the constitutional system acknowledged a different status for Ireland. Its representatives sat in the British Parliament, initially unreformed, later much more representative as the reforms in the English and Welsh, and then in the Scottish, electoral systems were also extended to Ireland. But Ireland was still governed by means of a Viceroy and a Chief Secretary, and its turbulence (chiefly on local agrarian grounds) dictated the maintenance of an armed police and occasional recourse to troops. At the back of most British minds was the legal possibility that if worst came to worst it might be necessary to govern Ireland as a crown colony: almost at the end of his life Arnold came close to advocating such a course.[2] In the meantime *habeas corpus* and various other protections of the subject were from time to time suspended for Ireland. It might be thought that British intellectuals would concern themselves with their government's failure to integrate the United Kingdom satisfactorily. The intellectual may be expected to see the ideal, and to remind others of their duties to strive for it. In fact very few creative writers did so. Some—Thackeray, Trollope, Tennyson, Stevenson, Kipling—were drawn to subjects with Irish reference. Others—historians chiefly but still creative—Macaulay, Carlyle, Froude—were drawn in for professional reasons; still others, such as Scott, were led from observation to important conclusions. But of all of these great men—I am speaking only of great men—Matthew Arnold was exceptional in seeking to remould the British mind such as to acknowledge identity with Ireland, to make the United Kingdom a reality. All of them believed in the Union and a few of them practised it: Scott's literary preceptress, Maria Edgeworth, was Irish; Thackeray's wife was Irish; Trollope first found professional, literary and social success in Ireland; Stevenson briefly contemplated dying, and even being killed, there; Macaulay made some great speeches about it in his Parliamentary capacity; Carlyle made it the text of several Jeremiads; Kipling committed treason because of it.[3] But Arnold was constructive. He was not content simply to integrate an Irish solution into his existing political beliefs, which in any case were much more naturally fluid than those of most of his literary contemporaries. He had restraints of upbringing, training, methodology, family traditions, family affiliations, class consciousness, regional preoccupation. Yet he put these things to his service in his fight to win Ireland a place in the British mind and heart, and thereby Britain a place in the Irish. He showed remarkable perception in his fight: he was not imagining some mechanical Ireland which would accommodate itself to Liberal dreams once a sufficiency of mechanical nostrums had been administered. He was, in the last analysis, concerned not with victories in the council chamber but in the world of art and creation. He was, as Chesterton said, the most cosmopolitan of his Victorian fellow-artists,[4] and his approach to Ireland was cosmopolitan also, in that he differed from most other English writers in placing Ireland in the context of Wales and Scotland (Froude admittedly tried, but the effects, while hilarious, are intellectually unimpressive).[5]

150

And he deserves one sad little epitaph: if the English had generally resembled him in seeking to make the United Kingdom truly united, it would probably have survived.

Matthew Arnold made the study of matters Celtic a respectable subject for the academic élite of Oxford and Cambridge, and their far-flung if somewhat embittered exiles. His motives were mixed, his apostleship was restricted, and his scholarly basis had decided limitations, and these things we shall examine. His impact was very great in this field, although the initial reception of his theses among the makers of English public opinion was rather cold.[6] He built the platform for the Celtic evangelists of the 1890s: the Oscar Wildes, the Bernard Shaws, the Grant Allens, the Fiona Macleods, the W. B. Yeatses, the R. Barry O'Briens, the Ernest Rhyses. Their attack on English literary orthodoxy was the bolder because of him; as the Americans say, he made them walk tall. He was in himself doing a very Hiberno-Scottish thing in that the original scholarly impetus for his evangelization was the work of Ernest Renan, much as Carlyle had preached German romanticism, and, in the future, Shaw, Wilde, Yeats, William Archer and James Joyce would call in forces of world literature to counteract the parochialism of English conventions against which their Irish and Scottish self-conciousness rebelled. What he said and did meant a great deal to him.

Yet there remained another legacy, and one from which he cannot be absolved. Arnold appeared to many people to be a profoundly serious man; Chesterton declared him to be the most serious of his times. Yet it was not the word his disciples in the 1890s applied to him. Ernest Rhys spoke of 'his light guerilla warfare with his contemporaries',[7] and of his Celtic concerns as 'brilliantly tentative . . . At times he appears confused . . . his adventure is apt to suggest nothing so much as Oxford in person trying to break into the wilderness.' Wilde saw Grant Allen as having superbly asserted 'that Celtic spirit in Art that Arnold divined, but did not demonstrate, at any rate in the sense of scientific demonstration, such as yours is'.[8] Shaw found in him the appropriate symbol for a philosophy which could not sustain its momentum beyond its own time, and as such an appropriate source for quotation by Hector

Malone in that great statement of revolt against the rebels of the previous generation, *Man and Superman*.[9] Wilde's pupil Max Beerbohm produced his famous caricature of a leering, whimsical Arnold being confronted by his temporarily diminutive niece Mary Augusta, the future Mrs. Humphry Ward 'Why, Uncle Matthew, oh why, will you not be always wholly serious?' The laugh is primarily against Mrs. Ward, as might be expected from a disciple of Wilde, who had so lightly demolished *Robert Elsmere*,[10] but it is not only against Mrs. Ward. Even she, or at least her father, had a vantage-point which questioned Arnold's depth of Celtic involvement; Thomas Arnold the younger settled in Ireland, adopted its majority religion and died in it.[11] Shaw subjected the English superstitions about the Celt to ferocious analysis and ridicule in *John Bull's Other Island*;[12] the more hostile racial theories came from Carlyle and Froude and other prophets against whom Arnold's gentler message was in part directed, but Froude would draw on him to some purpose, and subsequent popular writing owed its freedom and indolence in its depiction of what constituted a Celtic temperament to the relative lack of pains with which Arnold had prepared himself for his work. Granted that Renan and others had asserted the concept of the femininity of the Celt, it was Arnold who gave it magisterial currency.[13] And finally did he not also open a way for his beloved Oxford and its emigrés, down to the Trevor-Ropers and Rowses[14] of the latest generation, to engage themselves on supposed Celtic scholarship with equal sense of fitness for the task given by their academic birthright, and much less pains in arming themselves for their work? He enriched scholarship and letters; but did he not also increase the ranks of the ignorant armies?

What has been consistent in his critics, from Henry Stuart Fagan and Robert Giffen at the outset, through Andrew Lang and W. B. Yeats during the Celtic Renaissance, through Wyndham Lewis and Lionel Trilling in the iconoclastic interwar years, to John V. Kelleher and Rachel Bromwich in our own times, has been a sense of surprise, almost of awe, at Arnold's twin epaulettes of confidence and ignorance.[15] If there was much of Celtic literature and post-Celtic history that he did not know, he made claims so extraordinary for the

Celtic past, and appeared so dismissive or so hostile to the Celtic present, that it seems hard to escape the thought that he was coat-trailing. Yet he was not, save for a consistent desire to provoke the Philistine, who by definition knew less than he did. He may have been the ancestor of the modern Oxbridge exponents of abrasive and assertive ignorance; but unlike them he was not seeking to provoke the hostility of the philo-Celts. Even at his most enraged moments respecting Ireland, he always saw as his opponents the wrong-headed English. The Fagans and Giffens he left to themselves, and, since they decidedly had the advantage over him in point of specific knowledge, he was right. He was very frank about his poverty of knowledge—*On the Study of Celtic Literature* opens with a cheerful self-description as 'an unlearned bellettristic trifler'[16]—but it did nothing to diminish his certainty of his correctness in defining and analysing Celticism and Irishness. Was he simply a brazen Oxonian?

The answer, I believe, is that Arnold was so confident about what was Celtic and Irish because he believed himself to be both. Dr. Frederic E. Faverty in his fine study *Matthew Arnold the Ethnologist*[17] draws our attention to the letter Arnold wrote his Cornish mother from Paris on 8 May 1859:[18]

> I could not but think of you in Brittany, with Cranics and Trevenecs all about me, and the peasantry with their expressive, rather mournful faces, long noses, and dark eyes, reminding me perpetually of dear Tom and Uncle Trevenen, and utterly unlike the French.

The letter disposes rather effectively of Dr. Rowse's 'It is odd that Matthew Arnold should not have been aware' of his Celticness or Cornishness.[19] The *Westminster Review*, noticing *On the Study of Celtic Literature*, knew better:[20]

> He has done thorough justice to the Celtic genius, to which his own is so much akin. Like the Celts, he has no patience for science. Like the Celt, too, he loves idealism. Like the Celt, also, as may be gathered from his volume of poems which we have just noticed, he is imbued with a deep sense of sadness. Those who would understand Mr. Arnold's own temperament should certainly study this book.

But if Arnold would have agreed, it would have been partly because he felt in himself not only a Cornish ancestry, but an

Irish. Indeed his niece Mary Augusta—let us, after all, enable her to answer the question Max Beerbohm put in her mouth—saw his Celticism as

> derived . . . rather from an Irish than a Cornish source. Dr. Arnold's mother, Martha Delafield, according to a genealogy I see no reason to doubt, was partly of Irish blood; one finds, at any rate, Fitzgeralds and Dillons among the names of her forebears.[21]

Now, it is sufficiently improbable that Mrs. Humphry Ward's acquaintance with a genealogy documenting the origins of her great-grandmother was not shared by the previous generation: it had almost certainly been thence that she had learned of it. So Matthew Arnold thought of himself as Celtic from both sides of the family. The nonsense of his Celticism being undertaken in opposition to a non-Celtic father vanishes, and Dr. Thomas Arnold joins the sea-divided Gael in his son's estimation at least. Mary Augusta Ward went on to descry in Uncle Matthew's countenance similarities with Irish faces she had seen 'faces full of power, and humour, and softness, visibly moulded out of the good common earth by the nimble spirit within': Dr. Faverty is unkind about her remarks on the Celtic qualities of her father and uncle, which he sees as 'unwittingly illustrating . . . the snares and delusions into which Arnold's ethnological methods may lead'.[22] But for us the point is that she records a family tradition of paternal Irish ancestry, and probably another about its finding an outlet in Matthew.

It may be difficult to find a more apposite example of his disciple Wilde's dictum that 'the highest, as the lowest, form of criticism is a mode of autobiography.'[23] Arnold's assurance about matters Celtic and Irish arose because he was talking about himself; his conviction that the Celtic would only be of value if it were brought in to offset the duller qualities of the Saxon arose from his belief that it was doing this within himself, and by him in his influence on the Saxon world. His ultimate anger about Parnellite Ireland, then, had something akin to the anger of the Dublin crowd who protested against *The Playboy of the Western World* twenty years after; they resented this view of the society whence they had derived, they insisted its values were false, they objected to its depiction as typical things they denied to be true, they had a secret fear they were true. As to the last, Arnold might have questioned Parnell's status as a Celt, but he could not question that of John Dillon, who bore the same name as his own ancestors, and whom he quoted angrily and repeatedly.[24]

Granted that Arnold thought of himself as partly Irish, and that his niece, and possibly himself, saw this Irishness as expressing itself in his temperament and countenance, does this make him Irish? Does he qualify in Conor Cruise O'Brien's sense that to be Irish means that one identifies with Ireland to the point of ultimately being mauled or maimed by it? Anthony Trollope's long residence in Ireland made him Irish in that sense, I believe, although he had no Irish ancestry.[25] In Arnold's case I am more inclined to doubt it. He visited it briefly in his youth, and again during Forster's unhappy term of office in 1881, but for all of his influence on subsequent Irish writers he never seems to have seen himself as addressing it, although he did ultimately address the Welsh.[26] His Irish controversies always remain British controversies. Ireland, at the end, angered rather than hurt him; he remains didactic, even academic, rather than anguished in the way that Trollope shows himself to be in *The Landleaguers*. Perhaps the point may be that in relation to Ireland Arnold was 'the critic as artist', in Wilde's sense, but never a purely creative artist, as Trollope was. His poetry might use Celtic materials and means, even specifically Irish ones; but it was not torn from Ireland as some of Trollope's stories were.

But Irish or not, he remains the great Celtic evangelist *contra Gentiles* of his own and subsequent generations. He was courageous, he was noble, he was a tremendous advocate. And if he was dilletantish, although less and less so as Irish questions entered deeper into his soul, he possessed not only the wit of the popular professor, but also the laughter and the enthusiasm of a boy. Our first picture of Arnold as Celticist should be as he shouts his way happily around Llandudno with his children in 1864, or maybe we should look back thirty years earlier to another group of boys, in two opposing forts, and in the midst of them, hurling missiles and nicknames, while his eyes twinkled with pleasure, is Dr. Arnold.[27]

2

Sophocles long ago
Heard it on the Aegaean, and it brought
Into his mind the turbid ebb and flow
Of human misery; we
Find also in the sound a thought,
Hearing it by this distant northern sea.
('Dover Beach')

Before Matthew Arnold obtained status as apostle of Celticism, in the 1860s, crusader for Irish education, in the 1870s, critic of Irish socio-political revolt, in the 1880s, he had been a poet. The origins of involvement with Celtic themes at first were joyful associations for him: his parents, his children, his friendship with Arthur Hugh Clough.[28] But the strain which contemporaries such as the *Westminster Review* critic isolated as Celtic in his work was one of melancholy. This may be conceded; he might have agreed. Yet if there is a specific Celtic theme in his poetry, it is one which adds to that perception of melancholy a strange hope. Relatively little of his poetry is formally concerned with matters Celtic. But what is much more important is that it exhibits themes and hollows, contours and yearnings, to which the evangelization of Celtic culture offered a response. Professor Seamus Deane, in a brilliant essay, hits the nail very neatly on the head by describing Arnold's vision of the Celt as 'The Scholar Gypsy of Europe'.[29]

There are, first, the Celtic-related poems. Ironically, given the insistence of Andrew Lang and others that the qualities Arnold as a prose critic took to be Celtic were to be found in the folklore of surviving primitive cultures in general,[30] Arnold's poetry produces important instances of themes from other cultures which can be paralleled within the Celtic. 'Sohrab and Rustum', for instance, deals with a father's killing of his son in chivalric combat as representative of his people; one of the most famous counterparts of this Persian story is the Irish hero Cuchulainn slaying his son in similar circumstances. The most famous modern retelling of it is that by Yeats in his play *On Baile's Strand*; Yeats was fired by Arnold's prose apostleship of Celtic literature, whatever his specific reservations about it, and the Arnold parallel as well as the Gaelic original stand as his chief sources.[31] 'The Forsaken Merman' is of Norse origin, but the ideal of mortal union with praeternatural figures is found in Gaelic and Welsh literature alike, and usually turns on the ultimate dissolution of the marriage (Oisin or Ossian being the most famous example). But 'The Forsaken Merman' is also a metaphor for Arnold's view of the Celtic place in modern English literature. Conventional society rejects the more remote culture, but it has its own eminently justifiable logic. In fact, Arnold greatly enhanced the acceptability of the merman by Victorian standards. He shows no signs of physical difference from the mortals, and he is in protest against the destruction of his ideals of love, kindness and family fidelity which the demands of a more modern, regimented, legalist culture have set aside. The implication is present that the more modern culture is the worse for it. The timing of the merman story means that Margaret's Catholicism is the self-satisfied modern doctrine, whereas in Arnold's own day Ireland's Catholicism is the softer culture rejected (and, in part, wrongly rejected, in Arnold's view) by the dominant English outlook. The case for the merman is strengthened for its Victorian audience by being presented in what would now be termed male chauvinist priorities; it is as though we were hearing Torvald's version of *A Doll's House* after the defection of Nora, if the poem may be conceded a Norse successor as well as precursor.

The most directly Celtic of Arnold's poems is 'Tristram and Iseult', with its concentration on the two Celtic heroines, Iseult of Ireland and Iseult of Brittany. Here again Arnold is at great lengths to make them acceptable. There is nothing of the Irish Iseult's forcing her maidservant to take her place on the wedding night with King Marc and then seeking to have her murdered to ensure her silence, nor of the Breton Iseult's telling Tristram that the Irish Iseult has refused to return to him whence causing his death from what Théodore de la Villemarqué diagnosed as 'chagrin'.[32] Iseult of Brittany sees her dying beloved gasping for a sight of her rival:

Tristram
Soft—who is that, stands by the dying fire?

157

Matthew Arnold: Between Two Worlds

> The Page
> Iseult.
>
> *Tristram*
> Ah! not the Iseult I desire.

She nurses him through the vigil, witnesses his final embrace and death with Iseult of Ireland, and is finally discovered at the close of the poem a year later watching over her children—hers and Tristram's. She finds escapism in telling them stories.

> ... the tales
> With which this day the children she beguiled
> She gleaned from Breton grandames, when a child,
> In every hut along this sea-coast wild.
> She herself loves them still, and, when they are told,
> Can forget all to hear them, as of old.

Otherwise, 'Joy has not found her yet, nor ever will.' The example of her story-telling with which the poem closes, Vivian's imprisonment of the love-sick Merlin in a tree to rid herself of his aged and tedious courtship, has been condemned as irrelevant. But it is central in its message. Merlin's infatuation has destroyed him, as Tristram and the Breton Iseult have in different ways been destroyed by their different infatuations, and she can find surcease from her own pain in telling of the destructive powers of love. It is not an expression of desire that she had never loved; it is that her tragedy increases her artistic powers. It is important that her account of Merlin is from folklore, not from any personal acquaintance with the protagonists. Arthurian legend has Merlin living long into the life of Arthur, but Iseult's version is specifically presented as coming from long before her time. And, whether from his Cornish mother, or elsewhere, Arnold shows here a perceptive knowledge of the place of folklore in the Celtic culture, both in its strength and in its power to sustain the afflicted. As Mrs. Bromwich stresses, his lectures on *Celtic Literature* are insensitive to the oral tradition[33]; yet his artistic mind understood it, even if his critical mind did not.

These poems are from the late 1840s and early 1850s. Arnold turned to a Celtic theme for his last narrative poem, 'Saint Brandon', published in 1860. Its interest lies in the use of Celtic legend to imply a possible softening of the iron force of eternal damnation. Judas, encountered by the Irish saint, tells him that once a year he has a respite from the fires of hell to mark the one good action of his life, giving his cloak to a leper:

> That germ of kindness, in the womb
> Of mercy caught, did not expire;
> Outlives my guilt, outlives my doom,
> And friends me in the pit of fire.

It is an argument of greater mercy, justice and wisdom in the Celtic spirituality as against the conventional outlook of Arnold's contemporaries. It was not quite as comforting a message for the philo-Celt as it seemed, however; it carried the logic that if Arnold were to discover a Celtic merciless justice, as he ultimately found it in the Land League, he would not take it kindly.

Writing to his mother in 1852 after a few days in Wales with Clough, Matthew Arnold gave her loving birthday salutations[34]

> from a son to whom you have for nearly thirty years been such a mother as few sons have. The more I see of the world the more I feel thankful for the bringing-up we had, so unworldly, so sound, and so pure.

This search for the unworldly touches much of his poetry, and increasingly he associated it with Celtic culture, particularly in what he thought that culture could contribute to his own society. In certain non-Celtic poems, therefore, we find symbolism of the unworldly of the kind he would ultimately identify as Celtic. In 'The Scholar-Gipsy' the symbol of the unworldly influence is not the eponymous hero himself, but the gipsies and their civilization he feels impelled to join.

> . . . the gipsy-crew,
> His mates, had arts to rule as they desired
> The workings of men's brains,
> And they can bind them to what thoughts they will.
> 'And I', he said, 'the secret of their art,
> When fully learn'd, will to the world impart;
> But it needs heaven-sent moments for this skill.'

There is something of magic in this, and something of an old learning which the brash new greed, including scholarly greed, of the world is losing and rejecting. The scholar-gipsy is in part still possessed by the world's greed with his ambitions to publish a research scoop—how disgusted Arnold would have been to know he predicted the behaviour of modern anthropologists—and it is only when he has really failed by the world's standards, when the book does not materialize, when his appearances are confined to fleeting encounters with shepherd and fugitive solitary drinking in remote alehouses, and when he dies unknown, that he may be seen to have really succeeded—whether as ghost, or as case-study from Glanvil, or as principle, or as subject of a poem by Matthew Arnold. The scholar-gipsy's rejection of the world, at first during his intended fieldwork and then for good, sounds as though he had anticipated Wordsworth's complaints about the world being too much with us, and had taken steps accordingly. But where Wordsworth simply embraced Nature, Arnold's creation or borrowing from Glanvil wants something more human. The gipsies supply a fifth column in the deplorable world, a cultural, linguistic, sociological fifth column, such as the Celts on a larger and more oblique level might do. The gipsies were by definition not political, and hence the Celts ought not to be.

There seems a kind of death-wish at the back of the scholar-gipsy's resolve, an Empedocles throwing himself into a gipsy Etna. Arthur Hugh Clough seemed to die in part from a death-wish as well, and Clough is another part of Arnold's need for the Celts. Clough had some identification with them, and wrote his greatest poem about a scholar's escape into love for a Celt, 'The Bothie of Tober-na-Vuolich', which has recently been singled out as the choice of that modern philo-Celt, Mr. Tom Paulin, as his choice of forgotten literature in need of revival.[35] Clough encouraged Arnold in the pursuit of Celtic themes and scenes, and vigorously advised him on 'Tristram and Iseult'. And then he was dead in Florence in 1861, and supplied in Arnold's elegy for him, 'Thyrsis', a further element in symbolism of the refuge beyond the materialist world. The poem itself offers only a wan little smile of irony to the reader who seeks in it solace in his own bereavement. It is to the long, deep mourning of 'In Memoriam' we must turn for that; that is heartbreak, that is where a breaking heart must go. But 'Thyrsis', partly in its links to 'The Scholar-Gipsy', offers something quite different; dead Thyrsis becomes a further haven in which to renew defences against the world. The Victorians were frightened of Death. The Celts with their dying culture hailed it as one of themselves. And the comfort in Cumner's topography that Arnold found from memories of Clough was there to supply an echo when he saw the identification of place and Celtic being.

3

> The Sea of Faith
> Was once, too, at the full, and round earth's shore
> Lay like the folds of a bright girdle furl'd.
> But now I only hear
> Its melancholy, long, withdrawing roar,
> Retreating, to the breath
> Of the night-wind, down the vast edges drear
> And naked shingles of the world.
>
> ('Dover Beach')

It was April 1848 and to the reports of revolutions in city after city in Europe was added the English nightmare of rumours of revolt in rural Ireland. 'I cannot believe', wrote Arnold in London to Clough,

> that the mass of the people here would see much bloodshed in Ireland without asking themselves what they were shedding it to *uphold*. And when the answer came—1. a chimerical Theory about some possible dangerous foreign alliances with independent Ireland: 2. a body of Saxon landlords—3. a Saxon Ch[urch] Estab[lishmen]t their consciences must smite them. I think I told you that the performance of [Corneille's] Polyeucte suggested to me the right of large bodies of men to have what article they liked produced for them. The Irish article is not to my taste: still we have no really superiour article to offer them, which alone can justify the violence offered by a Lycurgus or a Cromwell to a foolish nation, as unto Children.—It makes me sick to hear [the Irish Viceroy] Ld. Clarendon praised so: as if he was doing anything but cleverly managing the details of an imposture.[36]

Ireland's first value for Arnold began what would continue; it was a means by which to demonstrate the inadequacy of the English élite. Beyond that, he was not very flattering; he was not even, given the omnipresence of the Irish great famine, particularly humane. But he had a decent common sense liberalism, the same which had ensured that his laudatory poem on Cromwell, which won him the Newdigate Prize for poetry at Oxford, contained no word in praise of his hero's brutal Irish campaign. It may have been English common sense; it was hardly English common sentiment. Professor Jump remarks that 'his views were already those which he advanced at length later in life.'[37]

Arnold was elected Professor of Poetry at Oxford University in 1857, and he delivered his four lectures entitled 'On the Study of Celtic Literature'[38] in 1865–66. And he began by touching on his holiday in Llandudno in August 1864, and the sparkle and excitement in which he described it is important. Arnold entered *happily* into the business of being the St. Paul of Celtic literature. Moreover, he had expected to find emotional fulfilment in that journey to Wales. 'I . . . long—quite long— for Wales—that is a country which has always touched my imagination', he wrote his mother on 22 July 1864, '—and', he continued, clearly in allusion to Clough, 'have been there from time to time, at long intervals, and have recollections connected with it.'[39] But if Arnold could be justified in making a plea for Celtic literature because he had enjoyed himself at Llandudno, this holiday of all holidays deserved such celebration; his children were there, and he cheerfully roamed afield with them, shouting lines from Gray's 'The Bard', travelling half way up Snowdon, and rollickingly recounting their adventures to Mother before going on to share them with Oxford. And it would be one of his very last occasions for unrestrained exultation. In 1868 little Tom would die, and Basil, and Budge would follow them four years later. Thus the lectures and resultant book were probably the happiest and most emotionally fulfilled cultural exercise of Arnold's life, and that high noon of discovery of Celticism, however much anticipated, would always remain in a perfection the day's decline could never subsequently sustain. Celtic culture could only go down after 1868, as Arnold's happiness went down, and his golden memories were clouded by intervening sorrow, and his ignorance lost its bloom with the consequence that he ultimately would vent some of his annoyance on his subject. Arnold had said on 6 and 7 December 1865, on 24 February and 26 May 1866 what the Celts were, and he was hardly ready to thank them if they went on to prove they were something else. But the private wounds hurt far more.

St. Paul had, so to speak, a few Stephens to unstone, or to whose deaths to repent his former consent, and for that he was not fully ready in 1865–66. The invaluable R. H. Super, his wholly admirable modern editor, points out that at the very commencement of Arnold's career as an education inspector, he reported on 1 January 1853 that linguistic barriers should be effaced between Wales and England, and that government aid should be tied to proficiency among the pupils in the English language[40]:

> Whatever encouragement individuals may think it desirable to give to the preservation of the Welsh language on grounds of philological or antiquarian interest, it must always be the desire of a Government to render its dominions, as far as possible, homogeneous, and to break down barriers to the freest intercourse between the different parts of them.

So his book began with some cheerful ridicule of the Eisteddfod at Llandudno as he had witnessed it, laughing about the essays read on such topics as punctuality, and Havelock's relief of Lucknow; pathetic little attempts to pay tribute to Caesar in his own coin, all the more because of the advice being poured into Caesar's ears by such as Arnold himself, but it is the privilege of the conqueror to mock the payment of tribute. And in his lectures he initially went for the laughs. He had no intention of placing himself in a position of seemingly uncritical fealty to his new evangel, and he demonstrated as much by hilarious relation of the absurdities with which extreme Celticists surrounded themselves, linking the story of Taliesin with Ceres and Noah. He offered his audience the pains of a little learning in exchange for a better laugh, much as Trevor-Roper would do. His intention was nevertheless markedly different; he now wished to extol Celtic culture if only to differentiate himself from the Macaulays who saw no laudable future save in assimilation to English and oblivion for the barbaric tongues of the past from the heart of the Empire to its Indian rim.

Arnold had more in common with Macaulay than he would have cared to admit. In a paper the previous year he had charged Macaulay with being 'the great apostle of the Philistines',[41] and some months later he quoted Spinoza to the effect that the true banes of humanity are self-conceit and the laziness deriving from it, apropos Macaulay's dictum[42]:

> It may safely be said that the literature now extant in the English language is of far greater value than all the literature which three hundred years ago was extant in all the languages of the world together.

Arnold could be comfortable in opposing this as 'both vulgar, and, besides being vulgar, retarding'.[43] Opposition to this crude Whiggism was easy to sustain, and, carried into the Celtic context, gave Arnold the logical situation of defending the great Celtic cultural achievement of the past while not as yet doing violence to his former record on the necessity for a monolingual Britain and Ireland. But he was crude himself; his strictures on Macaulay missed the great enthusiasm for past culture which perpetually roared into Macaulay's essays and *History* and questioned so much of the Whiggism. Macaulay wanted above all else to entertain and win applause, but he too did his work as a cultural evangelist, very notably by perpetual casual reference to cultural achievements, tangential to his argument, which yet illustrated the times of which he wrote and whetted his audience's appetite for making good its educational deficiencies. 'Every schoolboy knows' was a shrewd sheepdog shaming of those well beyond the schoolboy age who did not 'know' whatever it was. And in the search for an audience, Arnold was as zealous as Macaulay. Of the publication of his lectures on Celtic literature in the *Cornhill* before book form, he feared that only the first would have 'much that is light and popularly readable in it'.[44] He had been very conscious of selling his product in the hilarious fireworks with which he commenced his work, for all of his assertion at his first lecture's close that he did not mean 'to throw ridicule upon the Celt-lovers,—on the contrary, I feel a great sympathy with them'.[45]

Arnold's desire to be popular, and his conviction that English culture of his time could only save itself from complacency and Philistinism by embracing the past cultural achievements of the Celtic periphery, seem to have inhibited his work to a serious degree. He rightly found occasion in these lectures to castigate Macaulay for opposing the acquisition of important Celtic manuscripts by the British Museum.[46] But he was much less ready than Macaulay to master the array of literature at his disposal in a given subject. In his anxiety to wear his learning lightly, he wore relatively little of it. Mrs. Rachel Bromwich, in her magisterial centenary retrospect *Matthew Arnold and Celtic Literature*, makes formidable lists of what he had left unseen and in some cases unknown.[47] But she also points out that he and his master in Celtic enthusiasm, Ernest Renan,[48] had undertaken for the first time a comparative synthesis of the literatures of Britanny, Wales and Ireland[49]:

> . . . these two attempts, in French and in English, however insecurely and inadequately based, to synthesize and to bring together the records of the Celtic peoples and to assess what *literary* (as distinct from linguistic and institutional) features they shared in common, represented an entirely new enterprise. Even though in Arnold's case this was done chiefly from an ulterior motive—that of asserting the presence of these same characteristics in English literature—yet in this respect his work, even more than that of Renan, marks an important landmark in Celtic studies.

On the other achievements of the lectures, Mrs. Bromwich naturally notes, and scouts[50]

> . . . Arnold's attempts to isolate specifically Celtic traits in the work of certain major English poets . . . a direct outcome of his beliefs about the persistence of innate racial characteristics: the question of the existence of such subconscious Celtic undertones in English poetry—and it was these, rather than explicit literary influences, which interested Arnold—can be no more than a matter of speculation now as then, for such theories are not susceptible of proof.

She then examines the three features he singled out as peculiarly Celtic: a gift for style, 'natural magic', and 'Celtic melancholy', the last two of which—but not the first—he owed to Renan. And we can add, that if his motives were more mixed than he cared to say or perhaps fully realized, his placing of his enquiry on the clear foundation of knowledge for its own sake

Matthew Arnold: Between Two Worlds

reflected the best scientific principles of scholarship in his time, Zeuss's, which he acknowledged directly, and Newman's, more indirectly. 'I can have no ends to serve', he declared a little disingenuously at the close of his second lecture, 'in finding in Celtic literature more than is there. What *is* there, is for me the only question.'[51] The last sentence was the most valuable of all his trumpet-calls.

Whatever the reservations about Arnold's content and learning, his evangelism deserves all praise on two counts: the lectures are magnificent in their vivid and exciting quality, probably the best example of that art-form since Carlyle's *On Heroes, Hero-worship and the Heroic in History* in 1839, and they shared with them the European and Near Eastern sense which battled so strongly against what Chesterton somewhat opti-mistically termed 'a certain odd provincialism peculiar to the English in that great century; they were in a land of pocket; they appealed to too narrow a public opinion.'[52] He rightly praised Arnold's exceptionalism on this score, with a slight qualification:

> Even Matthew Arnold, though he saw this peril and prided himself on escaping it, did not altogether escape it. There must be (to use an Irishism) something shallow in the depths of any man who talks about the *Zeitgeist* as if it were a living thing.

Chesterton on his own record would have been less ready to censure another weakness, allied to the last, Arnold's noisy generalizations about nations and races, such as 'Style, then, the Germans are singularly without.'[53] Yet when Arnold's blood was up, the generalizations thundered against pro-vincialism to great effect, perhaps the more because he was using the nonsense of racial and national character to attack a provincialism which had hitherto sustained itself by them. On the Celtic influence in English poetic style, he provides a grand exhortation, magnificently grasping *en route* the nettle of Macpherson's *Ossian*[54]:

> Its chord of penetrating passion and melancholy, again, its *Titanism* as we see it in Byron,—what other European poetry possesses that like the English, and where do we get it from? The Celts, with their vehement reaction against the despotism of fact, with their sensuous nature, their manifold striving, their

166

adverse destiny, their immense calamities, the Celts are the prime authors of this vein of piercing regret and passion,—of this Titanism in poetry. A famous book, Macpherson's *Ossian*, carried in the last century this vein like a flood of lava through Europe. I am not going to criticise Macpherson's *Ossian* here. Make the part of what is forged, modern, tawdry, spurious, in the book, as large as you please; strip Scotland, if you like, of every feather of borrowed plumes which on the strength of Macpherson's *Ossian* she may have stolen from that *vetus et major Scotia*, the true home of the Ossianic poetry, Ireland; I make no objection. But there will still be left in the book a residue with the very soul of the Celtic genius in it, and which has the proud distinction of having brought this soul of the Celtic genius into contact with the genius of the nations of modern Europe, and enriched all our poetry by it. Woody Morven, and echoing Lora, and Selma with its silent halls!—we all owe them a debt of gratitude, and when we are unjust enough to forget it, may the Muse forget us!

Mrs. Bromwich finds the choice of *Ossian* 'unfortunate',[55] as from the point of view of exact scholarship it certainly was, but she notes the soundness of his instinct in going for what was most authentic in *Ossian*, specifically in the emphasis on Celtic fatalism and elegy. Yet, in his desperate struggle to awaken the English to the value of the Celtic inheritance both for the liberation of English cultural attitudes from complacency and provincialism, and for the value of recognizing Celtic cultural pride in making for a happier United Kingdom, Arnold could be forgiven for looking enviously at Macpherson's success in awakening Europe. And whatever Macpherson's sins, this was a great achievement, of incalculable cultural effects. Where Macpherson's influence was more inimical to Arnold was in leading him from time to time to confuse the purity of Celtic style with the great wash of romanticism which Macpherson's rendition undammed. Mrs. Bromwich also remarks on Arnold's failure to grasp the element of satire in ancient Celtic literature.[56] It is noteworthy that a much more severe critic of *Ossian*, Sir Walter Scott, illustrated in *The Antiquary* the vigour, bawdry and comedy of the original Fianna poems which Macpherson had looted so successfully.[57] Satire was an indispensable creative tool to Scott, the pupil of Maria Edgeworth. But it was a vein Celtic themes later opened up in Arnold.

It is fitting that another creative artist, very definitely from the Celtic periphery, should be allowed to sum up Arnold's work. The Irish short-story writer Frank O'Connor, wrote[58]:

> Most of Arnold's weaknesses as a critic come from an absolute acceptance of a contemporary racialism. . . . I am afraid I do not believe much in Normans, Anglo-Saxons and Celts. . . . Where Arnold deals with the subject he knew better than anyone else—English poetry—he is not easy to contradict. . . . That there is a strong Celtic strain in English literature is as likely as not, though I do not see how it can be proved or disproved. . . . It does not matter much whether or not we agree with Arnold, because *On the Study of Celtic Literature* is one of the really influential books of the nineteenth century. . . . It added greatly to the effect of German scholarship in making Ireland and things Irish dignified in the eyes of our people.

Perhaps O'Connor is eating the cake and still possessing it in saluting Arnold's valuable remarks on such poets as Milton and Byron within the lectures while questioning how far a Celtic element can be isolated in their work. But certainly Arnold can be hauled back within the realm of the plausible when it is acknowledged that he sought to show certain distinctive qualities in Celtic literature and noted some of these in great English poetry. In a sense, perhaps, he should be stood on his head, to the advantage of his own cause. He may not have proved Milton was a Celt; he did prove that reasons for admiring Milton also applied to Celtic literature. And on this he was unanswerable. Curiously enough, his own argument carried within it the seeds of its destruction in one respect. If Milton owed something of his greatness to a Celtic influence, then, contrary to what Arnold preached, Celtic literature needed to be maintained in a vigorous context of popularly spoken Welsh, Scots-Gaelic and Irish so that the frontier of English would always find itself challenged and renovated. Mrs. Bromwich makes an eloquent point on this.[59] The examples of Synge and, very differently, Dylan Thomas, illustrate the argument effectively.[60] But while Mrs. Bromwich and I would regard the need for such a permanent linguistic frontier as vital for English literature in any case, it bears even more strongly in the realm of what Arnold believed.

To return to O'Connor's argument, there must follow the question of how far in his description of the Celtic element in English literature Arnold was speaking of his own work. His cool observation of Nature and its effective symbolism are precisely what Professor MacEdward Leach wants us to think about in seeking to define 'Celtic magic'.[61] Arnold himself had in mind the fatalism, the melancholy, and above all the love which transcends both, asserting its necessity beyond simile and foreboding. Another trait present in much of his writing, though also left aside from his analysis of the Celtic element, is even more striking: its hortatory qualities. The Celtic bard wanted his audience to think, behave and act in certain ways. So did Arnold. There was decided identification in his love for the bard he knew best, in Gray's poem, of which he had written from Llandudno to his sister in his holiday of 1864:[62]

> The poetry of the Celtic race and its names of places quite overpowers me, and it will be long before [his brother] Tom forgets the line, 'Hear from thy grave, great Taliessin, hear!'— from Gray's Bard, of which I gave him the benefit some hundred times.

But as he learned the mass of the bards delivered most of their denunciations of the degeneracy of their times to their own people, not to Taliesin or Edward I. Arnold would increasingly follow their example, in dedication and vehemence. Consciously and unconsciously, then, his lectures in addition to all else have to be seen as a comment on what he now understood himself to have been doing in his own contribution to literature.

When this essay was in its final stage, I asked the greatest living Gaelic poet for his opinion of Arnold on Celtic literature. Sorley MacLean acknowledged all the weaknesses, the omissions, the ignorance, but pronounced it a great and valuable work. What he saluted above all else was its 'intuition'. Arnold looked into himself, and defined the Celtic.

4

Ah, love, let us be true
To one another! for the world, which seems
To lie before us like a land of dreams,
So various, so beautiful, so new,

Hath really neither joy, nor love, nor light,
Nor certitude, nor peace, nor help for pain;
And we are here as on a darkling plain
Swept with confused alarms of struggle and flight,
Where ignorant armies clash by night.

('Dover Beach')

On 30 November 1865, the trial of Thomas Clarke Luby for
Fenian activities commenced in Dublin, ending with his sentence of twenty years' imprisonment, to be followed by the trial
of John O'Leary, who met a similar fate. On 6 and 7 December,
Matthew Arnold delivered the first two of his lectures on Celtic
Literature at Oxford. On 9 December, Jeremiah O'Donovan
Rossa was sentenced in Dublin to imprisonment for life. On
17 February, a Bill suspending the Habeas Corpus Act in
Ireland was passed by both Houses of Parliament. On
24 February, Matthew Arnold delivered the third of his lectures. On 26 May, he delivered the fourth. On 2 June, the
Canadian Volunteers marched against a Fenian invasion and
drove it back to the United States, six of its number being
captured on Canadian soil where they were afterwards tried by
drum-head court-martial and shot. On 8 September, *The Times*
violently attacked Arnold's lectures. On 14 September, it
renewed the attack. On 11 February 1867, a Fenian raid on
Chester Castle was frustrated. On 5 March, a Fenian was shot
in an attack on police barracks at Tallaght, near Dublin;
Fenians briefly captured the police force at Glencullen; at
Drogheda and Thurles the telegraph wires were cut and the
railway torn up; at Kilmallock, police killed three Fenians and
took fourteen prisoners; a coastguard station was plundered
near Kilrush; the mail train from Cork to Dublin was sent off
the rails; the police station at Burnfoot was burnt. On 4 June,
On the Study of Celtic Literature was published with a new preface,
instalments having appeared in the *Cornhill* magazine in the
previous year in March, April, May and July.

Matthew Arnold and his contemporaries were exceedingly
conscious of this chronology. Towards the close of the second
lecture, in an excited discussion of philology, Arnold
demanded[63]:

Who does not feel his mind agreeably cleared about our friends
the Fenians, when he learns that the root of their name, *fen*,

170

'white', appears in the hero Fingal; in Gwynned, the Welsh name for North Wales; in the Roman Venedotia; in Vannes in Brittany; in Venice?

It would be easy to despise Arnold for the flippancy of this, delivered almost at the moment when Yeats's O'Leary of the 'lofty head', into whose grave he would consign 'Romantic Ireland', was receiving judicial sneer and savage sentence for his beliefs. It would also be easy to despise Arnold for the lightness with which he played with the threat of violent overthrow of lawful government. But our insouciant Oxford lecturer deserves, I think, a different response. The sophistication leads him to egregiousness in a minefield; but it stems from a very vulnerable innocence.

Insofar as Arnold had any political sense of what he was doing at all, his motives, where they were not frivolous in the manner of the topical allusion in a pantomime, were probably humane. The state was serving out brutal sentences on an organization it took to be terrorist; Arnold was telling his audience to keep its senses of perspective and humour. Although the Canadian raid, and the abortive insurrection lay in the future when he was speaking, he left the passage unaltered by them before book publication. But he was also exhibiting a rigidity of mind with respect to his data. It was nonsense for the modern Fenians to see themselves as the lineal descendants of the ancient variety and their votaries, but in Arnold's assumption of the survival of Celtic racial attributes down the millenia, their nonsense was his nonsense. Both Arnold and O'Mahony were the children of contemporary *English* racial views (which the English, for their part, had largely been taught by such Scots as Carlyle and Dr Robert Knox).[64] And Arnold cared little for any check the Fenians might give the theories he was so eloquently deploying about the Celts.

Dr. Thomas Arnold wrote of the Celts in his *History of Rome* published in the early 1840s:[64]

> The Kelts or Gauls broke through the thin screen which had hitherto concealed them from sight, and began for the first time to take their part in the great drama of the nations. For nearly two hundred years they continued to fill Europe and Asia with

the terror of their name; but it was a passing tempest, and if it was useful at all, it was useful only to destroy. The Gauls could communicate no essential points of human character in which the other races might be deficient; they could neither improve the intellectual state of mankind, nor its social and political relations. When therefore, they had done their appointed work of havoc, they were doomed to be themselves extirpated, or to be lost amidst nations of greater creative and constructive power, nor is there any race which has left fewer traces of itself in the character and institutions of modern civilization.

This passage is often cited as proof of Matthew Arnold's reacting against his father, and he had begun his lectures by citing his father's insistence 'on the separation between us and them' (the Celts) being greater 'than . . . the separation between us and any other race in the world', and subsequently told his mother that, unlike himself,

> I do not think papa thought of the Saxon and the Celt mutually needing to be completed by each other; on the contrary, he was so full of the sense of the Celt's vices, want of steadiness, and want of plain truthfulness, vices to him particularly offensive, that he utterly abhorred him and thought him of no good at all. . . . He thought our rule in Ireland cruel and unjust, no doubt. He was not blind to faults in the Saxon; but can you show me a single line, in all he has written, testifying to his sense of any virtues and graces in the Celt?[65]

Yet his mother, had she chosen, could presumably have covered him with confusion by producing evidence of his father's sense of any virtues and graces in at least one Celt. In fact, Dr. Arnold seems to have identified Celticism much more with the actual speaking of Celtic languages—he, if not his son, attempted some study of Irish to understand the Celtic mind (of the ancient Gauls)—and it was from Celticism thus renewed that he wished to separate himself, his Cornish wife and his Irish-descended mother. Matthew Arnold argued, more rationally than his father, that there really had been a mingling of Celt and Saxon with, as he felt, good literary results for the Saxon. But what this was doing was accepting the implications of a racial mixing within himself which his father sidestepped by identifying Celticism with linguistic fidelity. It was not that Arnold rejected his father; he simply

declined to accept his father's rejection of himself. The phenomenon is well-known to students of immigration; one generation
denies its cultural links to its ancestry, its more secure progeny
exalts them.[66]

But it is worth looking at Dr. Arnold's words again, to
notice with how much of them his son actually agreed. In his
third lecture Matthew declared[67]

> And as in material civilisation he has been ineffectual, so has
> the Celt been ineffectual in politics. This colossal, impetuous,
> adventurous wanderer, the Titan of the early world, who in
> primitive times fills so large a place on earth's scene, dwindles
> and dwindles as history goes on, and at last is shrunk to what
> we now see him. For ages and ages the world has been con-
> stantly slipping, ever more and more, out of the Celt's grasp.
> 'They went forth to the war', Ossian says most truly, '*but they
> always fell.*'

Without prejudice to the literary warfare to which the last
sentence gave rise, the significant point here, it seems to me, is
Matthew Arnold's proud maintenance of the Procrustean bed
devised by his father. It was central to his thesis, as it was to
his father's, that the Celts had failed and were vanishing. He
believed that they could nevertheless be of great service within
the Saxon world, or more specifically that their culture could.
But their political failure was as absolute in the modern United
Kingdom as in the ancient Rome to which contemporaries so
habitually likened it.

His conclusion was that Philistinism would be broken down
by the study of the Celtic cultural heritage, and his sense of the
pre-eminence of the English élite in education led him to the
practical deduction that the Celtic would receive a much
higher general respect in English cultural ranks if its cultural
respectability was asserted by a professorship at Oxford. But
he also had a humane political message entwined in his
reasoning, and his peroration at the close of the lectures
encapsulates both[68]:

> But the hard unintelligence, which is just now our bane, cannot
> be conquered by storm; it must be supplied and reduced by
> culture, by a growth in the variety, fulness, and sweetness of our
> spiritual life; and this end can only be reached by studying

> things that are outside of ourselves, and by studying them
> disinterestedly. Let us reunite ourselves with our better mind
> and with the world through science; and let it be one of our
> angelic revenges on the Philistines, who among their other sins
> are the guilty authors of Fenianism, to found at Oxford a chair
> of Celtic, and to send, through the gentle ministration of
> science, a message of peace to Ireland.

The humanity of the enterprise was clear and sensible
enough, that an obvious expression of respect to the Irish
cultural heritage would give the Irish a sense of having a stake
in the United Kingdom. Arnold might be naïf politically, but
he had, to reverse Chesterton, shown a depth in his super-
ficiality which went farther than almost all of his British
contemporaries. He had penetrated to the heart of the problem
which lay behind the failure of the United Kingdom to integrate Ireland. The trouble with the Union had been not that
the Irish did not want equality with the British, but that the
British did not want it. The revelation that Irish culture was
accorded honour, that the status of being Irish was admitted
to the British cultural pantheon, would have been the means
of grappling with the problem. The weakness of Arnold's case
lay not in its perception but in its execution. With the memory
of the great famine lying between the foundation of the Union
and this proposal for its cultural consolidation, it might be felt
the time was passed when a Chair in Celtic at Oxford would
settle everything. But of course Arnold was not offering a
panacea; he was offering a symbol and a start.

The Chair of Celtic was established in Oxford in 1877, and,
again following encouragement from Arnold, another was
founded in Edinburgh in 1882. It is a tribute to Arnold's
modesty to say that in cultural, though not in scholarly, effect,
the lectures were more important than the Chairs. The lectures
had their scholarly consequences, most of all, perhaps, in the
incitement they gave future scholars to correct their errors,
enlarge their scope of enquiry and respond to their challenge.
The Chairs certainly inspired much general cultural activity
as a result of their presence. But in the public arena of English
letters it was the Arnold lectures which affected creative and
critical writers, brought 'Saxons' to see what a wealth was
waiting for their discovery in their own archipelago, and

'Celts' to feel they were of cultural significance and had better do something about it. Appropriately, the martyrdom of O'Leary was also symbolic in its contemporaneity with the oratory of Arnold, and while O'Leary might seem as thorough a symbol of separation as Arnold of Union, the legacies of both mingled together in the Irish Renaissance, most conspicuously in the person of Yeats. If O'Leary offered Yeats the idealism Arnold gave him the audience, and perhaps also the inspiration of cultural apostleship. Yeats might ultimately carry his apostleship to Ireland where it would, with mutations, be applied to politics Arnold would have deplored; but Arnold told the Celts how to go about the business of cultural leadership and their own case was one of the best instances of his doing it. Yeats learned from this; and so, in Britain, would Wilde and Shaw and many others.[69]

The irony still remained that the Celts, as they saw themselves and were seen by Arnold, declined to admit their political ineffectuality. Arnold himself returned to the politics of the matter in the 'Introduction' which he published with his lectures in their book form. *The Times* had given him every reason for it. Indeed its editorials came close to his own earlier arguments in favour of the linguistic integration of Britain, and his own frivolities on the subject of the Eisteddfod were made the ammunition by which his whole thesis was denounced:

> An Eisteddfod is one of the most mischievous and selfish pieces of sentimentalism which could possibly be perpetrated. It is simply a foolish interference with the natural progress of civilisation and prosperity.

> The Welsh language is the curse of Wales. Its prevalence, and the ignorance of English, have excluded, and even now exclude the Welsh people from the civilization, the improvement, and the material prosperity of their English neighbours.

Arnold quoted these sentences from *The Times* of 8 September. But he did not care to give fresh currency to the brutalities of the editorial of 14 September when it spelled out its meaning of the presumed consequences of this exclusion:[70]

> We can only observe as a matter of fact that Welsh music and poetry have not had the slightest effect in civilizing the Welsh

people. So far from being more refined or polished than the English or Scotch, they are far behind them in the most elementary conditions of refinement and morality. There are practices tolerated and even cherished among the Welsh which are not known and would be put down at once in most parts of England.

The ominous vagueness of Delane's *Times* on the Welsh abominations let the English reader attribute common English assumptions of lying, thieving, 'welshing', to the barrier thrown by the Welsh language in the way of the purifying English linguistic civilization. But Arnold was quick to see that what was being ascribed to the Welsh had all too much relevance to the lowest caste among Delane's fellow-Irish. He mocked Delane, but having mocked went again to the heart of the problem:

> . . . I have made a study of the Corinthian or leading article style, and know its exigences, and that they are no more to be quarrelled with than the law of gravitation. So, for my part, when I read these asperities of the *Times*, my mind did not dwell very much on my own concern in them; but what I said to myself, as I put the newspaper down, was this: '*Behold England's difficulty in governing Ireland!*'

And the introduction concluded with a renewed call to cultural arms for the sake of the English, the Celts and, emphatically, the Union:[71]

> . . . we English, alien and uncongenial to our Celtic partners as we may have hitherto shown ourselves, have notwithstanding, beyond perhaps any other nation, a thousand latent springs of possible sympathy with them. Let them consider that new ideas and forces are stirring in England, that day by day these new ideas and forces gain in power, and that almost every one of them is the friend of the Celt and not his enemy. And, whether our Celtic partners will consider this or no, at any rate let us ourselves, all of us who are proud of being the ministers of these new ideas, work incessantly to procure for them a wider and more fruitful application; and to remove the main ground of the Celt's alienation from the Englishman, by substituting, in place of that type of Englishman with whom alone the Celt has too long been familiar, a new type, more intelligent, more gracious, and more humane.

176

And bravely he sent forth his beautiful and generous book.

He had been moving more deeply into the waters of Irish politics by that time. On 19 November 1866 the *Pall Mall Gazette* carried from him a comment on how far Ireland would be improved by Prussian Land Reform, in the course of which the symbolic Irish landlord to whom he was replying was described as 'that bloodsucker'.[72] His purpose was political— on 31 March 1865 his brother-in-law W. E. Forster had moved for a select committee of the Commons to investigate the conditions resultant from the Irish land system, and Arnold had been anxious for him to study the example of vom Stein's legislation in Prussia[73]—but behind his political agitation lay a sentiment which seems common to all his Celtic concerns, whether land reform, Fenianism, cultural acceptance or reinvigoration of the atrophying English: a desire to *protect* the Celts as well as their culture. Believing as he did in their political ineffectuality, half-persuaded by his father's vision of their inevitable doom, they became for him an endangered species for which he had to fight both for themselves and for the cultural salvation he was convinced they brought.

The same emotions were present in *Culture and Anarchy*, as a kind of subterranean sacred river making occasional appearances. Into that great work it is not possible nor necessary to enter in detail here, but he returned with characteristic courage to Fenianism, for all that January 1868, when it first appeared in the *Cornhill*, was far from a propitious moment to be forthright and playful on the subject.[74] (The Manchester rescue from the prison van had been accomplished by the Fenians, with the unintended death of Police Sergeant Brett on 18 September; five men were sentenced to death for it on 1 November; three of them were hanged on 23 November; twelve people were killed and 120 injured in an unsuccessful Fenian attempt to rescue prisoners from Clerkenwell on 13 December.)

> We are not in danger from Fenianism, fierce and turbulent as it may show itself; for against this our conscience is free enough to let us act resolutely and put forth our overwhelming strength the moment there is any real need for it. In the first place, it never was any part of our creed that the great right and blessedness of an Irishman, or, indeed, of anybody on earth

except an Englishman, is to do as he likes; and we can have no scruple at all about abridging, if necessary, a non-Englishman's assertion of personal liberty. The British Constitution, its checks, and its prime virtues, are for Englishmen. We may extend them to others out of love and kindness; but we find no real divine law written on our hearts constraining us so to extend them. And then the difference between an Irish Fenian and an English rough is so immense, and the case, in dealing with the Fenian, so much more clear! He is so evidently desperate and dangerous, a man of a conquered race, a Papist, with centuries of ill-usage to inflame him against us, with an alien religion established in his country at his expense, with no admiration of our institutions, no love of our virtues, no talents for our business, no turn for our comfort!

And he went on to point out how in contrast the law protected a venomous-tongued anti-Catholic agitator in Birmingham, for all the violence he might threaten and might occasion.

Without again directly invoking the need for Celticization of British culture, it was absolutely implicit in his

definition of culture, or the pursuit of light and pefection, which made light and perfection consist, not in resting and being, but in growing and becoming, in a perpetual advance in beauty and wisdom.[75]

More generally, the saving alien element whose quest haunts so much of his poetry, to be answered in part by his discovery and formal adoption of the Celt, was firmly asserted.[76]

Therefore, when we speak of ourselves as divided into Barbarians, Philistines, and Populace [his version of aristocrats, bourgeoisie and masses], we must be understood always to imply that within each of these classes there are a certain number of *aliens*, if we may so call them,—persons who are mainly led, not by their class spirit, but by a general *humane* spirit, by the love of human perfection; and that this number is capable of being diminished or augmented. I mean, the number of those who will succeed in developing this happy instinct will be greater or smaller, in proportion both to the force of the original instinct within them, and to the hindrance or encouragement which it meets with from without.

But he was beginning to give dangerous hostages to Celtic fortune. As Mrs. Bromwich reminds us, he had ignored, at least in his prose, the folk basis of surviving Celtic literature, and hence did not ask himself how alien such popular forms of transmission might be to his own attempts to preach his Celtic gospel from the élitist high places. He was sufficiently in tune with the principle of a bardic élite; he did not ask himself how much the culture of the bardic élite had owed to the populace of Celtic lands in intervening years, in their guardianship of it, furtherance of it and additions to it. One of the weakest moments of *Culture and Anarchy* is that in which his ignorance dismissed the universities of the United States, an expression of popular organization of higher education and cultural conservation if ever there was one.[77] He knew nothing of their obligations to the Scottish tradition of a 'democratic intellect', the product of Lowland Scotland in its university towns, but one reflecting influence from Highland migrants. In his appeals for Hellenism as against Hebraism, he was thinking in part of the Celtic tradition, and, whether he knew it or not, it had borrowed from the Greeks and Romans, but he was as ignorant of the male chauvinism in so much of Celtic and Hellenic culture as he was of the rôle of Deborah the prophetess in the first book of Judges when he declared:[78]

> Who, I say, will believe, when he [*sic*] really considers the matter, that where the feminine nature, the feminine ideal, and our relations to them, are brought into question, the delicate and apprehensive genius of the Indo-European race, the race which invented the Muses, and chivalry, and the Madonna, is to find its last word on this question in the institutions of a Semitic people, whose wisest king had seven hundred wives and three hundred concubines?

The strongest indication of where his peril lay was in his protest against the Disestablishment of the Protestant episcopalian Church of Ireland being enacted simply in response to Nonconformist pressure, which prevented the dispersal of established Church funds being distributed among other Christian sects, including the Roman Catholic. His principles were admirably ecumenical, but they showed little signs of understanding what the legacy of religious persecution meant to votaries of a religion therefore made dependent on the populace. He knew the latter fact; he does not seem to have

179

grappled with its implications. He sneered at the Nonconformist greed as well as the Nonconformist bigotry[79]—

> Look at the life imaged in such a newspaper as the *Nonconformist*,—
> a life of jealousy of the Establishment, disputes, tea-meetings,
> openings of chapels, sermons; and then think of it as an ideal of
> a human life completing itself on all sides, and aspiring with all
> its organs after sweetness, light, and perfection.

Yet his beloved Celtic Wales, sanctified by his visits there as a
boy, as the companion of Clough, as brother and father, was
saturated in that life.[80] And had it not much in common with
the rising Catholic bourgeoisie in Ireland, seeking for the
social position of the Church of Ireland, while haggling among
the preoccupations for which his emulator Yeats would later
charge it?[81]

The Church of Ireland was duly disestablished by Gladstone's first government in 1869, and in 1872 Arnold summed
it up as[82]

> the abolition of the Irish Church through the power of the
> Dissenters' antipathy to church-establishments, then telling
> ourselves in our newspapers we had done it out of a pure love of
> reason and justice, and then calling solemnly upon the quick-
> witted Irish, who knew that the Dissenters would have let the
> Irish Church stand for ever sooner than give a shilling of its
> funds to the Catholics entitled to them, to believe our claptrap
> and be properly grateful to us at last. . . .

Yet he reckoned without the satisfaction of the Catholics and
their prelates at the fall of their old enemy who had despoiled
and despised them in the bitter penal days of the eighteenth
century. Arnold may have been optimistic in seeing the Celtic
spirit as antipathetic to materialism, but in nurturing griev-
ances Catholics could readily forgo material considerations,
and the symbolic triumph far outweighed any pickings that
might, improbably, have fallen their way in a more enlightened
Act. Arnold was here fighting a hopeless battle, all the more
because it was for England his logic was really intended.
Ireland simply served him as a means for a paper conflict. As
Chesterton put it[83]

> while Arnold would loosen the theological bonds of the Church,
> he would not loosen the official bonds of the State. You must

not disestablish the Church: you must not even leave the Church: you must stop inside it and think what you choose. Enemies might say that he was simply trying to establish and endow Agnosticism. It is fairer and truer to say that unconsciously he was trying to restore Paganism: for this State Ritualism without theology, and without much belief, actually was the practice of the ancient world. Arnold may have thought that he was building an altar to the Unknown God; but he was really building it to Divus Caesar.

In fact he was once again seeking to tailor a new socio-political age to the doctrines of Dr. Thomas Arnold, modernized to suit his own taste. Ironically, Dr. Arnold had conspicuously enunciated them in agreement with Gladstone's *The State in its Relations with the Church*, that clarion-cry in 1839 for the state to show itself guardian of the Church in all things which had drawn such ferocious execution from Macaulay.[84] Matthew Arnold was attacking Gladstone for abandoning the tenets which had so rejoiced the heart of Thomas Arnold. But the Irish Catholics are unlikely to have cared more for the views of Arnold junior than they had for those of Arnold senior. Their political power was receiving its due deference at last, however much Matthew Arnold might choose to assume the deference was only being paid to the Nonconformists.

5

Arnold said little in criticism of the next victory that so rejoiced the Irish Catholics (hollow enough though it proved)— the Land Act of 1870. His wife was present in the House of Commons when Forster spoke on his Education Bill, and Gladstone hugged him with delight, murmuring afterwards of Education and Land proposals 'Well, I think our pair of ponies will run through together.'[85] This was implicating the family with a vengeance, but privately Arnold told his mother that

> while the Liberals lean so on the Protestant Dissenters and adopt all their prejudices without believing in them, and simply to get political power by their help, I have no desire for Liberal candidates to win.

He added sourly, 'Gladstone, who is always shifting, is this year in a much more Anglican mood, as I judge by a curious letter he wrote me a week ago.'[86] But when the third demand of the Irish Catholics, a satisfactory university establishment for their benefit, drove a wedge between their hopes and the taboos of the Dissenters, the Government fell, and Arnold publicly condemned its Bill propounded 'under the eye of' its 'Secularist and Nonconformist supporters' as

> simply ridiculous. Religion, moral philosophy, and modern history are probably the three matters of instruction in which the bulk of mankind take most interest; and this precious university was to give no instruction in any one of them! The Irish have a right to a university with a Catholic faculty of theology, and with Catholic professors of philosophy and history. By refusing them to Ireland our fanaticism does not tend to make one Catholic the less, it only tends to make Irish Catholicism unprogressive.[87]

This was no treason to the family: he was simply preferring the interests of his brother Thomas over those of his brother-in-law William. The younger Thomas Arnold had become converted to Roman Catholicism and had been for a time Professor of English in Newman's Catholic University in Dublin in the later 1850s. He later turned away from the faith, but was drawing back to it and would shortly be within the fold once more; he later returned to Dublin to play a part in the Jesuit institution which took the place of Newman's venture. He had polemicized for the cause of the Catholic University, but its degrees were never recognized. The brothers had recently been together at their mother's funeral, and Newman had written about her in terms which moved Thomas greatly.[88] Matthew's demands for the Catholics' university in the wake of the government defeat derived in part from the common loss and love between them. His major discussion of it appeared in a preface to the second edition of his *Higher Schools and Universities in Germany*, completed in the weeks after his mother's death.[89] It was fine polemic, and it took its line and its immediate occasion from the polemical argument that Bismarck's *Kulturkampf* against Catholic education in Germany actually involved a juster recognition of Catholic claims for university teaching than Britain was prepared to accord. There was a touch of sensationalism in this approach which suggested fighting the Philistines with their own weapons (although sales proved sluggish); but it was not a mode of defence likely to endear him to Irish Catholicism. He firmly remained its protector, but equally firmly continued to assume its political ineffectuality and hence need of his protection.

Much of Arnold's writing in support of a Catholic University of Ireland, whether in this preface, which appeared in 1874, in 'Irish Catholicism and British Liberalism', published in the *Fortnightly Review* for July 1878, or in his letter to *The Times* printed on 31 July 1879, repeats itself, sometimes in the same words, but there are important changes as both his argument and his conviction hardened. The last, written when Disraeli's Irish University Education Bill was going through the Commons, sums up his case.[90]

> The Catholic majority in Ireland is neither allowed the use of the old endowments to give it a University instruction such as it desires, and such as in England and Scotland we make the old endowments give us, nor is it allowed the aid of State grants. . . . We have waited until our Universities have become thoroughly of the character that suits us, and then, when the Anglican character of the English Universities, the Presbyterian character of the Scotch Universities, has got thoroughly established and is secure for the next generation or two, at any rate, we throw open our doors, declare tests and subscriptions abolished, pronounce our Universities to be now perfectly undenominational, and say that, having made them so, we are precluded from doing anything for the Irish Catholics. It is as if our proceedings had had for their very object to give us an arm against the Irish Catholics. But an Irish Catholic may say, 'All we want is an undenominational University just like yours. Give us a University where the bulk of the students are Catholic, where the bulk of the teachers are Catholic, and we will undertake to be open to all comers, to accept a conscience clause, to impose no tests, to be "perfectly undenominational".' We will not give him the chance.

The Disraeli proposal, successfully carried, simply created a Royal University which would act as an examining board whence degrees could be obtained; the unrecognized Catholic University of Newman now became an establishment in which students were trained for the exams at the Royal. Arnold's letter may have assisted to get the proposal enacted, miserably inadequate though he saw it; the letter was certainly so timed. But he made it clear that he had given more thought to the rôle of the past as midwife of Irish Nationalism in the present, especially when matters were so managed by the British Government as to assist the induction of such an activity[91]:

> It seems to me that the Irish have a very real grievance. It is a grievance to which I find no parallel elsewhere in Europe. It is a grievance which must perpetually remind Ireland that she is a conquered country. Finally, it is a grievance which must be the more irritating from the manner in which it is denied or excused.
>
> . . . To treat the Irish Catholics in this way is really to have one weight and measure for ourselves and another for the Irish. It is, however we may dress the thing up in our own minds, to treat Ireland still as a conquered country. It is a survival from the state of things when no Irish Catholic might own a horse worth more than £5. The Irish cannot but feel it to be so.

Let us at once acknowledge that Arnold's view of the question was noble and generous, and testified to the increasing hold which that Irish prophet of culture, of conciliation, and of the power of the past, Edmund Burke, was having on him especially where Irish affairs were concerned.[92] It does not detract to stress its familial interest; Thomas Arnold was by now firmly in the Roman Catholic Church once more. But there had been a strange development. Matthew as well as Thomas Arnold was by now beginning personally to identify with Catholicism. In 'Irish Catholicism and British Liberalism' (1878) he scouted Catholicism's dogma, as he scouted the Biblical fundamentalism of Protestants. But he accorded it victory in what interested himself:[93]

> I persist in thinking that Catholicism has, from this superiority, a great future before it; that it will endure while all the Protestant sects (in which I do not include the Church of England) dissolve and perish. I persist in thinking that the prevailing form for the Christianity of the future will be the form of Catholicism; but a Catholicism purged, opening itself to the light and air, having the consciousness of its own poetry, freed from its sacerdotal despotism and freed from its pseudo-scientific apparatus of superannuated dogma. Its forms will be

retained, as symbolising with the force and charm of poetry a few cardinal [*sic*] facts and ideas, simple indeed, but indispensable and inexhaustible, and on which our race could lay hold only by materialising them.

From this ideal future of Catholicism, truly, few countries can be farther removed than the Ireland of the present day. . . .

But in Arnold it was, in part, the logical development of his Celtic evangel. Modern Ireland lay outside it, and this was the fault of English rule in Ireland. Much though it would have horrified Arnold to know it, his logic was to inspire Alice Stopford Green, James Connolly and the other votaries of the doctrine of Ireland's Golden Age before the Norman conquest, and hence the philosophy of Sinn Féin, of the movement for Ireland's independence, and of the official creed of the new Irish state. But Arnold, as a Unionist, sought to relieve Ireland of its spiritual heritage of conquest[94]:

> Irish Catholicism is Ultramontane, priest-governed, superstitious, self-confident. It could hardly be otherwise. The Irish Catholic has no public education beyond the elementary school. His priests are educated in the closest of seminaries. The national sense has been so managed in him by us, with our oppression and ill-government, that national sense as a member of our nation and empire he has none. His national sense is that of a conquered people, held down by a superior force of aliens, and glad to conspire against them with Rome or with any one else. If we want the Irish to be less superstitious, less priest-governed, less Ultramontane, let us do what is likely to serve this end. The Irish will use Catholic schools and no other. Let us give them secondary and higher Catholic schools with a public character. They have at present no secondary schools with a public character. As public higher schools the Queen's Colleges have been offered to them; but they will not use the Queen's Colleges, any more than we, either, are disposed to use colleges of that type. The Catholic layman has, therefore, neither secondary nor higher school; the priest has for a higher school Maynooth, a close seminary. What an admirable and likely cure is this for Irish ignorance, sacerdotalism, Ultramontanism, and disaffection!

And he rejoiced that Joseph Chamberlain and Sir Charles Dilke seemed to agree with him.[95]

British opinion saw the controversy as one between Catholic

Bishops, demanding government support for a university they would control, and Protestant voters, refusing to give power to Catholic Bishops. Arnold's solution was that the Catholic University should have the best qualified Catholics appointed to its professoriate, under the ultimate control of a Minister of the Crown. He believed that if such an offer were to be made, the Catholic laity would accept it, even if the Bishops would not. It was the viewpoint of the supporters of Newman's ideal, such as his brother Thomas, and it gained some force with the death of Newman's great antagonist, Paul Cardinal Cullen, Archbishop of Dublin, in 1875. Thomas Arnold would sum up the conflict between those two in 1892 in terms he had doubt-less articulated years earlier to Matthew[96]:

> Cullen was a strong man, and not hostile to learning and culture on principle; and if Newman had been less shrinkingly sensitive, less English, less Oxonian, in short something differ-ent from what he was, the two might have worked together to some profitable account. As it was, no one who saw the blunt, sturdy, rugged peasant from the Co: Meath side by side with the half French banker's son from London and Oxford, could doubt that cordiality between them was impossible.

Yet Matthew Arnold was positing that an Irish Catholic laity, although up to now imprisoned in sacerdotalism, would sud-denly emancipate itself in the light of a generous offer. This optimism was as fundamental to his thesis as his pessimism about the present state of Irish Catholicism. And here, fortified by what he had learned from Thomas's Irish experiences, he was comprehending a pattern of effects from Catholicism's heritage of persecution solidifying its popular basis. His increase of knowledge, and indeed willingness to learn, meant that his diagnosis greatly improved. His prescription was much less likely to prove as sound as his diagnosis—in which situation he was but following the normal lot of humankind, led by the medical profession—but in any case it was never given the chance of being put to the test.

Arnold disliked what he saw of the results of Roman Catholicism's being driven to depend on the mass of the people instead of on the established structures of an ordered society. But he could not separate this popular dependence from what he liked about Catholicism, and even Celticism; and what was his own anxiety to bring education to the masses but following in the wake of Christianity's impact on them?[97]

> The Roman Catholic religion is the religion which has most reached the people. The bulk of its superstitions come from its having really plunged so far down into the multitude, and spread so wide among them. . . . Who, again, has seen the poor in other churches as they are seen in Catholic churches, or common soldiers in churches as they are seen in the churches of Rome? And why? Because the attaching doctrine of the equal share of Christians in the beauty and glory of religion, which all churches preach, the Church of Rome makes palpable; and the poor find in church, and free to them as to the rich, the 'gilded saloons' which with us they hear of but can never enter.

6

The bitter controversies on the Risorgimento, the Papal intransigence against Italian unification and the assertion of the doctrine of Papal infallibility between 1860 and 1870 had embattled British opinion against Pius IX in particular and Roman Catholicism in general. Garibaldi had become a great popular hero, and if Victor Emmanuel and not he had proved the real beneficiary, he too was popular as the ally of the United Kingdom during the Crimean War. Arnold had diagnosed the ails of Roman Catholicism as the product of persecution which brought in its wake a ghetto religious outlook. But it was natural that he should single out Ultramontanism, the adhesion to Papal politics as well as to Papal religion, as the 'worst' of the 'dangers'[98] of Roman Catholicism in Ireland. He saw as the alternative to it a 'national sense'.

> . . . practically, a church as wide as his nation, suited to his nation, nationally governed, is what a man should seek, and he does ill to run after the shadow of more and lose the substance of this. But the national sense is strong in every nation, and may be trusted to assert itself as time goes on. What hinders it from asserting itself in Irish Catholicism? What keeps Irish Catholicism Ultramontane? Our policy and our policy only. We will not let Irish Catholicism be instituted publicly; we will not suffer it to be national, to have the sense

of being the Church of Ireland, and independent; we keep it a private thing, and its only way of being great and public is by being Ultramontane.

But here his convictions, headed by his generous devotion to the cause of a Catholic University, impaired his analysis. Ultramontanism in fact was in its immediate political context reactionary, no doubt, yet it acted as a preventative against the dangers of Irish Catholicism becoming still more parochial, indeed it aided it to retain a European sense lacking in Britain and against whose lack Arnold was in perpetual protest. Ultramontanism might make Ireland's European sense a force on the wrong side, politically, but it kept some cultural links with Europe alive in Ireland where they were dying in Britain. And Arnold in 1874 still had difficulty in realizing the actual as opposed to the theoretical alternatives. The 'national sense' of which he spoke was present in Ireland, and was about to burst forth into new vigour, but it was not liable to increase its devotion to the United Kingdom. Cullen had, after all, stood as a bulwark against Irish Catholicism's acceptance of too much of the British-ruled state, but he had also stood against Irish nationalism in any form which might seem to recall Mazzini and Garibaldi, and he was not inclined to be cautious in his search for such tendencies. With Cullen gone, the 'national sense' reasserted itself in Irish Catholicism, and the United Kingdom would be the loser. Ironically, Arnold had seen so much of the several factors which would go to make new Irish nationalism—the rejuvenated enthusiasm for a Celtic past, the Fenian activities, the vigorous agitation for Catholic claims, the quest for an educated laity—but he still failed to appreciate that the nationalism he preached would take a form antithetical to what he sought. What may have blinded him was that when Irish nationalism emerged into the limelight, both in its Parnellite, and then in its Sinn Féin, phases, it would owe much to the United Kingdom nationalism in style and system of thought while taking its being in opposing it. It would also partake of the popular cohesion born of the civil and social disabilities of Catholicism. Arnold's gallantry had come too late.

But, as he pointed out, governmental remedial legislation

was smaller and later. As the land agitation in Ireland swirled into ferocious and sanguinary confrontation, Arnold went back to his basic insistence on seeking a justice for Ireland which was no more than what Englishmen might ask for themselves. His solution to the land question was that bad landlords should be ruthlessly expropriated and deprived of the property rights they were dishonouring. The idea was not chimerical; the sharp treatment of disgraceful offenders would have been a means of robbing the agitation of its strongest propaganda weapons and incentives to action, while showing the mass of the Irish peasantry that British justice was no abstract and remote concept whose only realization in practice was to bear down on themselves. It was the logic of his arguments on the university question. But, again consistently, he firmly denounced the idea of incompatibility of Britain and Ireland; Ireland was not a nation, in the sense of being opposed to the United Kingdom, any more than Scotland, Wales or Cornwall (at last his mother's origin was heard from).[99] Celticism could only play its part within the United Kingdom; a separate Ireland would simply have been left to self-destruction. So reasoned Arnold, determined to the last that as he had willed the Celtic world to be, so it should be, even though his concomitant theses on the political ineffectuality of the Celt was falling to pieces before his eyes and the iron politics of Parnell rose implacably from the ruins.

In Arnold's last years of bitter Unionist denunciation of the Parnell movement and demands for more and more coercion,[100] there is in part the anger of the intellectual who sees his theories variously ignored, thwarted and refuted. He had sought to be the advocate and friend of Ireland; the new Ireland wanted only acceptance of its demands, with no self-serving ratiocination whose twists would make for political unreliability. He had been the paternalist patron; he would never accept dictation, especially from sources whose nature he had defined and dictated. But there was a further dimension. Arnold, of all Victorian intellectuals, had most resembled the alienated Russian intelligentsia, in his cosmopolitanism, in his contro-versialism, in his contempt for politicians, in his conviction as to the wisdom of his political nostrums. He was a friendly and warm person; but in his reflections on politics he was also a lonely one. His diagnoses had been profound; they had also been perverse. He could provide one of the finest and most inspiring anatomies of British inequality and its evil social effects by contrast with European models[101]; and he could inveigh against the idea that the obsequies of a Dissenter in a village churchyard should be presided over by a pastor of the corpse's faith who might thus bring greater consolation to the bereaved relatives.[102] Ireland above all had drawn him into direct political controversy. Yet he almost gloried in the knowledge that his mixture of hostility to religious dogma and defence of the Anglican establishment left him a political anchorite, all the more when to the Anglican cause to which faith unfaithful kept him falsely true, he added his admiration for the poetry of Roman Catholicism. (The other part of Tennyson's couplet did not apply to him: his honour rooted in no dishonour stood.[103]) It was as though in one person he wedded Darwin's *The Origin of Species* and Dryden's 'The Hind and the Panther'.

But Ireland had another grim joke to throw at its evangelist, who had formally made so little of its traditions of satire, oral literature and anti-clericalism, for all of their links with the other Celtic, part-Celtic and post-Celtic lands on the English periphery. He had held the politics of his brother-in-law Forster at some remove, although being ready to use him as a means of turning an ideological screw in a Commons debate. Perhaps Forster's repudiation by the Quakers among whom he had been born, when he wedded Arnold's sister Jane, had deepened Arnold's readiness to believe the worst of Dissenter greed and Dissenter arrogance. But when Gladstone came back into power in April 1880, Forster was given the post of Chief Secretary for Ireland. The direction of affairs would supposedly be his; the Viceroy, Lord Cowper, was not expected to play any significant part. Forster was at this juncture the ablest of Gladstone's lieutenants, far abler, certainly, than the lackadaisical Hartington who had briefly replaced Gladstone during the latter's all too premature retirement in the mid-1870s. What followed for him was wholly tragic. The great statesman and philanthropist who had laboured so well for the starving Irish during the great famine and sought to advance democratic education for the United Kingdom, now degenerated into a hysterical, friendless wreck, whose troubles were endless and whose leaders seemed callous. The Gladstone-Forster correspondence in the British Museum Manuscript Room remains mercifully unpublished; it steadily deepens into cold, cutting contempt on one side, pathetic, wild despair on the other. Forster was in actual physical danger; his enemies in the landlord and tenant embattled forces seemed as inexhaustible as they were conscienceless; his superiors were at first indifferent (Gladstone during much of 1880 remained impatiently convinced that he had settled the Irish land question once for all in 1870), and later they made it plain that no serious negotiation would consider him. He would be thrown to the wolves; he would be the scapegoat, whatever the solution; he was expendable, bargaining counters being available in his office, his reason, perhaps even his life. Gladstone had returned to power with a new lease on life, and woe betide those near to him in succession! Forster resigned, wretchedly, on 2 May 1882, in protest against Gladstone's Kilmainham Treaty with Parnell, and his successor was assassinated before the windows of the Viceregal Lodge in the Phoenix Park four days later. The family saw all Forster's tragedy, among them the young Mary Augusta, taken by Forster to the House to see how Parnell would reply to his bitter attack on the Kilmainham Treaty.

> The figure of Parnell—the speech, nonchalant, terse, defiant, without a single grace of any kind—his hands in the pocket of his coat—and the terse silence of the crowded House, remains vividly with me.[104]

Well might Arnold feel that Culture had truly been confronted by embodied Anarchy.

7

He was wrong. Parnell was not Anarchy but a New Order, in all senses, but it was on Anarchy he seemed to rise. Forster could not see through his blind hysteria that the countless agrarian outrages and the Fenian-organized dollars had no power to control the new master of Ireland, who would abort the Land League revolution and rob the Irish-American incendiaries of their insurrection. He could only denounce, despair and die.

Arnold had not long before he followed him. But first he had his debts to pay; and never was he more Celtic than in the revenge he sought for the martyrdom of Forster. In America or in Britain, in private or in public, in speech or in print, he threw everything that was in him into the calls for coercion, the crusade against Home Rule, above all the cry against Gladstone. Increasingly Burke had been his great Mentor on Irish questions, and in 1881 he had faithfully edited Burke's *Letters, Speeches and Tracts of Irish Affairs*, the great storehouse of his own logic that Ireland must be given a sense of British concern for her welfare and an equal participation in the benefits of empire. Now he would turn to Burke again, to the Burke who broke remorselessly with old friends and party ties against the anarchy of the French Revolution and its British supporters and sympathizers. Was it not just such anarchy that he saw in Ireland? and were it not just such treason to mankind to permit it to flourish? Burke had not seen an Ireland in arms, but he had seen the dangers that his Ireland might fall into the hands of designing enemies of civilization and history, of truth and culture. That time had now arrived.

Unlike Forster, he went down fighting. Gladstone's declaration for Home Rule released him from the ambiguities created by Gladstone's continuing conflict with the Parnellites up to 1885 and Parnell's support for the Tories in their short-lived accession to power and election in that year. Thereafter, he had the pleasure of seeing what Forster never lived to see, his opponents solidly ranged on one side, and his rage burned against them with increasing vehemence. He still retained the perspective to admonish Chief Secretary Arthur Balfour for seeming to coddle the unregenerate landlords in contrast to the wise discrimination practised by his predecessor, Sir Michael Hicks Beach, in the choice of beleaguered property-owners to defend.[105] But for the most part he summoned up the spirit of Burke's final onslaught on revolution, and it was in that spirit he died, suddenly, on 14 April 1888.

'They went forth to the war,' Ossian says most truly, '*but they always fell.*'

Matthew Arnold's Fight for Ireland

NOTES

1. Arnold, 'Equality', a lecture delivered at the Royal Institution of Great Britain for the Promotion, Diffusion, and Extension of Science and of Useful Knowledge, on 8 February 1878, published in the *Fortnightly Review* (March 1878), in Arnold, *Mixed Essays* (London, 1879), and ultimately in R. H. Super (ed.), *The Complete Prose Works of Matthew Arnold* (Ann Arbor, Michigan, 1960–77), VIII. *Essays Relgious and Mixed* (1972), pp. 277–305, notes 450–59, 510–13. I am under the deepest of obligations to Professor Super's splendid edition. This essay has greatly benefited by a reading from Kenneth D. Mackay, and by conversation and advice from my mother (who died before its commission but whose assistance on the subject was lifelong), and from W. W. Robson, Sorley Maclean, Roger Savage, Terence Brown, Emrys Evans, George Shepperson, Colin Affleck, William Bell, R. Dudley Edwards, Bonnie, Leila and Sara Dudley Edwards and my long-suffering editor. My thanks are also due to the staffs of Edinburgh University Library, the National Library of Scotland and Ms. M. Wheelaghan.

2. Patrick J. McCarthy, *Matthew Arnold and the Three Classes* (New York, 1964), p. 157, and in general pp. 139–75. I differ from this valuable study on certain points, but in general it provides a useful summary of Arnold's coercionist crusade on Ireland in 1881–88, for which I have little space. For texts of the relevant material, see Super (ed.), *Prose Works of Arnold*, XI, *The Last Word* (1977).

3. I have published essays on a number of these writers in preparation for a book which presently has the working title *Ireland in British Minds*.

4. G. K. Chesterton, *The Victorian Age in Literature* (London, 1913), p. 74.

5. James Anthony Froude, *The English in Ireland in the Eighteenth Century* (London, 1881: 2nd edition), I, pp. 7–14. Dr. Terence Brown points out to me that this work was directly influenced by Arnold's *On the Study of Celtic Literature*.

6. 'Arnold's commentary has gone virtually uncontradicted since it was made, in 1866', declares the Harvard scholar John V. Kelleher ('Arnold and the Celtic Revival', in Harry Levin (ed.), *Perspectives of Criticism* (Cambridge, Mass., 1950), p. 198), speaking of *Celtic Literature*, but this has been seriously challenged in Super (ed.), *Prose Works of Arnold*, III, *Lectures and Essays in Criticism* (1962), pp. 497–98, citing Henry Stuart Fagan, notice, *Contemporary Review*, VI (October, 1867), 257–61, and still more in Frederic E. Faverty, *Matthew Arnold the Ethnologist* (Evanston, Ill., 1951), pp. 223–24, who states that 'the essay met with repeated criticism, often enough of the most severe and violent kind, from 1866 on', citing *The Times*, the *Daily Telegraph*, the *Saturday Review*, the *Pall Mall Gazette*, the *Fortnightly Review*, Fagan, and Swinburne. See also Carl Dawson and John Pfordresher (eds.), *Matthew Arnold Prose Writings: The Critical Heritage* (London, 1979), pp. 17–22, 153–70.

7. Rhys, introduction to Everyman's Library edition of Arnold, *On the Study of Celtic Literature and Other Essays* (London, 1910), pp. viii, vii. The whole

Matthew Arnold: Between Two Worlds

introduction is important comment for its time and ours (pp. vii–xiv).

8. Wilde to Allen, c. 7 February 1891, in Rupert Hart-Davis (ed.), *The Letters of Oscar Wilde* (London, 1962), pp. 286–87, commenting on Allen, 'The Celt in English Art', *Fortnightly Review* (February 1891), on which see also Holbrook Jackson, *The Eighteen Nineties* (London, 1913), Ch. X, 'The Discovery of the Celt'.

9. Dan H. Laurence (ed.), *The Bodley Head Bernard Shaw: Collected Plays with their Prefaces* (London, 1971), II, p. 602 (i.e. *Man and Superman*, Act II).

10. Rupert Hart-Davis (ed.), *A Catalogue of the Caricatures of Max Beerbohm* (London, 1972), p. 24 (37): it appeared in Beerbohm, *The Poet's Corner* (London, 1904), originally.

11. James Bertram (ed.), *Letters of Thomas Arnold the Younger 1850–1900* (Auckland, N.Z., 1980), *passim*.

12. Kelleher, 'Arnold and the Celtic Revival', p. 199, admits this as 'the only plain opposition to' Arnold's thesis, arguing that 'Shaw proves that every characteristic Arnold thought of as typically Celtic is typically English, and, of course, vice versa. And Shaw does not mention Arnold either in the introduction or the play.' This is certainly unfair to Shaw whose dramatic genius was far too strong to be shackled by anything as mundane as 'proof', especially since his argument in part depends on climate as a determinant. See esp. Act I, and the preface, esp. 'Our Temperaments Contrasted', where Shaw has a lot of fun with the hard-bitten Irishman Wellington and the romantic Englishman Nelson (Laurence (ed.), *Shaw: Collected Plays*, II, pp. 813–19, 893–921). It is certainly Arnold whom Shaw is standing on his head. See also Faverty, *Arnold the Ethnologist*, pp. 146, 226; and a nice little linkage particularly telling in its inaccuracy: 'Like the later satirists, Shaw, Wilde, and Viscount Haldane, he is regarded by his countrymen as un-English', 'he' being Arnold (p. 8). Shaw and Wilde were Irish; Haldane was Scots.

13. I have not entered into discussion of Arnold's great inspirational pre-cursor, Ernest Renan, *La Poésie des Races Celtiques* (Paris, 1854), belatedly translated for inclusion in his *Poetry of the Celtic Races, and other Essays*, intro. William G. Hutchison (London, 1896), but have largely dealt with material original to Arnold. A fine balance on Arnold's debts to Renan and personal contribution is struck in Rachel Bromwich, *Matthew Arnold and Celtic Literature: A Retrospect 1865–1965* (Oxford, 1965), *passim*, esp. p. 8 (Renan's 'knowledge of Irish literature was in fact so slight as to be almost negligible; where Ireland was concerned he drew his information from ecclesiastical legend rather than from the native literary tradition'). See also Super (ed.), *Prose Works of Arnold*, III, pp. 494–95. Renan made more of the femininity of the Celts than Arnold, who extols the 'Titanism' of the old heroes, making too much of this as a peculiarly Celtic quality, but his equation of the Celts with a recessive rôle in history makes the same point. See also L. P. Curtis, Jr., *Anglo-Saxons and Celts: A Study of Anti-Irish Prejudice in Victorian England* (Bridgeport, Conn., 1968), p. 61, as well as pp. 39–45; Faverty, *Arnold the Ethnologist*, p. 146: 'In Arnold's account, the Celt is unquestionably the weaker vessel.'

14. Hugh Trevor-Roper, 'The Invention of Tradition: The Highland Tradition of Scotland', in Eric Hobsbawm and Terence Ranger (eds.), *The Invention of Tradition* (Cambridge, 1983), pp. 15–16, is a particularly appalling example of Oxbridge ignorance and arrogance in which the author announces that 'Racially and culturally', the Highlands and Islands were 'a colony of Ireland' whose 'literature, such as it was, was a crude echo of Irish literature. . . . It had—could have—no independent tradition.' The eighteenth-century Irish writer John Toland is cited as stating 'that the Scottish bards were the rubbish of Ireland periodically cleared out of Ireland and deposited in that convenient dump'; what Toland actually said was that in late sixth-century Ireland lesser bards were transported to Scotland, a very different matter from asserting that they constituted the bardic population of Scotland 1,100 years later (Toland, *History of the Druids*, ed. R. Hudleston (Montrose, 1814), p. 76, reprinted from *A Collection of Several Pieces of Mr. John Toland* . . . (London, 1726), I, pp. 27–8). It is probably somewhat unfair to A. L. Rowse to place him on a level with this performance; there is much more to be said for expressing admiration for poetry one has read than for denouncing poetry one has not, and Rowse's stress, however self-gratifying, on the Cornish background of Arnold's mother is useful, but his 'Matthew Arnold as Cornishman', *Welsh Review*, IV (March 1945), 39–49, enlarged into his *Matthew Arnold Poet and Prophet* (London, 1976), is greatly weakened by the constant substitution of arrogance for industry. It is a pleasure to salute by contrast the O'Donnell Lecture at Oxford delivered by the Lecturer in Celtic Language and Literature at Cambridge, Rachel Bromwich, which in its impeccable scholarship and insights fulfils Arnold's highest hopes as opposed to his worst faults.

15. Further to earlier citations of some of these critics, for the Scots economist Giffen see Dawson and Pfordresher (eds.), *Arnold Prose: Critical Heritage*, pp. 166–71, reprinting Giffen on *Celtic Literature* from *Fortnightly Review*, 1 July 1867, 124–26; for Lang see his 'The Celtic Renascence', *Blackwood's Edinburgh Magazine* CLXI (February, 1897), 181–91; for Yeats see his 'The Celtic Element in Literature' in his *Ideas of Good and Evil* (London, 1903), pp. 270–95; for P. Wyndham Lewis, his *The Lion and the Fox: The Rôle of the Hero in the Plays of Shakespeare* (London, 1927), pp. 299–326 ('Arnold . . . has supplied us with a superb "celtic" nonsense book'); for Lionel Trilling, *Matthew Arnold* (London, 1939), pp. 232–43 ('In 1866 Ireland, under Sinn Fein leadership, was becoming violent'). One might add 'see also' Hugh Kingsmill, *Matthew Arnold* (London, 1928), pp. 206–15, if only because of its author's advantage in part-Irish parentage, but it might be kinder to his memory if one did not.

16. Super (ed.), *Prose Writings of Arnold*, III, p. 305. Actually, the passage is a very Celtic lament for Eugene O'Curry: 'Obscure Scaliger of a despised literature, he deserves some weightier voice to praise him than the voice of an unlearned bellettristic trifler like me; he belongs to the race of the giants in literary research and industry,—a race now almost extinct.' The inspiration of the passage may be Byron, *Don Juan*, Canto III, Stanza 86: 5 ('And must thy lyre, so long divine,/ Degenerate

into hands like mine?'): Arnold would identify Byron in his lectures with what he termed Celtic 'Titanism'. The antecedent lines are also suggestive as to his vision of the Celt: 'On thy voiceless shore/ The heroic lay is tuneless now—/ The heroic bosom beats no more!'

17. Faverty, *Arnold the Ethnologist*, p. 116.
18. Matthew Arnold to Mary Penrose Arnold, 8 May 1859, in George W. E. Russell (ed.), *Letters of Matthew Arnold 1848–1888* (London, 1895), I, p. 85. The caution must be made for any quotations from this edition that Russell admitted having made 'some slight excisions; but, as regards the bulk of the Letters, this process had been performed before the manuscript came into my hands', which is ominous in general but unlikely to affect the argument of this essay.
19. Rowse, 'Matthew Arnold as Cornishman', 39.
20. *Westminster Review*, XXXII (October, 1867), 605.
21. Mary Augusta, Mrs. Humphry Ward, *A Writer's Recollections* (London, 1918), pp. 40–42.
22. Faverty, *Arnold the Ethnologist*, pp. 116–17.
23. In his Preface (in response to critics) to *The Picture of Dorian Gray*. On Wilde's discipleship to Arnold, see Ernst Bendz, *The Influence of Pater and Matthew Arnold in the Prose-Writings of Oscar Wilde* (Gothenburg, 1914).
24. Super (ed.), *Prose Writings of Arnold*, XI, pp. 136–38, 140, 142, 190, 196, 253, 346; he also cited him without naming him, as in *ibid.*, pp. 192–93. Even in his darkest moments of hostility to the Parnell movement, there is evidence of some sneaking sympathy for Dillon (see p. 140). Had Dillon made his case by powerless prayers instead of powerful threats, Arnold would have been his zealous advocate. But while Dillon's emaciated, tubercular frame looked like that of a suppliant, his words were those of a power-broker, and an effectual one.
25. O'Brien, 'Irishness', in his *Writers and Politics* (London, 1965), pp. 97–100. Owen Dudley Edwards, 'Anthony Trollope, the Irish Writer', *Nineteenth-Century Fiction*, XXXVIII (June, 1983), 1–42.
26. Despite his criticisms of the Eisteddfod, he attended and (twice) addressed it in 1885 (Super (ed.), *Prose Writings of Arnold*, III, p. 497).
27. Matthew Arnold to Mary Penrose Arnold, 7 August, 20 August, 1864, and to Frances Arnold, August 1864, Russell (ed.), *Letters of Arnold*, I, pp. 233–39. Thomas Arnold, *Passages in a Wandering Life* (London, 1900), p. 9.
28. Clough was of Welsh antecedents and wrote his major poem, 'The Bothie of Tober-na-Vuolich', about what he took to be the lure of Celtic Scotland. Arnold visited Wales with him (Matthew Arnold to Mary Penrose Arnold, 19 August 1852, Russell (ed.), *Letters of Arnold*, I, p. 19; Arnold to Clough, 27 July, 3 August, 25 August 1853, Henry Foster Lowry (ed.), *The Letters of Matthew Arnold to Arthur Hugh Clough* (London, 1932), pp. 137–41).
29. Deane, *Celtic Revivals: Essays in Modern Irish Literature 1880–1980* (London, 1985), p. 25: the essay is entitled 'Arnold, Burke and the Celts'.
30. Lang, 'The Celtic Renascence', 181–84. MacEdward Leach, 'Matthew Arnold and "Celtic Magic"', in Ray B. Browne, William John Roscell

Matthew Arnold's Fight for Ireland

and Richard J. Loftus (eds.), *The Celtic Cross: Studies in Irish Culture and Literature* (West Lafayette, Ind., 1964), pp. 78–9.

31. Tom Peete Cross, 'A Note on "Sohrab and Rustum" in Ireland', *Journal of Celtic Studies*, I (November, 1950), 176–82.
32. C. B. Tinker and H. F. Lowry, *The Poetry of Matthew Arnold: A Commentary* (London, 1940), pp. 106–24.
33. Bromwich, *Arnold and Celtic Literature*, pp. 23–7.
34. Matthew Arnold to Mary Penrose Arnold, 19 August 1852, Russell (ed.), *Letters of Arnold*, I, p. 19.
35. Paulin, contribution to symposium on 'Neglected Fictions', *T.L.S.* (18 October 1985), 1188.
36. Arnold to Clough, early April 1848, Lowry (ed.) *Letters of Arnold to Clough*, pp. 78–9.
37. J. D. Jump, *Matthew Arnold* (London, 1955), p. 27.
38. Super (ed.), *Prose Writings of Arnold*, III, pp. 490–94.
39. Quoted ibid., p. 491. The letter is not in Russell.
40. Quoted ibid., p. 500.
41. Arnold, 'Joubert', Super (ed.), *Prose Writings of Arnold*, III, p. 210.
42. Arnold, 'The Literary Influence of Academies', ibid., p. 232.
43. Ibid., p. 257.
44. Matthew Arnold to Mary Penrose Arnold, 28 February 1866, Russell (ed.), *Letters of Arnold*, I, p. 319.
45. Super (ed.), *Prose Writings of Arnold*, III, p. 313. But Kelleher, for one, has some unanswered charges as to the way in which 'Arnold stacked his cards' to raise a laugh ('Arnold and the Celtic Revival', p. 207). Such a fault is an occupational disease of the inspiring lecturer.
46. Super (ed.), *Prose Writings of Arnold*, III, p. 385.
47. Bromwich, *Arnold and Celtic Literature*, pp. 9–10.
48. Super (ed.), *Prose Writings of Arnold*, III, p. 405 points out that it is in *Celtic Literature* that Arnold's chief indebtedness to Renan has been noted. It is a little disingenuous in Arnold that his sole reference to Renan in this work is a critical one, on Renan's view of the Celt as timid, shy and delicate which 'will never do for the typical Irishman of Donnybrook fair' (ibid., pp. 342–43). But Kelleher notes that Arnold's own emphasis on sentiment, spirituality, ineffectualness and sensuousness make for the same effect. See also Faverty, *Arnold the Ethnologist*, pp. 120–24, which argues that Arnold's greatest debt is to Henri Martin 'for his analysis of the Celtic race'.
49. Bromwich, *Arnold and Celtic Literature*, pp. 8–9.
50. Ibid., 11.
51. Super (ed.), *Prose Writings of Arnold*, III, p. 335.
52. Chesterton, *Victorian Age in Literature*, pp. 159–60. See also Chesterton's introduction to Arnold, *Essays Literary and Critical* (London, 1906), the selection for Everyman's Library; it was later reprinted in his *G.K.C. as M.C.* (London, 1929), pp. 18–28, ed. J. P. de Foseka.
53. Super (ed.), *Prose Writings of Arnold*, III, p. 364.
54. Ibid., pp. 370–71.
55. Bromwich, *Arnold and Celtic Literature*, p. 30; also pp. 20–2.

56. Ibid., p. 21.
57. '. . . Do you compare your psalms,/ To the tales of the bare-arm'd Fenians?'
    'Are you sure you are translating that last epithet correctly, Hector?'
    'Quite sure, sir', answered Hector, doggedly.
    'Because I should have thought the nudity might have been quoted as existing in a different part of the body.' (Scott, *The Antiquary*, Chapter Thirtieth.)
58. Frank O'Connor (*pseud.*, i.e. Michael O'Donovan), *The Backward Look: A Survey of Irish Literature* (London, 1967), p. 160.
59. Bromwich, *Arnold and Celtic Literature*, pp. 32–3.
60. Synge and Thomas founded much of their art on their reporting skills, and their sensitivity to grammatical construction and inflection. Both are dealing with post-Celtic language structures in English. Had the Irish and Welsh languages perished in 1865–66 as a (Celtic) magic response to Arnold's lectures, there would have been no place in English literature for either writer.
61. Leach, 'Arnold and "Celtic Magic" ', pp. 77–8: 'concrete and specific detail, . . . pictorial composition with constant and vivid use of color, close integration of the physical world by way of symbol and figure of speech . . . a tendency toward understatement, abstraction translated into terms of action and symbol, and animism.' These qualities are not constant in Arnold, but they figure frequently, though seldom simultaneously, in his poetry and his prose. I omit Leach's 'no difference between natural and supernatural, rational and irrational', although in one sense Arnold's enthusiasm for religion while eliminating its supernatural elements makes for the former, and is sustained by the latter, of these.
62. Matthew Arnold to Frances Arnold, August 1864, Russell (ed.), *Letters of Arnold*, I, p. 238. His spelling of Taliesin improved in time for the lectures.
63. Super (ed.), *Prose Writings of Arnold*, III, p. 333.
64. Quoted in Faverty, *Arnold the Ethnologist*, pp. 117–18.
65. Matthew Arnold to Mary Penrose Arnold, 10 March 1866, Russell (ed.), *Letters of Arnold*, I, p. 310. Super (ed.), *Prose Writings of Arnold*, III, p. 300.
66. Dr. Thomas Arnold was in some respects a much more enlightened commentator on race than his son Matthew, who seems to have interpreted his views as much more racist than they were; this is in keeping with the deepening racism of the English-speaking world during the nineteenth century. Dr. Arnold is saluted for his advanced views by a specialist on race relations in history: Richard K. Barksdale, 'Thomas Arnold's Attitude to Race', *Phylon*, XVIII (April, 1957), 174–80, particularly citing Thomas Arnold, *Introductory Lectures on Modern History* (Oxford, 1842), pp. 162–63: 'The whole character of a nation may be influenced by its geology and physical geography.' Perhaps Shaw had more in common with father than son.
67. Super (ed.), *Prose Writings of Arnold*, III, p. 346.

68. Ibid., p. 386.
69. One way in which Yeats, Wilde and Shaw showed their debt to Arnold in strengthening themselves as cultural evangelists would be in the confidence with which they learned to criticise him.
70. Quoted in Bromwich, *Arnold and Celtic Literature*, pp. 36–8.
71. Super (ed.), *Prose Writings of Arnold*, III, pp. 392, 395.
72. Super (ed.), *Prose Writings of Arnold*, V. *Culture and Anarchy with Friendship's Garland and Some Literary Essays* (1965), 64.
73. Ibid., pp. 393–98.
74. Ibid., p. 121.
75. Ibid., p. 130. See also p. 94.
76. Ibid., p. 146.
77. Ibid., pp. 149, 241–45 (quoting Renan!), 254.
78. Ibid., p. 208.
79. Ibid., p. 103.
80. He came to terms with it in some degree when he attacked the proposal for Welsh disestablishment, linking with it the continuing Irish crisis, in his 'Disestablishment in Wales' (Super (ed.), *Prose Writings of Arnold*, XI, pp. 334–49), published in March 1888, six weeks before his death. See F. J. W. Harding, 'Matthew Arnold and Wales', *The Transactions of the Honourable Society of Cymmrodorion* (1963), 251–72. He did suggest some subvention of Dissenters.
81. See esp. Yeats, 'September 1913', where the Catholic bourgeoisie's fumbling 'in a greasy till' is so forcibly contrasted with the past ideals of the deceased John O'Leary.
82. Super (ed.), *Prose Works of Arnold*, VII, *God and the Bible* (1970), pp. 44–5, in a review of Renan, *La Réforme intellectuelle et morale de la France*.
83. Chesterton, *Victorian Age in Literature*, pp. 76–7.
84. Thomas Arnold, *Lectures on History*, pp. 45–77.
85. Ward, *A Writer's Recollections*, p. 181.
86. Matthew Arnold to Mary Penrose Arnold, 16 June 1870, Russell (ed.), *Letters of Arnold*, II, p. 34.
87. Arnold to the editor, *Pall Mall Gazette*, 6 April 1875, Super (ed.), *Prose Writings of Arnold*, VII, p. 136.
88. Bertram (ed.), *Letters of Thomas Arnold*, pp. 108, 110, 113, 173–74.
89. Super (ed.), *Prose Writings of Arnold*, VII, pp. 423–25.
90. Super (ed.), *Prose Writings of Arnold*, IX, *English Literature and Irish Politics* (1973), pp. 58–9.
91. Ibid., p. 58.
92. He edited Edmund Burke, *Letters, Speeches and Tracts on Irish Affairs* in 1881 at what was evidently his own suggestion (Super (ed.), *Prose Writings of Arnold*, IX, pp. 286–89 (Arnold's preface), 417–19 (Super's notes)). He made one reference to Burke in *Celtic Literature*, coupling Burke with Shakespeare and Addison as revelatory of Celtic influence 'with the English basis', in Burke's case the characteristic being 'a largeness of view and richness of thought, not English' (Super (ed.), *Prose Writings of Arnold*, III, p. 358). By 1881 the references were coming thick and fast. Super's text of 'The Incompatibles', Arnold's essay

calling for the expropriation of bad Irish landlords and (once more) for a Catholic university, covers forty-seven pages of text of which twenty-one refer to Burke (Super (ed.), *Prose Writings of Arnold*, IX, pp. 238–85). The parallels are very close in some ways; Burke was of Irish Celtic origins, he was Anglican or Church of Ireland but defensive of the historic place and beneficial influence of the church of his ancestry—Roman Catholicism, he believed in a recognition of the self-respect of Irish Catholics by Britain, he saw a restoration of order as prerequisite to reform in a time of crisis. Arnold's Irish Catholic ancestry was relatively small and remote, but otherwise he is Burke's follower in these as well as in many non-Irish respects.

93. Super (ed.), *Prose Writings of Arnold*, VIII, p. 334.
94. Ibid., pp. 334–35. Arnold is here broadening the question to include the problem of Irish secondary schools, with all the authority of his own career and experience as an educationist. He resumed the schools question in 'An Unregarded Irish Grievance', published in 1881 (Super (ed.), *Prose Writings of Arnold*, IX, pp. 295–311).
95. Super (ed.), *Prose Writings of Arnold*, VIII, pp. 326–28.
96. Thomas Arnold to Lord Acton, 29 January 1892, Bertram (ed.), *Letters of Thomas Arnold*, p. 229. Newman was writing directly to Matthew Arnold on the question by 1876, for which together with discussion of his influence see David J. DeLaura, *Hebrew and Hellene in Victorian England: Newman, Arnold and Pater* (Austin, Tex., 1969), pp. 123–34.
97. Preface to the Second Edition (1874) of his *Higher Schools and Universities in Germany* (Super (ed.), *Prose Writings of Arnold*, VII, pp. 108–9).
98. Ibid., pp. 112–13.
99. Super (ed.), *Prose Writings of Arnold*, IX, p. 239. The idea of the expropriation of unjust Irish landlords put forward in this essay, 'The Incompatibles', in 1881, when his view of Ireland was still that of an advocate for an ineffectual suppliant, was reiterated down the years despite all his anger at the new and unwanted success of Irish agrarian agitation under Parnell. He asserted it in 'The Zenith of Conservatism' (1887), 'Up to Easter' (1887), 'From Easter to August' (1887) and 'Disestablishment in Wales' (1888), for which see Super (ed.), *Prose Writings of Arnold*, XI, pp. 138–42, 206–9, 262, 348.
100. To other summations and critiques may be added the useful summary and discussion in Benjamin Evans Lippincott, *Victorian Critics of Democracy* (Minneapolis, Minn., 1938), pp. 107–9. The justification for the demand for coercion was expressed in 1887 in 'From Easter to August': 'Until the Irish are convinced that the law is stronger than they or we, until they have had to renounce and forgo this temper of "insolence, refractoriness, defiance", not only they cannot be governed, they cannot be sane, they cannot be settled, they cannot be happy' (Super (ed.), *Prose Writings of Arnold*, XI, p. 256). Arnold was as much a victim as all other crusaders for the restoration of the rule of law in his inability to uphold the law without the abrogation of its provisions for civil liberties. But we do get a fine sense of his Irish priorities in the rhetorical emphasis placed on what he saw as the most important

point, that without the law the Irish 'cannot be happy'. He retained his priority to the last, in contrast to most English writers to whom the question was one of vindicating English honour and order. For this reason, and for the view of Gladstone's relations with Forster presented below, I cannot share the hostility of Patrick J. McCarthy, *Arnold and the Three Classes*, pp. 139–75, towards his final Irish phase, however much I may disagree with it.

101. 'Equality' (1878), Super (ed.), *Prose Writings of Arnold*, VIII, pp. 277–305.
102. 'A Last Word on the Burials Bill' (1876), ibid., pp. 87–110.
103. Tennyson, *Idylls of the King*: 'Lancelot and Elaine', ll. 871–72.
104. Ward, *A Writer's Recollections*, p. 179. On Forster's later career, see T. Wemyss Reid, *Life of the Right Honourable William Edward Forster* (London, 1888), II. But its quotations from the correspondence with Gladstone contain very little of the hysteria which charges so much of the unpublished letters in the Gladstone MSS.
105. Super (ed.), *Prose Writings of Arnold*, XI, p. 348. Certainly Arnold's campaign against the bad Irish landlords was in part activated by the ammunition which they gave to Parnell, Dillon and their followers, but equally certainly he was deeply angered by the injustice and suffering they wrought.

Notes on Contributors

DAVID AMIGONI is a graduate of University College, Cardiff, where he read English Literature and History. He is currently doing research in Victorian Studies at the University of Keele. In line with an interest in the theoretical and practical relationships between the disciplines of literature and history, he is presently working on the late Victorian novelist and Tory ideologist, W. H. Mallock, setting him in an historical and critical context.

ALAN CHEDZOY graduated in Philosophy and Literature at the University of Reading in 1963; after teaching in various schools he was Senior Lecturer in English Literature at the Dorset Institute of Higher Education. He is an authority on Dorset literature and has edited several novels by Hardy and poetry by William Barnes. His biography, *William Barnes: A Life of the Dorset Poet*, was published in 1985.

OWEN DUDLEY EDWARDS is Reader in History at the University of Edinburgh, where he has been teaching since 1968. He studied at Belvedere College, University College Dublin and the Johns Hopkins University. He has also taught at the Universities of Oregon, Aberdeen, South Carolina and California State University at San Francisco. He has written various books and articles of which the most recent are *The Quest for Sherlock Holmes: A Biographical Study of Arthur Conan Doyle* and *Burke and Hare*.

ROBERT GIDDINGS was educated at the Universities of Bristol and Keele, where he specialized in the study of Victorian literature. He has published on Dickens, Smollett, Mark Twain, Tolkien and contributed to several volumes in the Critical Studies Series, including those on Auden, Scott, Poe, Johnson and Smollett. He was co-author with Alan Bold of *True Characters: Real People in Fiction, The*

Book of Rotters and *Who Was Really Who in Fiction*. He has contributed frequently to *New Society*, the *Listener*, *New Statesman*, *Tribune* and other journals, and his autobiography, *You Should See Me in Pyjamas*, was published in 1981. He is now Senior Lecturer in English and Media at Dorset Institute of Higher Education.

WILLIAM KAUFMAN grew up in New Jersey and was educated at Montclair State College. His experience includes banjo-making in Nashville, music-making and teaching, working in graveyards, airports and Wall Street. A Marshall Scholarship took him to the University of Wales, Aberystwyth, where he was awarded his doctorate. He contributed an essay on the comedic stance of Mark Twain to the Critical Studies volume *Mark Twain: A Sumptuous Variety* (1985).

CHARLES SWANN is Senior Lecturer in the Department of American Studies at the University of Keele. He has published on Scott, Hawthorne, Eliot, Rutherford and Crane. He has contributed to two previous volumes in the Critical Studies Series, *American Fiction: New Readings* (1983) and *James Fenimore Cooper: New Critical Essays* (1985). He is at present engaged on a study of English literature, 1830–80.

JOHN WOOLFORD was born in 1946 and educated at Dover Grammar School and Christ's College, Cambridge. He was Research Fellow at King's College, Cambridge, 1969–72 and Teaching Fellow and Director of Studies in English at Fitzwilliam College, Cambridge, 1972–79. Since 1979 he has been Lecturer in English at King's College, London. He has published on Robert Browning, Elizabeth Barratt, Wordsworth and Basil Bunting. His book *Browning the Revisionary* is to be published in 1986.